Hives in the City

Keeping Honey Bees Alive in an Urban World

Alison Gillespie

CROYDON HILL

Croydon Hill
Silver Spring, MD
www.croydonhill.com

Cover design by Denise Reiffenstein

Book Layout © 2014 BookDesignTemplates.com

Hives in the City Alison Gillespie. -- 1st ed.
ISBN 978-0-9960259-0-4

To Sam and Grace.

CONTENTS

Introduction

Like a lot of other people, I was horrified in 2006 when Colony Collapse Disorder began to make the headlines and reports flooded in from all over the world, telling of beehives which were suddenly empty. The bees were dying, and even the nation's leading experts didn't know why.

It was as if someone suddenly pulled the rug out of the gardening world. I saw no issues in our own garden but the bees, which had once seemed as common as house dust, were elevated to the status of threatened and vulnerable. I found myself standing by the flowers for long periods of time, thankful for every bee I saw on every blossom. Bees provide about one out of every three mouthfuls of food we eat, including berries, nuts, and many vegetables. To contemplate their complete disappearance was terrifying.

For years I had been tending my garden as a wildlife sanctuary of sorts. In the 1990s I fell in love with the words of nature writer Sara Stein, who told how we could restore the ecology of our own backyards in order to offer birds, bees, butterflies and other kinds of wildlife a place of refuge. By planting native species and using organic gardening methods on my fruits and vegetables I sought to increase the biodiversity of my own piece of the planet.

Even though my gardens had always been in urban locations, I had always had great luck attracting bees, both native and non-native. The more I learned about the honey bees' struggles, the more curious I became. Most reports said that feral hives were a thing of the past, so if I was seeing honey bees among my flowers it meant that someone living within two or three miles of my house was tending them in hives. Who was this person that I shared a pollinator connection with each day?

I found myself peering into other people's backyards as I walked my dog, hoping to get a glimpse of that unknown beekeeper. I wanted to thank them, tell them I was grateful, or at least know who they were and why they kept bees. It was as if someone else had the other end of a long, imaginary string that connected our yards – and our lives.

Meanwhile, everywhere I went beyond my own neighborhood, I seemed to meet newly-minted beekeepers. Stay-at-home-moms, postal carriers, lawyers, college students, waiters serving me at restaurants and even my own dental hygienist –

people of all walks of life were suddenly telling me about their new love for the bees.

I decided it was time to write a book. We are all drawn to using the tools at our disposal in a crisis, and I was disturbed that there was still no real answer to the honey bee's problems. I was also fascinated by beekeeping's newfound stardom and popularity. The story of large-scale migratory beekeepers who were driving across North America's farmlands with thousands of bees in closed beehives on the back of flatbed trucks had been well-chronicled. But little had been said of the people keeping a hive or two in the city.

It was that story I wanted to research and tell. I wanted to know more about people who had a few hives tucked away in their backyards, sometimes in unlikely locations, desperately trying to keep those creatures alive against all odds. What drives someone to invite thousands of stinging insects into their garden, their balcony, their roof top, I wondered. What motivates them to stay with it, even though the bees can cost hundreds of dollars and can demand many hours of time in the spring, summer and fall? Are they drawn in because they see something familiar in the way the insects live, or was there something more primal and biological drawing people to these amazing social insects? Did people think they could save the bees in their own backyard hives, or was something more going on behind the trend?

I immersed myself in the beekeepers' world throughout the entire 2013 bee season, attending workshops, travelling to beekeeping meetings and shadowing many in their backyards and rooftops as they worked their hives throughout the urban and suburban corridor of the Mid-Atlantic US. Although it would be impossible to tell every beekeeper's story, I was honored to get a glimpse of their bees and grateful for the chance to be let inside their realm for a while.

The selection of beekeepers chosen here was based mostly on where luck and fortune led me as I went exploring. The inclusion of particular individuals in the book should not be seen as an endorsement of any one way of beekeeping over another. My intention in these pages is not to validate or in-validate any one beekeeping methodology. Instead, I would ask that readers consider the stories offered here as slices of life, snapshots of our current relationship with pollinators.

It is always important to me that science provide the com-pass for navigating a crisis, so I have also included a lot of research in the pages of this book and lean heavily on biolo-gists as interpreters of the natural world. Many were generous, allowing me to get a view of their science and an explanation of their investigations into bees living in our current, highly-urbanized environment here on the East Coast.

I have chosen to write mostly about urban and suburban bees in the Mid-Atlantic region of the eastern US; specifical-ly, this book mostly follows beekeepers in the metropolitan areas of Washington, DC, Baltimore, Philadelphia, and New York with brief examples drawn from Connecticut. Bees here share a similar climate, and have experienced similar weather cycles in the last few decades. They also feed from the same types of plants and trees, and experience similar pollution issues, and the cities they live in have undergone somewhat similar urbanization patterns in the last century. Some of these patterns are very different from the metamorphoses taking place in other regions. Astute readers may notice, for example, that there is no discussion of Africanized honey bees, because it has yet to be an issue in the Mid-Atlantic.

Attitudes toward beekeeping in the cities of this region have also experienced similar evolutionary patterns, and the laws regarding beekeeping here have changed dramatically in the span of just a few years. It was fun and interesting to be present as the beekeepers around me became politically empowered. Some of what happens in the Mid-Atlantic is unique to this region, but I think that anyone who has ever kept a hive anywhere in the world will be able to relate to issues regarding grouchy or fearful neighbors, pesticide overuse, and resistant or restrictive regulations. Bees everywhere have suffered from unearned bad publicity, and people remain innately afraid of stinging insects in all locations.

There may be disagreements about the best way to proceed into the future when it comes to the management of bees, their diseases and their environs. But those differences are dwarfed by a shared passion for keeping the bees alive.

As one beekeeper told me, the bees have a lot to teach us about our world. We just need to remember to stay calm, slow down, watch, listen and learn – from the bees and from each other.

1

Capital City Bees

The first challenge I face as I set out to learn about beekeeping is traffic. The second is parking.

To find out what motivates people to become urban beekeepers, I asked if I could sit in on Jeff Miller's beekeeping class, in March at his house in the heart of Georgetown.

Parking is hell in this neighborhood. Decades ago, when the rest of Washington, DC was drilled for Metro tunnels and equipped with underground subway stations, the residents of this historic enclave balked. Bordered by college campuses and treasured for its colonial and Victorian-era townhomes, driving the narrow streets of this beautiful place in search of an open piece of curb to snuggle up to can feel like moving through the levels of Dante's purgatory. Everything's tight and bumpy, and the thought of scraping one of the expensive cars parked in this neighborhood gives me pangs of anxiety. As the clock ticks closer to starting time, I bail out on a cold, windy corner where a valet service offers to keep my car under lock and key for a premium while I'm off learning about propolis, honeycombs, and queens.

Running in the freezing cold day, I trip on a piece of brick sidewalk that's been pushed up by the roots of an ancient linden tree growing between the houses and the street. Its brunch time, so I have to politely thread my way through well-dressed people perusing menus posted on the doors of some very fine restaurants and people taking selfies outside of a cupcake shop which offers a dozen of its treats – seen often on a popular reality TV show – for $29. A sudden snow squall begins, cascading flakes onto my eye lashes, and I shove my hands, numb with cold, into my coat pockets.

I'm wondering who Miller's students will be. Hipsters with chunky glasses and tattoos? Young? Old? Students from nearby Georgetown University? City-dwelling foodies? Or people like me who just like to geek out on nature?

As I approach the front door of Miller's pretty townhouse, I wonder what they will think of me. Georgetown and its posh stores and wealthy shoppers have had their usual effect of rousing my insecurities. But when Miller throws open the door and shouts hello, all of my worries melt away. Despite the cold he's in bare feet, jeans, and a bee t-shirt. Under an unruly shock of gray and sandy hair he's got a devilish expression – enhanced by a slight space between his teeth that makes him seem like a boy who's bought a new football and needs other kids to make a good game of it.

He shakes my hand and offers wine as he leads me past a gorgeously decorated living room where a wood fire is burning.

We pass through a dining room where pieces of fresh cut pine lumber are stacked on top of an antique dining table. A contemporary chandelier is throwing sparkles of light across frames of empty honeycombs made of plastic or wax. A huge toolbox is open on the floor next to oodles of extension cords coiled up like snakes on top of the antique wool rug on the hardwood floors. I'm wondering if it looks like this all the time – if beekeeping has completely taken over Miller's life – or if he's put all of this out for us to use later when we learn about constructing a hive from a kit.

I do not plan to keep bees. I will remain an observer, shadowing others beginning here with people learning about it for the first time. I know some basic bee facts, but want to steep myself in the biological details before I begin visiting anyone's apiary, and Miller has promised there will be ample info given today.

We wend our way into the kitchen where several people are standing around talking animatedly. He shouts out my introduction to the others and steps over to the stove where he's got a frying pan full of chicken wings already cooking. "They've been coated in a sauce made with some of the honey from my hives," he tells everyone.

The tiny gourmet kitchen is warm, and everyone is friendly. A well-dressed man with a clean shaven head and a Ralph Lauren merino wool sweater introduces himself and asks if I want some cheese. He explains how some of the offerings on the platter in front of us will pair better with honey than others.

"I'm already a cheesemaker. Now I want to be a beekeeper. When I do something, I tend go all in. I like stuff I can get obsessed with."

I don't know what I was expecting, but it wasn't this – this feels more like a party than a beekeeping workshop. Altogether there are seven of us huddled around a huge kitchen island munching on snacks and sipping wine.

Miller is telling everyone how excited he is to get started with a new bee season. It has been cold, much colder than last year, and so it has been hard to know when to put new queens out or start new hives. When it warms up, though, he'll be busy all the time.

During the week he's the Director of Real Estate for DC's Deputy Mayor for Planning and Economic Development. I assume that it's a stressful job. Politics can get steep in this small but power-filled town, and open properties are hard to find and often fought over. Although the recession has hit hard, there isn't much open land to be had, tucked so close to the Potomac River. Some parts of the city are also undergoing a huge revitalization, and everywhere you turn it seems like the sky is dotted with construction cranes.

Miller doesn't talk much about his job with his beekeeping friends, though. He likes to keep the two worlds separate. Over the last couple of years as beekeepers began to challenge a confusing and archaic law which seemed to prohibit beekeeping in DC, Miller never did any advocacy for bees while at work. Today it's obvious he's put himself in weekend mode.

When someone asks where he keeps his own hives, Miller takes a gulp of wine, points toward the ceiling, and grins. "My bees are up on the roof. It was the only space I had here at home. It works out great, except that the only way to get up there and do bee work is to put a ladder up in my bathtub and climb through the skylight. Its a real pain when I have to carry stuff up and down." He promises to tell us more about his other hives in locations all over the city once we get started with the class.

After a few more moments of chatting, we are shepherded into the living room where we assemble ourselves on various couches and chairs. I am incredibly grateful for the warmth of the fire, and try to get a seat close to the mantel to keep my hands warm.

Miller asks us to go around the room and tell why we want to learn about beekeeping.

Monica is a thirty-something woman from Chevy Chase, an area of DC that's almost as fashionable and desirable as Georgetown.

Brendan, the cheesemaker, says he's planning to put bees on the top level of a two-tiered porch in Palisades, an affluent neighborhood bordering the C&O Canal and the Potomac.

Katie is an energetic twenty-something. She's also the most experienced among the students. She's already got a hive that is doing very well in the trendy, club-filled neighborhood of Adam's Morgan where she rents, although she doesn't think that either of her neighbors knows about her bees. Her land-lord is cool with it. Beekeeping is a huge change from her job at a think tank downtown.

Lori, sitting next to me, says that she and her teenage son are hoping to install hives at the school where she teaches. He seems shy and a bit awkward sitting next to her – I never even catch his name – but his interest in the bees is quite apparent and sincere. He thinks maybe it would be cool to also have bees at their house in the Bethesda suburbs.

Kate Lee introduces herself last; she's hoping to find a place to put some hives this year. She kept bees, when she lived down in Georgia, but never here in DC. She's here to find out if there are any differences between the two locations regarding bees, and also to meet people and get a "brush up" from Miller on her bee facts. Later I learn that Kate is actually a bona fide urban farmer with a degree in urban horticulture from the University of Georgia. She's also the founder of the Capital City Farm Company, which aims to connect residents in the city with local produce. She sometimes offers onsite gardening services to clients, and she's hopeful she'll find a homeowner willing to host bees.

One of the first things Miller tells us is that bees are actual-ly not much work once you get a hive started.

Lee laughs and registers a gentle disagreement.

"Okay, okay," Miller says. "Are they harder or easier than a pet? Harder or easier than a goldfish?"

"I would say easier than a cat, but harder than a goldfish. Sometimes what's hard is keeping them going, keeping them alive after you get started."

Mid-spring, Miller says, is sort of like Christmas time for the bees. The nectar is flowing and the bees are busy. March – when it warms up – is like "the high holy days of beekeeping" and a really busy time for him. The rest of the year is much quieter, and the bees are less demanding of their keepers.

He begins a PowerPoint presentation on his widescreen TV. There are bee facts to be learned, he says, but a lot of that can be picked up through reading. In addition to the info he gives in this morning's lecture, he also provides every student with a copy of *The Backyard Beekeeper*, a how-to book by Kim Flottam.

Some info, Miller says, can also be learned once you have your bees already installed. He dismisses the idea that anyone would need to take a seven-session beekeeping course with a wave of his hand. Today's objective is to learn about the bees and their biological needs. Tomorrow, he'll work more with the class on products of the hive like soap, wax, and of course, honey. He thinks it's best for people to just get started.

Honey bees, Miller reminds us, are not native to the US. They were introduced by European colonists who valued the honey as a sweetener and the beeswax as an alternative to animal tallow for candle making. They have co-existed here fairly peaceably with the native bee populations, such as bumble bees and mason bees, for the last three centuries, helping to increase the return on vegetable crops and orchards as they go from flower to flower gathering nectar and spreading pollen.

There are many species of native bee, but they don't produce honey and most don't live in colonies. Honey bees, in contrast, are social and can produce enough honey to feed both their offspring and a beekeeper.

In order to keep a hive healthy and thriving, a beekeeper must understand how the colony orders itself and how the bees reproduce. Beekeepers must regularly inspect a hive and look for signs of ill health in their bees, so knowing what a healthy hive looks like and how the bees normally set up housekeeping is essential.

Bee colonies are divided into three castes: queens, workers, and drones. Every colony has only one queen who will lay as many as 2,000 eggs in a day.

The female worker bees comprise about 95% of the hive. They take care of feeding the young and also tend to the needs of their queen. Most of the honey bees you see in any garden are workers.

There are also drones, male bees whose only purpose in life is to mate with a queen. During the act of mating they actually lose their reproductive organs, and then die. Despite these differences, all bees actually start from the same type of eggs, which are laid into a special area the bees set aside as a so-called "brood chamber."

Each cell of honeycomb that is used gets just one egg. Eggs that are not fertilized will mature to become drones.

Eggs that are fertilized as they are laid by the queen become females. Some of these become queens, but most become workers. The third day after being laid, each egg dissolves and a tiny larvae is then released into the cell. For the next two or three days, the workers will visit thousands of times a day to feed the larvae a special "royal jelly." This food is made from a combination of enzymes from the bees' glands and the forage they have collected in the world outside their hive – pollen which is full of protein, and nectar which is full of carbohydrates.

On day four, however, the workers start to feed some female bees less often and giving them food which is not so rich in protein. These bees will become workers, living for a total of about five weeks, taking on a variety of roles before they die. Among the thousands of workers in any hive, some are nurses, some are house cleaners, some are guards, some are foragers, and some are mortuaries, removing the bodies of their fellow bees when they die.

Drones are fed a mixture even less rich than what the workers receive.

The bees that remain on the diet of royal jelly will become new queens, developing reproductive organs and glands which can produce hormones and pheromones. Only queens can lay fertilized eggs.

Developing queen larvae need more room than workers and drone bees, so it is relatively easy to find the larger queen cells in a hive – they hang down from the frames and are peanut-shaped.

Hatched and matured queens are also easy for an experienced observer to spot – they are much larger than the workers or the drones and they often lack the striped coloration.

Queens only leave the hive during brief periods of their lives. One of those times occurs shortly after a queen reaches maturity, when she goes off to find mates – about 16 days after she emerges from the brood cell. On her first few times away from the hive, she conducts short practice and reconnaissance flights to learn the lay of the land around her home. She'll need to know all the important landmarks around the hive in order to make it back safely after her mating flight.

After about a week of exploring, she heads out to find drones from other colonies.

Her successful mating flight may involve as many as 15-20 drones and usually takes place in an open meadow, park, or field. The sperm she gathers in her spermatheca during this time will have to last her the rest of her life, and a large amount of sperm cells gathered from a diverse group of bees will ensure her own longevity, as well as the health of the hive. Once her sperm supply has been depleted, she no longer gives off pheromone signals to the other bees, and she will be ousted and replaced by her hive mates. A strong queen who has the good fortune of gathering a large amount of sperm cells during her mating flights can live as long as six years, says Miller. (I also learn later that a good commercial breeder will make sure a queen has a lot of sperm cells; queens that are lacking them can cause a hive to fail very quickly.)

Unlike workers, a queen can sting multiple times – but rarely is found outside of a hive where she could sting humans. She will instead use her power to kill other queens that may emerge as she emerges from her brood cell.

Miller tells us that he often goes without a protective veil or gloves when doing bee work. He finds them annoying. His fingers, he says, are often swollen during spring from working his hives, but he's used to getting stung now.

Pheromones are key to the hive's orderliness and strength. The odors that each queen gives off are unique complex chemical compounds that present a kind of news brief to the other bees in the colony. They also act as a perfume tag that lets bees differentiate their own colony from another that may be in close proximity.

A healthy, vigorous queen gives off lots of these odorous pheromones as she is groomed and fed by her workers. The workers then further distribute those odors throughout their colony. If workers cannot detect that a queen is present through such pheromones, they will begin the process of nurturing a new queen from the existing eggs and larvae.

According to some researchers, bees have one of the most complex chemical communication systems in nature. The various processes which must happen in order for the new queen to emerge and acclimate to the colony demand a great deal of cooperative effort among all members of the hive.

The architecture which bees use to built their homes is also incredibly complex. The brood chamber is usually at the bottom of a hive. Above it, foraging worker bees will stash a supply of pollen they gather from plants. This pollen will be fed to the newly emerged workers and drones as they grow and mature.

Honey is usually stored just above the pollen, in capped cells of wax. The bees can build the wax on their own, but modern hives often include a pre-formed foundation which is believed to give the bees a head start, and therefore believed to shorten the time it takes to fill a hive with honey.

I'm shocked by the number of well-educated adults who mistakenly believe honey is something bees excrete – like a waste byproduct they produce as they poop. The reality is much more beautiful. Honey is a combination of nectar and enzymes extracted from their guts.

As honey sits in the warm hive, it is gently fanned by the bees' wings, causing moisture to evaporate, condensing the honey so its sugar content is intensified. Like wine, honey takes several weeks to cure, so it is essential that the bees gather a large amount of nectar early in the season – usually mid-spring in the Mid-Atlantic part of the US. Unlike wine, however, honey is not a product of fermentation, but rather evaporation and enzymatic actions.

Bees continue to need pollen and nectar all summer. Without a big deposit of nectar early in the season, there will not be enough surplus honey ready for either the bees or the beekeeper to enjoy by the time the cooler months arrive.

For this reason, it is optimal to get a new hive up and running at the very earliest part of the spring. Beekeepers often dream of having a beeyard near large tracts of trees that bloom and produce nectar in the spring, such as plums, lindens, or tulip trees to take advantage of peak nectar flows.

Miller thinks urban beekeepers often have a real advantage, for in a city the nectar can flow earlier and longer than other locations due to the urban microclimates. There's often lots of food available in the form of tree blossoms and weeds, but there aren't always a lot of other pollinators at those flowers.

Bees can also make combs in hollowed trees instead of hives maintained by a human beekeeper, setting up colonies that sometimes last for decades. When tree hollows can't be found, they also use empty attic spaces or hollow walls in buildings. In the US, where honey bees are not native, these colonies are referred to as "feral" and their discovery almost always causes a stir. People find it discomforting to discover that several thousand bees have set up housekeeping in their building, and removal can be very expensive.

As the afternoon workshop continues on at Miller's house, my brain feels saturated. It is a lot to take in for one day, and I suspect that if I were going to keep bees myself, rather than just be an observer from the sidelines this season, I'd actually need a seven-session course – if only to give myself a rest in between topics.

As if sensing our growing fatigue, Miller offers a piece of advice from his three years of experience. He's set up 30 hives around the city through his business, and helped a hundred people in DC get started with beekeeping so far, with hopes of helping another hundred in the coming year. The secrets to success, he thinks, involve a blend of patience, confidence, good sources of information, a bit of intuition, and sometimes laziness. It is possible, he says, to fret too much over a hive.

Someone asks him if he treats his hives with chemicals. Sometimes, he responds. Bees can get sick, and just like when you have sick kids, sometimes you treat them with needed medicine. But he tries to be as chemical-free as possible.

"Our view is to do it sparingly and responsibly."

For our break, snacks are served. Some members of the class go out to move their cars or fill their meters. Kate Lee brings out a mixture of red wine and mead which tastes like port with a bit of a zing. When I ask her why she loves bees, she says with a smile, "I find them very relaxing to watch."

I agree emphatically. Also, I think they look somewhat like teddy bears, although I can't explain why.

She laughs and says, yes, they do look kind of snuggly somehow.

In the dining room the piles of wood and the tools and cords are waiting. Miller reconvenes to start building supers for Langstroth-style hives, which is what the majority of backyard beekeepers in the US use. Some people say Langstroth hives look like layered wedding cakes. To me they are more like mini-skyscrapers made of wood. Each layer or story of the beehive is called a super. The bottom super holds the brood chamber. Above it, in slightly smaller supers, the bees will store their honey on hanging frames of pre-pressed foundation made of wax or plastic. Beekeepers monitor their bees through the season and add more supers as they see fit – keeping up with the bees' progress but not getting too far ahead of the colony's needs.

Another hive style known as the Kenyan top-bar is slowly gaining in popularity, but remains controversial. Some feel top-bars are harder to manage adequately and their shape may provoke more swarming. Others argue that top-bar hives allow the bees to live in a way that is closer to how they might live in their native habitat – the interior space is less restricted by prescribed dimensions or the pre-pressed foundations. The small amount of research does not show a significant difference to the health of the bees.

Everyone grabs tools and begins to piece together two supers which they will take home. Miller's lovely dining room, which belongs in a home design magazine most of the year suddenly feels like the New Yankee Workshop, as hammers and power screwdrivers are noisily put to work.

Monica finishes hers first. She laughs when she realizes she'll have to carry the 15" x 20" wooden boxes home via the Foggy Bottom Metro stop, several blocks and two neighborhoods to the east. She had ridden the Metro to that nearest stop and walked several miles to get to Miller's house in order to justify skipping the gym that morning. "It's going to be a long awkward walk and ride home for me!"

Others talk about how excited they are to get started – Miller will be travelling to Georgia to get bees for everyone, and they all are dreaming of the day when they can fill their supers with packages containing a new queen and her workers.

Before I leave, Miller uses a kitchen knife to slice off an enormous chunk of beeswax soap he's made. "You are more than welcome to come again tomorrow." He hates for anyone to miss out on the fun.

Back in 2012 Miller was featured in a documentary called *Capital Buzz*. On camera, his two school-aged daughters told the filmmaker that their dad began beekeeping because he was having a midlife crisis. He delights in showing people the film and the scene where his daughters, seated on the front steps of their town house, emphatically repeat how much happier he's been since he started his hives. It strikes me that perhaps keeping bees has become a way for him to connect with people in a city that can sometimes seem focused on intense and high-pressure work. As I walk out the door and down his front steps I hear the rest of the workshop members laughing and talking. This is, I think, how Miller keeps it "real" in a city often known for insincerity and political distrust.

I look back to see if – from half a block away – I can spot his beehives on the roof of his historic townhouse. I can't. I regret that we weren't able to climb the ladder from his bathtub to the bees today.

Only a few weeks before Jeff Miller's workshop, the legality of keeping bees in DC was still unclear. Regulations stated that you couldn't keep bees or a hive within 500 feet of a place of human habitation. But an addendum also stated that the regulation did not apply to bees confined to a hive or property.

Debates ensued: What did confined mean? Did the one part of the law totally negate the other? Were there contraptions which would confine your bees without harming them? Would that make a beehive legal? Was this law unfair to working-class beekeepers who often live on smaller properties and favor some wards of the city over others?

If you ask her about it today, Toni Burnham is quick to say she was one of many in the nation's capitol who wanted to keep bees in the city. But a lot of people in the DC government and DC beekeeping will tell you that she was the one who forged relationships with those in power. She was the one that presented it as something that would benefit the entire city. She was the one that led the charge to make beekeeping legal.

"It was a rising tide," she reflects. "But I charged a lot."

Seven years ago, Burnham was stuck in a traffic jam listening to a BBC broadcast about beekeepers working their hives on a rooftop in London. Intrigued and excited by the prospect of beekeeping at her Capitol Hill home, she signed up for a course in a nearby suburb and within weeks found herself placing two stout Langstroth hives on her rooftop deck.

"Everything changed in 2005," she says with a grin and a sigh. "Everything."

Bees, she quickly realized, gave her a new perspective on life. Before, she had no sense of what was happening in the outside environs. After she put up her hives, she felt every temperature change and smelled each new type of blossom as it perfumed the air of the city's streets. She felt grounded by the flying insects. She felt connected to her neighborhood in a whole new way. And she also made thousands of new friends – both in insect form and human form.

"I really believe that bees go a long way toward taking the fear and guilt out of our relationship with the environment. Bees are messengers between animal and plant life. They are the great connector between two kingdoms, and our only insect partner."

The dearth of information on urban bees is hard to imagine in the present day, when every beekeeper seems to know web design, and Googling the word "bees" fills your screen with hits. But in the days when blogging was still a new idea and high-speed internet access often a rare commodity, Burnham found scant resources on the world wide web about honey bees – urban or otherwise. She was forced to buy books or call people or attend classes and meetings to ask questions in person.

In order to fill the knowledge void she began to blog, keeping a diary-style site called City Bees. Her inaugural post began quietly enough with a photo of the bees exploring the inside of her new, empty frames. "I am in awe of the girls," she wrote reverently at the top.

At first, she wrote her words anonymously, refusing to reveal the name of her city or the exact location of her neighborhood.

"We are not trying to be cute but just now we aren't telling. We are in a city, and have lots of neighbors, some of whom may not be thrilled by their 20,000 new community members (too many killer bee movies, I think). Plan is to: 1) make two colonies survive and thrive through this year and next winter; and 2) tell the neighbors about this project when we can hand them a bottle of honey as well as the news that they have safely lived a whole year with it."

Although she set out to become neither a celebrity nor an advocate, she knew right away she wanted to work on legalization. Her idea may have been to discuss beekeeping online without revealing her true identity, but her enthusiasm for the bees drew a new community of people to her both online and off.

She quickly became very bad at staying secret, especially since she was repeatedly asked to talk to garden clubs, church groups, and neighborhood associations about the importance of urban bees. In 2007 she was even interviewed on a local radio show. She began to do bee programs for kids at a local elementary school. She taught classes on beekeeping in the city and just outside it, working with associations in the counties surrounding Washington's urban core. She had trouble keeping her love of beekeeping to herself.

Rather than offer advice, she confided to her readers about her nervousness, often posting shout-outs for help and input from more experienced beekeepers of the world. They answered her questions, and their posted responses helped many who were beekeeping for the first time.

"You know, at some point it must be possible to get to know this beekeeping business well enough not to fear the worst with every move, or suspect that every step taken is a Terrible Mistake," she wrote in her third week of beekeeping.

As Burnham's adventure progressed and her confidence grew, so did the problem of Colony Collapse Disorder (CCD). Mainstream news coverage of the bee deaths increased, and people searched the web looking for info, answers, comfort – all of which could be found on Burnham's blog. She wasn't writing about CCD, but she offered a window into a world where bees were thriving in spite of the problem. Even people who had no interest in beekeeping were drawn to read what she wrote. And the beekeepers themselves found a way to connect with each other and the public.

She formed a strong network of beekeepers in her own city and beyond. Through that network her desire to teach others became strengthened.

Burnham is a tall, slim woman with a soft, raspy voice, dark, wavy hair, and a tendency to get poetic and philosophical about her hobby – even when talking about the technical and scientific side of things. "I'm not any better beekeeper than the people who've been here forever, I'm just noisier," she jokes.

Although she dismisses any kind of romantic or spiritual notions about her bees, she seems to find inspiration in their sense of order.

A really big change occurred in Washington in 2008 when Barack Obama was elected to office and brought his wife and children to live with him in the White House, just a short distance from Burnham's own neighborhood.

Anyone who has ever lived in DC will tell you that a change of presidents can mean a change for the whole city. New staffers are hired to work at lobbying firms, new initiatives are started based on the new administration's interests, and there are lots of new ways to network and interact for those who are lifelong residents. Politicos who love jargon describe these changes as being times of "new cross-pollination."

What no one realized – including Burnham – was that this time the change of administration would also mean similar changes and opportunities for DC's honey bees. They, too, were about to have a lot of new opportunities and share some moments in the limelight – and Burnham was going to get a front-stage, inside-the-hive view of the whole thing and share it with her readers.

Throughout Obama's campaign, his wife Michelle had repeatedly emphasized the importance of eating healthy, locally-grown food. As soon as she arrived at the presidential residence, she began to carve out a thriving victory garden in the midst of the White House's enormous green lawn to showcase the importance of eating fresh vegetables for the public – especially for families with young children. Eleanor Roosevelt had planted one herself, during World War II. This time, however, the war was against childhood obesity.

When plans for the garden were unveiled to the public in early March of 2009, Mrs. Obama told the *Washington Post* that although the garden would provide food for the first family's meals and some of its formal dinners, its most important role would be educational. Honey bees, which would be brought in to help pollinate the 55 planned crops, would be tended by Charlie Brandts.

Brandts was selected because he was already a known entity at the White House; he had been a staff carpenter there for several decades. He is a very shy man, and at the time was relatively new to beekeeping.

"Every beekeeper in the world wanted to help Charlie. But I just happened to be local, and could be available at a moment's notice in the middle of the week. If they were going to gather honey on say a Thursday, I could be there – even at a moment's notice." Burnham's friendly, open willingness to face the tough questions about the safety of bees, their bounty, and their limitations attracted the attention of White House staff members, and she was asked to draft talking points on urban beekeeping.

She wasn't sure what to expect of the White House as a place for bees to live, but was pleasantly surprised to find upon her first visit to the grounds that the White House lawn is actually not all grass. There are many historic and mature trees – oaks, maples, hollies, lindens – and lots of perennial and annual plants available for bees to use as forage. "Turns out it's a 20-acre reserve of proper plants that need pollination – a profoundly rich environment for the bees."

Although she never got to see the official residence nor meet the first family, she did get to see a lot of the backstage areas, like the florist shop, the conservator's office, and the seamstress's studio. Once, the staff had to ask her to wait inside until the president's helicopter had finished departing the grounds. To make up for the inconvenience she was given leftover cookies and pastries from the kitchen.

"What's to complain about?" she recalled thinking as she ate the goodies. "It is fun to go to the White House."

In addition to the little perks of the task at hand, the White House was also full of Burnham's favorite thing: people who wanted to learn about bees.

"You know what's really funny," she says with a giggle, "you have these people walking around with belt-fed weapons, and every once in a while one of those is sort of interested in the bees but they aren't allowed to pay attention, and of course I want to teach anyone who comes within ten feet."

Even so, there were the sharp reminders that security was serious business. Once she accidentally took a wrong turn down a hallway – putting her on course to enter the private areas of the building without proper clearance.

"Suddenly I was face to face with these two enormous Secret Service guys the size of the Twin Towers and I actually squealed a little high pitch noise and ran away," she laughs.

That March she posted pictures of the White House hives to her blog, wanting to share the excitement over the "First Bees" with the world's beekeeping community. Most of the photos had been taken by Brandts from inside the grounds – places where Burnham herself did not have clearance to walk.

Some revealed interesting particulars – such as the fact that hives placed on the White House grounds have be secured in place by ratchet belts in order to prevent accidental tip-overs during helicopter take offs.

Brandts also made education a priority – making sure to paint the outside of the hive supers in two different colors. Burnham wrote on her blog that he "felt it could be education-al for the public to observe the process of reversing, as he manages the hive for swarm control."

That bit of info would soon prove helpful as swarms de-scended upon a tree at the opposite, northwest end of the White House lawn in April, just behind where the press corps set up their cameras each day to do their reporting. It was im-mediately obvious to beekeepers that this swarm was not from the official hives. Those bees had settled in to take care of their new queen and were happily working the frames. The swarm, some believed, was possibly from a feral bee colony living close to the White House.

As the workers busily surrounded their new queen on the shrubbery, Brandts emerged from the building wearing his official White House beekeeping veil and shirt and carrying a large, cardboard box. He carefully used a pair of scissors to cut the branch where the swarm had balled together and gath-ered up the bees for safe delivery to a new hive.

I would wager that no other swarm in history has been more photographed than that one. Some of the world's best news photographers were standing by, waiting for political news from the White House Press Secretary. Reading through news reports about it online now, I wonder just how slow a news day that must have been; it was as if no one had ever known a swarm could happen in an urban area.

Soon they would all learn just how common swarms could be, though. Burnham herself was present when yet another ball of bees appeared a few days later. She had been at the White House helping Brandts check on the health of his new charges. Opening the supers that April day, they saw only minimal presence of Varroa mites and a gentle, contented queen at work, which was pleasing. As they tidied up and were making their goodbyes, Brandts received a staff call − near the north gate a small swarm had taken up in a bush and needed immediate attention. Burnham offered to take it and re-home it with a friend who had been seeking a replacement queen.

When a third swarm was discovered sometime later that spring at the White House, Burnham was again called and asked to assist. Although she wanted to be helpful, she was slated to volunteer elsewhere. She suggested that they call another local beekeeper instead.

Her beekeeping colleagues and friends ribbed her. "They all said, 'Oh! Its got to be old hat to go help out at the White House!'"

In truth, celebrity beekeeping on Pennsylvania Avenue wasn't always fun for Burnham and Brandts. Being in the limelight meant having every beekeeping decision questioned by veteran keepers, sometimes publicly. The swarms weren't helping either; although all the beekeepers knew those swarms would have happened even without the erection of the new hives, many in the general public just didn't understand what was happening with each new occurrence. At one point several far-right religious organizations took the opportunity to note that President Obama's arrival in the White House was being marked by bad omens and biblical plagues, implying that he might just be the antichrist.

The combination of the much-publicized swarms and the much-publicized beehives made a lot of veteran DC beekeepers very nervous. When the White House beehive was first erected, questions about its legality emerged very quickly, and the beekeeping law was dissected carefully in the local news. Those who hadn't realized beekeeping was illegal in the city were suddenly talking about it. Beekeepers in all wards began to squirm under the scrutiny.

Still, there were some very good things that came out of the increased attention, no matter how uncomfortable it made the beekeepers themselves.

The Obamas were a family with young children, and although Mrs. Obama had developed the garden to educate the public about healthy food choices, the inclusion of the bees made a statement about both the insects' importance and their relative safety. Not too far away from the hives stood a swing set the Obamas had installed for their girls to use. Honey was natural, and yummy. Bees were important. But bees were *also safe*. That message was only further reinforced later when numerous school groups were asked to help tend and then harvest the vegetable garden with the First Lady. If it was okay for the President and his family to be around bees, it must be okay for other families, too.

The hives also proved that bees were popular with the public, capturing their attention in ways that no one had anticipated. Instead of fear or dismay, many expressed envy, wishing that they, too, could have hives in their own backyard. Many inquired about buying the honey as a souvenir when they visited the city. Eddie Gehman Kohan, author of the Obama Foodorama blog, noted that "White House Honey" was one of the top ten search terms used on her blog, ranking even higher than "Barack Obama eating."

In June of 2009 a popular columnist named Petula Dvorak wrote a long article about Burnham for the *Washington Post*, describing her as "bucking the furtive, don't-ask-don't-tell ethos of city beekeeping by lobbying for legislation that protects and encourages beekeeping."

Although she had already "come out" to the mayor and other officials in the city earlier that year, Burnham still hadn't really told her own neighbors what she was doing up on her roof. Dvorak's piece caused her a lot of worry, but also eventually brought a sense of relief. She could finally talk about the bees openly and begin to discuss new possibilities for beekeeping with the city at large in an honest, frank manner.

The post she made to her blog that day might be one of the most beautiful essays ever written by an urban beekeeper:

> *Whether we planned on it or not, one of the windows that the bees seem always to open looks out on a world of natural miracles and wonder. And worries*

and responsibilities and joy as we try to help them thrive in a world that seems just packed full of challenges and threats and flowery opportunities.

Newspaper articles appearing now will perhaps make many more thousands of people aware of the bees on my roof and in yards and in flowers all over this city. My own personal hives have never been so exposed, and I hope I have not done wrong by them in sharing them with you. We live in a world that is full of fear, and I can certainly understand why something so unknown and seemingly out of place could cause concern. But we are in so much more danger without ties to the world and each other, without a community to turn to and ties that reach all the way into the world of bugs, plants, and critters.

I cannot tell you how good it feels to have a relationship that links me to a world of flowers and sunshine.

By that fall, more than 140 pounds of honey had been harvested from the White House hives. Special glass jars were made for it, filled, and distributed to the spouses of leaders attending the G20 Pittsburgh Summit in September.

But while the honey gleaned from hives at 1600 Pennsylvania Avenue shone under the spotlight, the legal status of honey production elsewhere in the capital still remained in question.

Rather than be discouraged by the legal ambiguity, Burnham felt fueled to teach even more. By 2010 she was openly advertising DC Parks and Recreation classes about the topic throughout the city, even though she had to admit to her blog followers that "beekeeping in DC is in an ambiguous, unprotected legal environment." She never turned down an invitation to speak – if she herself couldn't make it, she'd find the group requesting information another beekeeper.

People were out there beekeeping either way, she figured. They sure had better be doing a good, careful job to keep it safe. Bees that aren't tended carefully can sometimes cause incidents, and if a child or some other vulnerable person were stung badly, or an unsteady hive fell on someone from a rooftop, she knew it could really be hard to undo the bad publicity.

"I was on pins and needles," she says. "I was worried that we were going to have some horrendous incident before we even got started."

Outside the realm of beekeeping, urban attitudes about all kinds of agricultural activities were changing. Locavore eating became chic. Several articles decried the more impoverished neighborhoods in DC as "food deserts" – places where there was no way to obtain healthy groceries. Activists called for the formation of community gardens and better access to locally grown food. Some wanted chickens, but the laws regarding chicken coops in the city turned out to be just as contradictory and confusing as those regarding bees.

Burnham strongly suspects that anger over the outcome of some legal wrangling regarding chicken coops was an embarrassment to some city staff members, especially since Mayor Vincent Gray had announced in July 2011 that he wanted to make the city "the healthiest, greenest and most livable city in the United States."

"For years there's been kind of contest among DC's mayors to see who can be greener-than-thou," Burnham notes, so when the mayor began working on his "Sustainable DC plan, a renewed effort was made to include urban farming with other popular environmental ideas.

"There's a little bit of dry cleaning, and a little bit of day care centers... and it was like what else can we put in this? And bees went in."

The plan was ambitious, aiming to put 20 acres of land under cultivation for food in the city by the year 2032. It included the development of five acres of orchards and the installation of educational gardens at half of the city's schools But farms, the city's planners realized, need bees. So the plan also included discreet language to make beekeeping legal as of Earth Day, April 22, 2013.

"We want to create a holistic understanding of where food comes from, and erase some of the separation between the producer of food and the person who consumes it," says Karim D. Marshall, a Legislative and Regulatory Analyst for the District's Department of the Environment.

Urban farms and access to fresh food can be an equity issue and urban farms – even small ones – can be transformative for neighborhoods. Georgetown might have ample food available for its prosperous residents, but there are other neighborhoods where poverty remains a stubborn problem. And in those areas, food – especially fresh produce – is almost impossible to find for sale at any price. But farms, the city's planners think, need bees.

"There has been a greater understanding of how bees work with the urban environment," Karim says. "Urban agriculture depends on urban apiculture and beekeeping. You can't have a crop without something to pollinate it."

There was never the large legal battle that some had feared and almost no backlash from the greater community. In total there were three full pages devoted to the bees' new legal status. They would need to be confined to Langstroth-style hives, and keepers would be limited to having four per one-quarter acre. All hives would also have to be registered with the city, and anyone found to have Africanized honey bees would be subject to having their hives and equipment impounded. The law, Burnham thinks, is a great start.

For her, the bees also help to validate her city as livable and lovable. It annoys her greatly that some will call her "crazy" for living downtown. Many still think of the city as it was 20 and 30 years ago – when corruption and violent crime were more pervasive. There are still some problems, but the city has changed and evolved and there's good to be found. Neighbors who care about each other, who make connections. People still think of it as a place where you can't walk the streets safely, but she points to the beauty of things like the linden trees lining Massachusetts Avenue or the 200 year-old maple that stands in front of her townhome.

Burnham also notes with pride that while scores of bees in the Maryland and Virginia suburbs struggle to survive, her bees and the bees in many other urban DC hives stay relatively content and healthy. She has not replaced a queen to date.

"My girls take care of it themselves, and remain wickedly healthy." Her honey continues to be plentiful and delicious, too. She thinks that very fact that the bees can find health and vitality on her roof is proof of the city's new found vibrancy.

Besides covering urban beekeeping for *Bee Culture* magazine she's training members of the District's Department of Transportation to form a swarm response team to re-home bee colonies found in city trees already slated for removal by arborists. Although other places throughout the US report almost no feral hives are being found in hollow trees, Burnham finds many colonies found throughout the city's trees every season. Those colonies often show evidence of having survived for four or five years without management – which she noted is more like it was in the US before the advent of the Varroa mite. She suspects the feral bees have evolved to match the local urban environment and are making very strong, healthy and resilient queens. "It seems like something is happening around communal choices that makes it possible for a normal feral bee to live. That means that's a lot of things that people are doing right."

She hopes to continue making the US into more of a "pro-pollinator environment." She tells the story of a community center in one neighborhood where they had done a lot of work over the years educating the staff about the importance of bees and their value to the city. If a kid wanted to know more she'd let them try on her veil, and at the end of the season she'd drop off jars of honey for the staff to enjoy. In 2012, when a monster swarm erupted just behind the center's well-used and crowded basketball courts she was called. The amazing thing, she realized, was how much the community trusted her.

"They stood back and waited for us to take care of it. Everyone's there with their phones up taking pictures, and what could have been a moment of urban terror and screaming instead became like Marlin Perkins' *Wild Kingdom*." It's those kinds of moments that prompt her to keep telling anyone and everyone about the bees and beekeeping.

2

Women in Backyard Beekeeping

My friend Laura Elkins has kept bees for six years – first behind a very small, tidy garden at the back of her urban row home in DC and now in a much more suburban new house just outside the Capital Beltway. I've stopped by her house to ask what its like to be a woman keeping bees these days. A surprisingly large number of women are taking on the hobby, and I'm wondering why.

It's a funny thing to interview a close friend. There are things you assume about one another, but never directly ask. To know Laura is to know her bees, but I never really talked to her about how it felt to be a beekeeper nor how she got started.

Laura, who was a middle school teacher before deciding to stay home with her own kids, confesses that she used to feel like a bit of a conversation killer at parties. "I'd go some where before I started beekeeping and people would say, 'What do you do?' and I'd say, I'm a mom. And then people would say, *oh*." Then there'd be a long pause.

Now a lot of people – including her own husband – introduce her as a mom who keeps bees, and the reaction is totally different. "It's like I have a little bit of a coolness factor now."

I argue that it isn't the bees that made her cool. Quite the opposite, Laura makes the bees seem cool.

The bees take work. In some seasons she spends hours doing "bee stuff" – checking for problems, monitoring the bees' needs and their health, and providing fresh frames or extra supers. Her commitment to the bees and the way she incorporates them seamlessly into her family life are both impressive. At her house, your kids inevitably end up playing outside around the bees. In the summer you might decide to pick raspberries from her bushes, where the bees also like to forage. You might find yourself in a costume at Halloween, milling around in the garden eating Frankenstein cookies just a few feet from the hives. Even sitting here this morning at her big rustic kitchen table, we can see the beehives out the window, two small rectangular towers packed in for their winter rest. She's always aware of what's going on out there, always aware that her bees are working away at the honeycombs.

Beekeeping, she says, has some similarities to parenting. "My first year I would just sit out in the winter and look at them and think: I am responsible for those 10,000 lives, and I would get so overwhelmed."

Had she done everything right to prepare for the season? Was the queen inside doing what she needed to do? What if something in there was going terribly wrong? "And all my male friends who were beekeeping would be like: They're bees. They don't care, *you're not their mother*."

It did remind her of being a mother, because in the beginning everything was so new and unfamiliar.

Over time she relaxed, learning to follow the lead of both her bees and her children. Now her children are bigger, and her bee colony is bigger. Maybe it's easier to worry less about older kids and established beehives.

Who knows, she says with a shrug. Maybe beekeeping taught her to worry less about life in general.

Laura had never intended to be a beekeeper, but another mom asked to station a colony in Laura's yard because hers was too shady. Laura's yard, which was just blocks from Walter Reed Medical Center, was tiny and urban but it was sunny and her vegetable garden would benefit greatly from the bees' presence.

As a doctor, Laura's husband worried about safety. What if someone had an allergic reaction to a sting? He insisted they buy an EpiPen in case anyone had a reaction and needed immediate care. Over time, though, he got more used to the bees.

Nothing bad happened and it wasn't a big deal. Besides, the honey was great.

The woman who owned the bees seemed to often forget they were there, coming only rarely to check on them. Laura was pretty sure they needed more attention than they were getting. Another friend's husband who was a beekeeper seemed to be working in his hives a lot.

"I didn't want the bees to die. I kind of knew that some stuff needed to be happening with them, I just didn't know exactly what."

Eventually, the owner announced she was getting out of the hobby and intended to sell her supplies. Laura took over, leaving the bees in place.

She's learned to better distance herself emotionally from the bees. Although her parenting style and her beekeeping style may have evolved in tandem, the comparison stops when it comes to healthcare. She uses no chemicals on her bees. She tried it the first year but found that working with the stuff made her miserable, and she wasn't sure it was necessary. Bees have lived for thousands and thousands of years without any help from humans. They innately know what they need to do, Laura thinks. So, for the past five years she's gone for a natural approach: No chemicals.

People make the analogy that they treat their bees with chemicals just as they'd treat their kids with medicine or vaccines, justifying their use of chemicals. Others say it to justify not using chemicals. One beekeeper we both know foregoes both chemicals for her bees and vaccines and medicines for her children, believing neither is healthy or necessary.

Even thinking about that makes Laura shake her head. "I'm really big into vaccines for my kids. If I lose a beehive, I'm sad, but its okay. But if I lose one of those guys," she says, pointing towards her children's photos, "that is not okay."

Is that ironic somehow, she asks me, or a kind of philosophical disconnect? Maybe, but bees aren't kids. They just aren't.

Perhaps how one keeps their bees is more about gender than parental status. In general the men she knows often derive a different kind of pleasure or take a different kind of pride in their bees than the women, as if some men are more into it for the numbers.

In the fall, when everyone comes to that first meeting after the honey's been harvested, men in the local beekeeping club swagger in announcing "I got 200 pounds!" as if they are talking about weight lifting or the girth of their muscles.

The women, by contrast, ask each other, "So how are your hives doing?"

Beekeeping courses, Laura notes, are still more often taught by men. Women come in to do the session on the "products of the hive," like making candles or lip balm. Men are more likely talk about their use of wooden shims, or some new contraption they've built to improve their hive, especially if it involves power tools.

The women are keeping bees in a different way because of what they're physically able to do. Frames of honey can get heavy, so women sometimes buy smaller frames or have fewer colonies of bees.

It just feels different when you talk with another woman about beekeeping, she says. Less competitive and more supportive.

One night in early April of 2013, I meet up with Laura and her good friend G. at a meeting of the Montgomery County Beekeeping Association (MCBA) whose Master Beekeepers are "there to help you with your beekeeping problems, or even to simply give moral support when needed, and promote better beekeeping," according to their brochure.

The MCBA holds its regular meetings at the Brookside Nature Center, just outside of Washington, DC in Wheaton, where a large forested regional park is surrounded by urban sprawl. To the north, horse farms and huge suburban lots dominate the landscape. To the south, it is high rise apartments, aging post-war neighborhoods with small lots, and the Capital Beltway. The beekeepers who join MCBA are drawn from a variety of environments.

G., Laura tells me, is one of the exceptions to her statements about some of the macho tendencies among some male beekeepers; he's often provided invaluable advice and help to her as she learned beekeeping, even helping her move her hives from the city to the suburbs earlier in the year. Like Laura, he and his wife homeschool, and like Laura his beeyard is relatively urban.

I ask the two of them what "better beekeeping" means to the MCBA members. They both laugh. It can mean different things to different people, my friends warn. Standing next to the snack table munching on carrots, Laura explains it to me this way: "They say if you ask three beekeepers for advice on a problem, you'll come away with five opinions on how to solve it."

G. chortles with sarcasm, puffing up his shoulders and pointing his thumbs at his chest in mock bravado. "Yeah, but no matter what everyone else tells you, I'm the only one doing it the RIGHT way."

Even so, when the meeting is called to order the atmosphere proves extremely collegial. As one man passes around spoons and some "homestyle" honey he brought back from a recent vacation in Brazil, about 50 people take their seats for discussion. I note that about a third of the people present are women.

"Okay, so what's everyone seeing in their hives?" the club's president, George Meyer, calls out to the crowd.

"Losses, lots of losses!" A show of hands provides evidence that man is not the only one. About half of the room have lost some of their bees over the winter.

"It makes me sad," says Meyer. "Here it is April and everything's going crazy out there... It's all bursting into bloom out there and it's awful to not have your bees doing their thing."

As many of the club members groan in agreement, one woman in her mid-twenties raises her hand tentatively.

She tells the room, "I'm new, and I made it through the winter. My first hive, it survived. They made it!"

"Yay! That's great!" calls an older woman who looks to be about 60, reaching across the aisle to pat the younger woman on the shoulder. The two immediately switch seats to be next to each other and trade names, quietly beginning a lengthy conversation in whispers about the newbie's success and her bees.

"Not me, and I have no idea why, but my bees – they all left," says a man up front despondently. "Is that Colony Collapse?"

A discussion ensues about how to diagnose the problem, its definitions, and how to get his hive up in time for coming nectar flow. Someone offers him "a split" of their bees – some of their own hive's surplus – provided he can come pick them up at the right time.

"Is it worth it to wrap the hives to insulate them in the winter?" someone else calls from the back. "I've heard they do that up north where it gets really cold every year."

"I do it," says another man up in the front row, taking off his baseball cap and running his hands through a shock of white hair. "But I don't know if it's really helping anything. I have had good luck with my hives this year, though."

The nature of the questions asked at the MCBA – and other meetings like it all over the country – point to the changing nature of beekeeping. What was once a fairly certain outcome has become a cause for celebration. Keeping bees used to be a much easier task, with bees regenerating themselves fairly regularly and plentiful honey flows a sure thing each summer. Now bees are dying in huge numbers. One group from the

University of Maryland found that roughly one-third of all the managed honey bee colonies in the US are being lost each year. Meyer describes the research to the group, and urges people to get in touch with those taking bee loss surveys so their losses can be counted, too.

Listening, I wonder, if the women bring a more supportive atmosphere to these clubs, or if people who beekeep suddenly find themselves more humbled by these mysterious bee deaths. Maybe *everyone* here needs more support and encouragement.

Although the female bees very much outnumber the males inside the colonies, outside it used to be almost all men doing the human side of honey bee work.

In her well-known memoir about beekeeping, *A Book of Bees,* Sue Hubbell noted that she was very likely the only woman beekeeping in all of Missouri in 1988, although she could not figure out why, since it was such a profitable and rewarding full-time job.

Women beekeepers were so unknown in the areas where Hubbell kept her hives, many of the people in her own county never even called her by name, preferring instead to refer to her simply as Bee Lady, because a "middle-aged woman in baggy coveralls who smells of burnt baling twine is a standout in any crowd," she wrote. Now, I doubt anyone in Missouri or Maryland would even blink at the sight.

Kim Flottam, editor-in-chief of *Bee Culture* magazine, tells me there are no official statistics to mark the changing demographics of beekeepers. The University of Maryland has estimated that there is a total of approximately 2.62 million colonies in the country. Rough estimates note that about 100 of those are large-scale commercial beekeepers and about 5,000-7,000 are people who have anywhere from 50 to 300 or 400 colonies as a business. There's an unknown number of hobbyists who have anywhere from 1 to 20 hives.

Very little is known about the people behind those statistics, although Flottam's staff is always interested in following the beekeeping trends. His publication, which has been around since 1873 and calls itself "The Magazine of American Beekeeping," currently has a subscription base of about 16,500 readers. Staying relevant is a top priority for both the publisher and its advertisers, so they send out a survey each year to their readers. But Flottam confesses this is self-selecting, and is far from being a comprehensive accounting of all of the people who beekeep in the US.

Beekeepers in most states are required to register with their state departments of agriculture, but no one pulls those numbers into an aggregate. People pick up beekeeping in a myriad of ways and no one – not the USDA, nor beekeeping associations, nor professional groups – keeps official demographic numbers for the whole US.

Flottam recalls that when he first learned beekeeping back in the '80s, about 95% were male, and mostly over the age of 50. Now, there are a lot more people in their thirties and forties who are taking up the hobby, and about 70% of them are female. A large part of the growth has come from cities.

"The number of women getting into beekeeping has increased dramatically and the age has dropped and that has changed a lot of things." The changes, he tells me, are positive.

For one thing, women are demanding better protective gear from the industry.

"When I started keeping bees I'd go out with a keeper and he'd say put on this veil, and I'd put on a veil that didn't work very well, and a hat that didn't fit very well, and he'd say: Tough it out. It was a macho kind of thing."

Now, he says, those teaching beginner classes, including Flottam himself, stress the need to feel comfortable and remain calm. A good sturdy veil that fits well is integral, because someone who feels safe and secure is also going to feel more confident, even as a beginner.

"If you don't feel safe when you go out to work your bees – if you are reluctant to go out there – you're not going to go out there and you're not going be a beekeeper. So now the protective gear is wonderful compared to when I got started. You can literally be bulletproof if you want to be."

He also notes that those who sell wooden supers for the Langstroth-style hives have seen a huge increase in the demand for smaller boxes. A major super with 10 or 12 frames can weigh 120 pounds once the bees have filled it with honey, and lifting such a thing can be hard. A smaller super with eight frames can be much easier to manage.

The smaller hives may not allow someone to harvest as large a crop of honey, but that is often less of a concern to many joining the hobby now – those not intending to make money from selling a crop in the fall.

"Thirty years ago, a lot of people who got into bees it looked as, 'I'm going to start slow, I'm going to build it as a sideline business, and when I retire I'm going to have it going, and it is going to pay for my retirement. It was a serious business. People took it seriously. People who are doing it now are doing it just as seriously but they aren't looking at growing it as a business for the most part."

In fact, in his how-to book *The Backyard Beekeeper,* Flottam notes that many successful beekeepers often come to rue a surplus of honey, comparing it to a garden full of zucchini. It can be hard to live with dozens and dozens of bottles stacked high for months on end – especially in urban houses lacking pantry space.

Newer beekeepers of both sexes are often seeking not income, but a connection with nature. They also want control of what is going on their table. Bees and chickens and lots of other urban agricultural trends are all a part of a movement toward food independence, he says.

"The trends of smaller boxes and urban beekeeping have fed off of each other."

A full-size 10 or 12-frame hive can weigh somewhere between 500-600 pounds by the end of a successful season. Many urban rooftops can't support that much weight but do fine with a smaller hive of reduced proportions and eight frames per super.

There are also more pre-made, fully assembled boxes of varying sizes being sold now, which appeals to city dwellers who have less time or space for woodworking.

A century ago, when Langstroth hives were being sold by mail to middle class farm families, it made sense to sell hives unassembled. People who wanted to beekeep had down time in the colder seasons. They had space for woodworking projects in their barn or backyard, and they were used to working with their hands and had tools hanging in their sheds. Manufacturers were also able to keep costs low by shipping the hives unassembled. So over time premade boxes largely fell out of favor and became pretty hard to find from any source in the US. People ordered the parts and put the boxes together themselves.

But now, at the beginning of the 21st century, beekeepers often don't have the time, the tools, or the skills for putting a hive together from the ground up. People living in a three-room apartment in New York City, for example, haven't got the room for assembly. They also don't have large families full of children who can help. So companies have responded to a market demand for pre-assembled hives, which makes Flottam – a busy man who confesses he has no woodworking skills – rejoice.

"I'm not a woodworker; I don't want to be. I want to be a beekeeper," he says.

"All the manufacturers will tell you this in a heart beat: 'I'm not making the stuff I used to make and I'm not make it the same way.' What's changed it has been the new people who are getting into beekeeping, and from my perspective it has been very fun to watch."

There are a few women who have taken the idea of protective bee clothing and pushed it to new realms. Bobbie Meyzen, a beekeeper working on a thirty-four acre antique apple orchard in Connecticut, is one of those. She sells a kind of bee couture online.

Meyzen's hats are striking for their feminine appeal. Hand-sewn onto a base of a classic pith-style straw hat, they seem unapologetically girly, about as far from the old style of macho of beekeeping described by Flottam as one could imagine – festooned with colorful ribbons and silk flowers on top of tulle which she uses to keep the bees out. Meyzen assures me, however, that they are made to be functional for the truly serious beekeeper. They promise to seal out the bees while leaving full vision intact – something many canvas-clad bee veils and zippered shirts cannot provide. They are also lighter, an asset to those who beekeep in hot, humid locations.

Meyzen says that although she favors romantic or old-fashioned looking equipment, bees and beekeeping tasks are not to be taken lightly. The bees, she assures me, are absolutely essential.

Meyzen and her husband Robert use both the honey from her hives and the apples from her orchard in La Cremaillere, the French country restaurant they own in Bedford, New York. When she first bought her property many years ago, the trees were languishing, their fruit poor. Her seven trees produce russets, a prized, sweet, antique apple rarely sold in the modern market which is known for its slightly rough skin in green or yellowish-brown. It was one of the oldest apple types grown in the US, prized by the likes of Thomas Jefferson. She wondered what she could do to bring in a good crop without using chemicals.

Then Meyzen read a fictional book by Sue Monk Kidd called *The Secret Life of Bees,* about a young teenage white girl who runs away from home and her abusive father in 1964 and finds refuge in a large apiary owned by three African American sisters in rural Georgia. The novel, which became a *New York Times* best seller in 2002 and a movie starring Queen Latifah in 2008, features honey as balm – both metaphorically and literally – for all kinds of problems including racism, mental illness, economic disparity, and romantic heartbreak. Perhaps most significantly to beekeepers, it showed the women making a prosperous income from their bees without assistance from any men, a motif many female readers said they found refreshing.

Meyzen says the story charmed her, but also sparked an epiphany. Did she even know what a honey bee really looked like, she wondered. She knew the yellow jackets, but how did they differ? She began to read nonfiction books on the topic, and spent long hours searching for pollinators in the flowers of her trees and fields.

"I fell completely in love with the bees."

After three years of beekeeping classes and meetings, she decided she was finally ready to give it a try.

"Within one year of having the honey bees, the apples were round again, and stayed on the tree longer, and were delicious, delicious, delicious."

Meyzen says she proudly donates ten percent of each hat sale she makes to the American Bee Federation's fund for research on CCD, along with a portion of money earned from her bee-themed jewelry and gloves.

She now leads courses on some very technical topics, such as the microscopy of bees – by examining specimens at very close magnification. She also has served as Vice President of her local beekeeping group, the Back Yard Beekeepers Association (BYBA).

Tammy Conley, the BYBA's president, tells me the group is celebrating its twentieth anniversary in 2013. Although based in southwest Connecticut, its three hundred members live as far east as urban New Haven and suburban Westchester, New York. Women aren't just members of the BYBA but take on leadership of the group in great capacity – on the board, leading bee talks, and running mentor programs. The BYBA is also enormously proud of having the state's four certified Master Beekeepers among their ranks.

Conley has been beekeeping for about 15 years. She began after helping a coworker capture a feral swarm at the New Pond Farm, the non-profit environmental education center where she works in Redding.

Now, as president of BYBA, she reflects on the changes she's seen. Bees are much harder to keep alive now, she says with dismay. As a result, more people – including herself – are choosing to go chemical-free in their hives. Everyone is worried about helping the bees survive.

But also, when she first started there weren't that many women at the meetings. There were a lot of older gentlemen, she says, who had been doing it for years and years.

"It was not really not as scientific then. They were mostly people who had grown up doing it or had been keeping them for years and it was kind of a sideline or how they made their living. But then within the past ten years there's really been a flooding in of women, to where now we're definitely fifty-fifty as far as membership."

Many of the new members of both sexes have no background in the topic, no inherited traditions or passed down methodologies, so they often crave information. The club hosts lectures from nationally-known speakers about research or the biology of the bees. The BYBA has also started a program to pair new beekeepers with more established ones.

Between her work with the BYBA and her job at New Pond Farm, Conley spends a lot of time teaching both adults and kids about bees. When I ask her if she's noticed any differences between how men and women approach a hive, she pauses thoughtfully before answering.

"I notice that I can go in with children and get them to go in nice and slow, but I can't get the men to slow down some-

times. I think they are used to muscling things, you know –
kind of a 'I can get this out of here' kind of thing."

Reconsidering, she says some of the men in the club are as
patient and methodical as the women, and some are more
brusque and hurried. "I don't know any men who work with
beekeeping who don't respect bees, I think that's pretty uni-
versal. And you can't not respect the bees. You can't have a
colony and not respect them."

*****

Out of the thousands of blogs posted about beekeeping on
the internet, perhaps none is more followed than Rusty Burlew's Honey Bee Suite. Burlew, unlike most of the beekeepers
I interviewed, keeps her hives in the western part of the US,
near the 47th parallel in Western Washington State. A lot of
what she writes, though, is not geographically limited and
could be applied to beekeeping anywhere in North America.

Burlew makes me laugh, plain and simple. I love reading
her stories online and love her sometimes curmudgeonly approach to beekeeping. She's an excellent writer and a darned
good storyteller. Her posts are an entertaining combination of
humble and pissed-off. I'm sure she can hold her own in a
room full of opinionated men, and though I don't agree with
her on every topic, I find myself cheering at her willingness to
take on the bullies of the agricultural world.

In a classic post written in February of 2013 entitled "A
Personal Note to Cranky Old Beekeepers," for example, Bur-

lew writes that it is difficult to be equitable to people who make ridiculous comments, including those who say they do something in their hive or to their hive simply because it was how their grandfather did it back in the day. After adding that many such comments come from people in their sixties whose grandfathers kept bees more than a hundred years ago, Burlew retorts:

"If you belong to this group, your grandfather probably heated bathwater on the stove, got the news from a crotchety radio with hot tubes inside, and made calls from a telephone forever attached to the wall. If he had a car at all, he started it with a hand crank. Fast food meant it was running when shot. Heck, your grandfather needed a tool just to open a bottle of Coke. But hey, if you think the old ways will work for you, knock yourself out."

Her conclusion: the landscape has changed and so has the way to deal with the bees. We learn, she adds, from the triumphs and failures of those who worked the bees before us. Cranky and old is not about a number or an age, but about attitude and willingness to learn from both our mistakes and the mistakes of others.

"So," she admonishes readers, "take care of your bees by remembering that this is not your grandfather's planet. This is the environment we've provided for our bees and ourselves and it's often not pretty."

Burlew represents a new face in the beekeeping world. She's not afraid of telling you she's a woman and how that impacts her beekeeping reality – such as in posts made about bees getting stuck in very awful places in her bra or about how much she hates wearing ill-fitting bee gear made for a man twice her size. But she's also got the experience and research to back her thoughts.

Ironically, Burlew's own bee adventures began many decades ago with her grandfather, who led her through the forests and fields of rural Pennsylvania hunting for feral beehives in the hollows of old trees, and showed her his hives at the back of cemeteries behind ancient church yards.

Years later, after graduating from Oregon State University with a degree in agricultural science, she landed a position teaching job skills to soon-to-be-released prisoners in a minimum security prison, where her convict students prepared themselves for life outside of jail. Beekeeping was a way to teach both science and augment confidence. Prisoners who had demonstrated good behavior and were not labelled a security risk were allowed to travel briefly outside the fence, where state-owned tree farms bordered riparian areas and beehives thrived along the edges of deciduous forest.

Many of her students had quit school long before getting through high school biology. Some did not believe her when she explained the pollination process.

"They had no idea there were sexual systems in plants as well as animals and it was incomprehensible to them that plants were reproducing," she says. They sometimes giggled when she talked about the male and female parts of the flower.

Burlew doubted that any of her former students from that time went on to be beekeepers, but what mattered to her was that they were learning about life and life systems. They were engaging with the world around them in a new and positive way, learning biology for the first time and often surprised by their own new-found curiosity in the environment. When it came time to extract their honey at the end of the season, the men were ecstatic. "The honey tasted good, but to the guys it tasted incredible. They would just glow when they tasted it."

Inspired by the experience, Burlew went to Evergreen State University in 2010 for a masters in environmental science. The world of agriculture had changed dramatically since she first went to school during the "green revolution," when DDT was still being sprayed on crops and chlordane was still being applied to yards all over the US. Now, she says, the chemicals are even deadlier, and the kind of hollow trees filled with feral bees in the lush forests are long gone.

"The world was different back then. Most of these assaults on bees are relatively recent. When I was young and I was learning beekeeping, there were no mites, there were no hive beetles, there were no viruses. Birds sometimes got in your hive and mice sometimes got in your hive and there was foulbrood [a destructive bee disease]... and that was the big threat, but there wasn't this onslaught of hundreds of different things."

People are telling her through emails and conversations that their bees are dying very suddenly. It used to happen every once in a while, she says. But now it seems like all the time

– and many say their bees that were healthy just a few weeks before. Then, they go out to do a routine check on their hive and the bees are dead.

"It's happening to people in the city, it's happening to people in the country, it's happening to people in the suburbs," she says.

Burlew, who is director of the Native Bee Conservancy, suspects that the deaths are due to poor genetics. "So many hives are dying every year that there's a huge push to breed and produce as many queens as possible so that we can supply as many people as possible with bees all over again. I think that not enough consideration is going into the genetic variability of those queens."

"I get upset with the groups that say let the bees be bees, or let nature take its course. To me, that's cruel. What we've done to the bees is we've provided them with an environment that it's almost impossible to live within…If you decide to care for an animal, any animal, and you decide to keep that animal than you have a moral responsibility to take care of it. I really do believe that. So when someone who buys a box of bees and puts it in a hive and then abandons it and says let nature take its course, I think that's immoral. I really do."

Bees, she tells me, are a lot like farm animals. They have been taken out of the wild and domesticated here in the US, and now depend upon us for survival. "You take a cow or a sheep or whatever you have on a farm and you put it out in the wild, its going to die. Same thing with the bees," she says. "They no longer can survive in the wild."

She also thinks there's a danger that the whole species is in danger of collapsing.

"We may have to go back to native bees as pollinators in the future if we can't keep the honey bee alive. That might sound overly negative, but I think it's a real possibility that even if they don't go totally extinct we might not be able to keep them going in the numbers that are needed to pollinate crops all across the world."

That's not to say the native bees don't have their share of troubles and challenges in the current environment. Pesticides and diseases are taking their toll on those species as well. But diversifying farms and understanding the importance of natives in the agricultural sector is likely to be central to the future of farming. Monoculture farms are just about the worst possible environment for bees she can imagine.

The current interest in beekeeping is a fad, she thinks, whose timespan is likely limited. Eventually, something new will capture people's attention. There was a similar spike in beekeeping in the 1970s when people were swept up in the back-to-the-land movement. But while the bees and the beekeepers have the public's attention, there's a lot that can be gained which may prove lasting in society.

"To me the big value of this interest in beekeeping is that it makes people aware of the environment, and aware of the problems in the food supply and the environment. You can't be a beekeeper in a vacuum. The climate change is related, the number of freeways near your hive is related, the plants that grow near your hive, late spring, early winters or whatever, or the guy spraying chemicals next door to you. It makes people very aware."

*****

If it turns out that beekeeping's popularity does amount to just a fad, it seems as if the lasting legacy may be left via parents – both male and female. Many who are brand new to bees are out there suited up and learning the craft along with their sons and daughters, teaching them not just to make honey and beeswax candles, but imparting a love and respect for the insect world that only first-hand experience can provide.

My beekeeping friend Laura, is one of those. Shortly after she took over the management of the hive stationed in her backyard, her young son decided he'd like to try beekeeping, too. Not until you are six, she told him. Then you can help me with the bee chores.

Once the important landmark birthday had passed and she saw he was ready to begin learning a few basic things, the excitement was incredible. They ordered him a child-size suit and he would come out to stand next to her and watch – sometimes finding the work rewarding, and sometimes finding it tedious or hot. Her younger daughter, meanwhile, claimed she wasn't interested in helping, but would watch from a safe distance or from behind the window – intrigued but coy, and anxious to differentiate herself from her older brother.

Then one day her daughter announced that she, too, wanted to join in, and from her very first time out she demonstrated a cool confidence around the hives, even having the good fortune of spotting the queen almost immediately.

"She was over the top about it," Laura tells me with a proud grin. "She kept yelling 'I saw a queen laying an egg!' "

Although children can sometimes find bee stings traumatic, beekeepers' children often learn to take stings in relative stride. And so it was with Laura's son – who has been stung a few times on his feet and once on his face. The tears have not deterred his love of the insects – perhaps because he's seen Laura and her friends get stung so often he realized the pain would pass. (Her daughter has yet to be stung, and Laura wonders with some trepidation about what the reaction will be once that first sting occurs.)

Neither child has really mastered the full craft, even though they are now eleven and nine. Mostly they assist or watch while she takes care of her hives.

They may not have colonies of their own, but they have a pride in the family apiary and have lapped up information about the bees' special biology. They love teaching others about it, even accompanying Laura while she volunteered at a booth about bees at the Smithsonian Folk Life Festival on the National Mall. She recalls the pleasure and pride she felt watching them teach other kids and even adults about the differences between the queens, the workers, and the drones as the bees wriggled around next to children in a glass observation hive. They also go with her to teach kids at nearby schools, especially enjoying the sensation of telling older kids about bees.

"They have a little celebrity status," she says.

Like Laura's kids, Tobias and Sebastian Wiggins (ages nine and eleven) overcame their fear of being stung when they began beekeeping with their mom, Susanne, in suburban Gaithersburg, Maryland in 2012.

Prior to taking a beekeeping class together, no one in the family had ever been a beekeeper, and they knew almost nothing about the bees they hoped to host. But getting a hive seemed like a natural extension of their Waldorf homeschooling curriculum, and a great way to augment the brimming wildlife garden behind their townhouse. They worked with a friend to build and install a top-bar hive made from old scrap lumber.

"We made our bee suits out of old clothes and hats we already had," the boys told me proudly one day in February of 2013. "And the gloves just came from the grocery store."

They hadn't intended to start their colony with feral bees, but when the bees they ordered through the mail didn't arrive, they pounced on the opportunity to bring home an early spring swarm that a more experienced beekeeper had found behind an empty house.

Sitting in their house, the Wiggins clan gets me laughing as they describe their team work in that swarm capture. Somehow emboldened by the thought that they wouldn't have to wait a whole extra year to fill their empty hive, they set off with gusto and confidence. The experienced beekeeper was already there, watching the bees congregate on a branch.

"The tree branch was just dipping down with the weight of the bees," Tobias tells me. "When she cut the branch it just went *thunk!* down into the bucket, and that was it."

The experienced beekeeper, Susanne says with a laugh, had on "her moon suit, the full nine yards kind of thing, and here we were in our homemade jackets and veils and hats!" They put the bucket into a large copy paper box.

"Then we put them into the back of our little tiny Honda Fit," Susanne says. "And I have hardly ever driven so carefully as I did that stretch. It probably wasn't even ten miles, but if felt like an eternity! And you hear them buzzing: *buzz buzz buzz* – you've got to imagine the Honda Fit, the trunk is filled with bees and the whole family is piled into the car."

"You could hear their wings flapping, trying to cool the queen down," Sebastian says of the bees. "They were loud!"

Once home, they began the delicate process of unloading and trying to acclimate the bees to the waiting hive. It was a moment that Susanne had been dreaming of, fantasizing about for weeks, as she poured over every available You Tube video on the topic.

"I kind of felt like I was preparing for this surgical operation. So that when the bees came, I would rehearse in my mind each of the steps I would go through... I really wanted to do this right." Now, faced with the reality of a feral swarm, she and her sons had to improvise.

It was at that moment, their next door neighbor came out and in a friendly voice asked from the next deck over, "Are those bees?"

"And we just tried to act all calm," the boys tell me with a laugh. "Yes, that's right!" Like everything was going along as planned, even though none of it had been planned this way.

Eventually, their found bees would die. Maybe the queen was too weak. Maybe she had gone feral after being ousted by a younger, more fertile queen. They never quite knew, and once the colony was gone it was far too late in the summer to begin again. But as they tell the story, I find I am simultaneously envious of their adventure and sad for them. They seem to have bonded over the shared escapade and the eventual heartbreak that followed.

We missed the bees once they were dead, the boys tell me. The remaining days of summer seemed a bit emptier. It strikes me as we talk in their living room that even if these boys stop beekeeping and their interest in the hobby does fade, these two will probably still grow into teenagers who are very aware of the environment around them, and men who have great respect for pollinators and the needs of the bees. This, I think, may be the best investment any of us can make in the coming years, and the biggest gift we can offer the bees: getting kids to understand and care.

We are waiting for a call tonight, Susanne says with a twinkle in her eye. Someone closer to DC, in the Kensington neighborhood, has told her she can get bees from his apiary this year, and he is known for being chemical-free and producing strong queens.

And this time, Sebastian tells me pumping his hands into fists with excitement, we are going to try a Langstroth-style hive, not a top-bar.

"I got stung a few times," Tobias says softly, flipping through colorful close-up pictures of the hive on the family's tablet computer. But mostly the bees didn't bother anyone, he insists, and he and his brother really liked to sit on the deck in the sunshine and watch them come and go.

"When you get them to land on your leg or whatever, " Sebastian tells me, "they're just cute, fluffy things. You just brush them off."

"The bees are nice," Tobias says wistfully.

3

NYCBee: From the Rooftops of Chelsea to the Bottom of Hell's Kitchen

"Just remember, what we do here is not going to save the bees," Andrew Coté tells us on the rooftop high above the streets of New York City. "This is something we do for ourselves."

And with that the nine people around me – including a former chef, an architect, a design student, a poet, a freelance communicator, a non-profit organizer, and a construction worker – all suit up to learn about urban beekeeping, zipping canvas shirts and slipping on tight gloves.

Coté is the rock star of the beekeeping world, the man who got famous for keeping hundreds of beehives on rooftops all over the city of New York – even during the years when the practice was illegal.

The group up on the roof today in the Chelsea neighborhood first met him when they attended an intense, 15-hour course he taught in the cold days of February as president of the New York City Beekeepers' Association. In the painfully early hours of this Saturday in May under his supervision they will use flat metal tools to crack open lids on six hives and check on the bees inside.

They want to become better at beekeeping, but I want to find out what drives someone to start the hobby. Beekeeping's popularity has exploded; all over the country people are learning how to buy bees and set up hives in unlikely and unconventional locations. The bees, struggling with Colony Collapse Disorder, have become incredibly charismatic in American culture.

It's a cloudy day, yet the skyline remains impressive, and from the top of this ten-story building in Manhattan the iconic red letters of the New Yorker Hotel's sign look like a caption, framing out the crisp point of the Empire State Building.

Most of the other buildings are empty, the city still shaking off its Friday night. People are groggy, downing giant cups of coffee and shaking off sleep, but in front of us the bees are already hard at work, searching for nectar in mysterious corners of the city below.

Two blocks over I see a possible source of forage; right at eye level to us there's a rooftop restaurant surrounded with planters of flowers. A waiter is silently inspecting carefully laid table settings, though the tables are all empty. I wonder if he knows what we are up to over here. I decide not to wave hello when he glances in our direction.

We look like a team of Imperial Storm Troopers from a *Star Wars* movie, with our white suits and faceless mesh masks. Supposedly this will help us stay safe from the bees, who are instinctively predisposed to sting intruders who look like bears with eyes, ears and mouths. I like the protection, but hate that I lose most of my peripheral vision. On the other hand, the costume forces me to walk slowly and deliberately, which is probably good for avoiding a crash with the bee-keepers or their tools.

A special device called a smoker is placed on the edge of the roof and opened. It looks like a coffee can with a bellows and a conical nose on top. Coté takes a piece of burlap out, lights it, and places it inside.

Smoke is used to keep bee stings to a minimum when working a hive. Bees communicate alarm signals among themselves via pheromones, and the strong smell of smoldering burlap interferes with signals. There are theories that it also causes bees to ingest some of the honey they are storing as food for the colony – perhaps as an instinctive response to protect their stores in the case of a forest fire. Either way, a bee with a full belly cannot easily bend its abdomen to sting.

Some rural beekeepers use pine needles in their smokers, but those are hard to find ten stories up in a neighborhood of art galleries. Coté has learned to make an inventive city substitution, repurposing bags used by food retailers for coffee. Potatoes sometimes also come in burlap bags, but are to be avoided, Coté warns his students, since those crops are often sprayed with chemicals such as fungicides that can harm bees.

Coté stands out from the rest of this rooftop crowd since his bee shirt is khaki. But even without the color difference, he's as easy to pick out of the faceless crowd as the queen bees in the hives, since everyone waits for his direction before beginning a task. His apprentices hover around him, awaiting instruction. He's still worried about the hives that seemed to be struggling last week.

This is the first season they've put bees on this particular roof, and getting the new colonies established and strong is proving difficult. Approaching the first hive, he loosens the ratchet belt and gingerly inserts a metal hive tool underneath the lid, breaking the seal of sticky propolis which the bees use to glue the lid to the hive. Bees begin to emerge in great number, and the apprentice at his side carefully swirls a bit of smoke around as he and Coté both lean over and peer inside. The hives seem like patients spread out for surgery. There's a precision to the work, and calls are made for tools. Once opened, each of the hives' innards are examined and diagnosed.

"Shitty queens!" Coté sighs in disgust, leaning his gloved palm against the edge of the open hive. "Ugh! That guy gave me some shitty queens!"

Healthy queens are everything to a hive, since the colony of bees spends its life satisfying the needs of this singular leader. Coté doesn't reveal where this queen came from, but to get a new hive up and running, most keepers on the East Coast turn to apiaries in the southern states, and buy packages of bees from places like Georgia. These include a queen bee and attending female worker bees which are either shipped or picked up in person and then driven north in mesh and wood packages.

A queen is usually larger, and mostly brown, although spotting her among the 30,000 or more bees in a healthy hive can be challenging. Some keepers mark the backs of their queens with a spot of bright paint. Others say they have learned to find the queen by watching the workers carefully: those diligent female attendants always circle in a knot around the queen, fanning her constantly.

Coté points out to the crew that there is no queen in the first box he's opened. She may have died recently, and the workers have reacted by laying eggs which, if left to mature, will turn into massive numbers of male drone cells. These will need to be removed to make room for a new, strong queen and her eventual offspring. (In a normal healthy colony, only a queen will lay the eggs in the hive.)

The building where we work seems to be in the path of a helipad; a half dozen large helicopters fly over head in an orderly line and the echoes reverberate off the bricks all around us. The Hudson River sparkles below, and in between helicopter passes I can hear the bass notes of tug boats that are beginning to work the water, pushing barges into place along the piers. The city is waking up.

"Ew, God, this is funky," says one apprentice as he peers into another hive. "Something is going really wrong in here." Coté walks over to offer his assessment: another dead queen, more layers of drone larvae that will need removal.

As he climbed up to the roof this morning, Coté carried along two replacement queens and their attending worker bees – which were collected as they swarmed on Friday. One was found in New Jersey, the other in a schoolyard in Brooklyn. The swarm bees sizzle and hum inside ventilated buckets making a sound like steaks on a hot grill.

"These in here look calm, but those look impatient," says one apprentice, holding the two containers of captured swarms at eye level for comparison.

"They seem ready to get to their new home!" someone else agrees behind her.

Swarms often scare the hell out of people in this city, but beekeepers know that's when bees are at their most docile. There's a skill to capturing swarms, and a certain blend of showmanship and level-headedness needed to keep the bees happy as they are gathered for relocation to a new, pre-built hive.

"Half of handling urban swarms is figuring out how to get up there to do it," says Coté, who is often called in to help with swarms since he's president of the New York City Bee-keepers Association. This city is an unforgiving landscape of glass, steel, powerlines, and constant traffic. You have to work with whatever resources you have in the moment. One time he had to flag down a guy driving a refrigerated beer truck and offer him fifty dollars to pull up under a swarm so he could climb on top and gather the bees quickly.

Sometimes he gets calls from the city engineers – those people you can see in hard hats climbing in and out of man-holes and up and down ladders on busy streets to repair street lights. "They are pretty tough guys, and they are moving away from the problem, and I'm moving toward it calmly – it does kind of give you a certain sense of satisfaction."

Coté is one of only two people city officials regularly use to gather swarms; although he's got his apprentices on alert to help whenever a call comes in he thinks its too hard to simul-taneously handle crowds of people and hordes of bees and he's hesitant to ask anyone else to try just yet. "There's not a lot of on-the-job training when you are talking about these heavily populated civilian areas," he says.

Coté often uses the word "civilian" to describe people who aren't trained as beekeepers. He's got the air of a former mili-tary man, too. He briefs and then later de-briefs his keepers, like an officer gathering field reports. His closely cropped hair also looks like an officer's cut. Over the years he's been branded as a bit of a short fuse, although he confesses that he's puzzled by the label. He thinks of himself as simply keeping up with the high-energy city that surrounds him. He likes people. He thinks this is the greatest city in the world and he readily embraces its vibrant, fast pace.

Bees demand physical fitness, they demand focus, and in New York they often demand climbing loads of rickety stairs with heavy loads of honey or equipment. If you are going to be a high-profile keeper like Coté, you also have to be a bit brash and ready to answer when cranky New Yorkers get in the way. You have to be ready to defend your opinions and judgment at all times. He stays ready, alert, attentive.

Today on the roof, he's disappointed by the "dud queens" that died so early in the season, but he's also enjoying the company of his new apprentice team. He needles one team member, a student at Parson's School of Design, for confessing to partying during final exams. He compliments another on choosing cheerful paint colors for the new hives they installed up on this roof. There's a lot of laughter and an obvious esprit de corps.

"Look at the great job Tim did on this observation hive, everyone!" Coté calls out, holding up a frame full of bees boxed in by glass. "From nothing but a magazine picture. He figured out how to do it just from a picture. He is *that* good!"

Tim Cerniglia, the apprentice being complimented, takes it with a wide smile. A contractor who owns his own business in Greenwich, Connecticut, he enjoys making things with his hands but working with bees is different from building gas stations, highway rest stops, and custom houses in the suburbs. He poses for photographs, revealing muscular arms and a few tattoos as he raises up the observation hive for others to see. Any tough guy persona that the 40 year old might otherwise exude is quickly offset by a warm, boyish smile and his desire to talk about things like sustainability, green building materials, and low-VOC paint choices for beehives.

Although still only an apprentice to Coté, Cerniglia already has 16 bee colonies set up in Connecticut. He bravely began to take care of his bees as a self-taught keeper only one year ago, but found that one of his first two hives died of starvation. It was then he found Coté and his intensive class and apprenticeship program.

"It was such a sad thing when that happened," he says about his bees dying. "I knew I needed to get more educated."

He hopes to have 50 hives by next year, including a few in the Bronx and Manhattan if he can find suitable locations. He also wants to put one close to his niece and nephew's house so he can teach them about the bees. He admires the way Coté has taught so many people about beekeeping, and calls him generous. "Taking the class and doing the apprenticeship has also been an incredible way to meet and network and start relationships with new and different people."

Coté says he's wanted to put a team like this together for a long time. In the last few years the demand for training has been intense in the city and he hasn't always been so good at saying no to giving instruction on the fly. Now that he's got a specialized team that he can trust he can be more proactive, more organized. Anyone who wants instruction can sign up for next year's class, and then apply for the apprenticeship program, which costs $500. He hopes it will add some sanity to the crazy life of professional urban beekeeping he has taken on full-time.

The two hives which are queen-less need straightening before the queens captured from yesterday's swarms can be added. The process demands patience, skill, and an iron nerve; the worker bees don't like to see their work undone. Once the frames are put back, however, the new queens can settle in and the work of making honey can begin.

There's a giant buzzing sound next to my ear. One of the apprentices assures me that the bee which crashed into my veil is gone now. But actually, I am finding I need no reassurance. My suit makes me feel safe, and the bees are circling us like electrons. I like it.

One area of the rooftop where we stand holds two massive water cisterns which loom 20 or so feet above our heads. Coté tells the apprentices to do the shaking of the drone-filled frames on the other side of these – far away from the rest of the hives. The frames containing layers of drones are then handed in bucket-brigade style over the guywires that criss-cross the roof around us, and the scraping and shaking begins.

The bees are becoming more agitated now, and one of the apprentices gets stung on the arm when a bee finds its way up his sleeve. Earlier, before Coté's arrival, this same apprentice had been wondering if he should get stung today on purpose – he's never been exposed to honey bee venom and he is worried he might be unexpectedly allergic. After he calmly announces his sting, a fellow apprentice escorts him to the opposite side of the roof. There, out of the line of action and far from the hives, they use the smoker to prevent further stings when the veil is removed. When a bee stings it gives off a strong scent – some say reminiscent of bananas – an alert to the rest of the hive which can sometimes cause female worker bees to sting aggressively.

The sting barely registers with the apprentice; there is no swelling and he says it hardly hurts once the stinger has been removed from his skin. He and his first aid escort put their veils back on and return to work shaking the frames, with slight ribbing from his fellow beekeepers. It will remain the only sting that occurs that day.

"Hey, was that on purpose?" someone asks the stung apprentice with a laugh.

"Naw," the apprentice grins back.

It is harder to hear what's being said since a construction crew set up a jackhammer on the street below. Along the other side of the roof, far in the distance, the city's newest outdoor attraction, the High Line, is already filled with people who've come to enjoy the morning on this elevated promenade. I watch them taking pictures. Although they are so far away I cannot make out faces, sometimes the light of their flashes go off in the low light of the morning, like bright, daytime fireworks. I wonder if the balcony blanketed with Japanese wisteria vines next to those photographers is used as forage by the bees on this rooftop – probably, since bees will travel as far as three miles in search of reliable, sweet nectar.

Apprentice Melissa Lam bends over to work on the inside of a hive, scraping away excess propolis and wax from the frames and then pulling them out to carefully inspect them. Some of these will be moved to new, freshly painted supers today.

"Look at her back!" laughs Coté, pointing to bees which have blanketed her like an oozing sweater vest.

She laughs too, and asks someone to please take a picture so she can see what it looks like. I step over closer, careful to keep out of the path of work. Why is it so mesmerizing? I snap and snap, and snap again – taking dozens of digital photos of Lam's back and the inside of the hive box where she works.

Suddenly, a shout of surprise can be heard emanating from behind bee veils all around as Coté and three of his apprentices surround one of the hives and begin to hustle. Something large and brown has been found – a two-inch long cockroach. The bees inside are corralling the invader in a formation that looks like ten thousand people doing "the wave" at a sports stadium – and a flat metal hive tool is used to flick the alien out of the waxy frames.

Alex Batkin, an apprentice in skinny jeans, chases it across the rooftop and stomps on it with his toe. A cheer goes up from the beekeepers.

"Got it!"

"Man, that's a big sucker, too!"

"Way to go, Alex!"

Cockroaches might be the norm in this city, but later Coté tells everyone, "I have never seen that before – not in more than 20 years keeping bees in New York."

He has actually been keeping bees even longer than that – starting 30 years ago at his father Norman's side in nearby suburban Connecticut when he was about ten. Norman – like Andrew – had a brush with celebrity when he kept hives on the property of Martha Stewart, eventually teaching the famous TV personality to keep bees on her own.

Coté says his favorite thing in beekeeping is being with his dad. "We don't have to speak. We can anticipate each other's moves."

Both Cotés are continuing a long family tradition by keeping bees – there are at least four generations of keepers in their history. But even so, it wasn't the career Andrew initially chose.

When asked about his professional background, he tosses out words like polyglot and vagabond and educator to describe his career. For a while he studied Japanese literature, and was a Fulbright scholar in Moldova. He came home to the US when his mother became ill, and began a PhD at Yale in Middle Eastern studies. He taught at a community college. Eventually, the bees presented themselves as a profitable possibility, and he decided to open the Silvermine Apiary in Connecticut, selling honey wholesale to local grocery stores in the early 2000s.

Slowly, the hives Coté managed increased and their locations became more and more urban. He moved to the Lower East Side when city honey turned out to be surprisingly easy to sell at farmers markets near landmarks like City Hall, Rockefeller Center, Union Square, and Thompkins Square

Park. Customers loved buying honey from Queens, Hell's Kitchen, and Brooklyn, and the taste was as unique as the neighborhoods where it was gathered.

New York's foodie set noticed, including high profile writers like Mark Bittman. In 2009, Annemarie Conte of the *New York Times* "Diner's Journal" called Coté's "seriously local honey" smooth, and noted it had "distinctive caramel and fruit flavors."

The article never mentioned that beekeeping had been outlawed during Rudolph Guiliani's term as mayor, but when a reader asked point-blank about it in the *Times'* online comments section, Coté brazenly admitted it: Yes, he had hives in New York, and No, he wasn't going to tell anyone where. Suddenly, he was the face of the underground movement that had become city beekeeping.

Behind the boldness, Coté says he was working closely with city officials to change what he saw as a regulation that had no merit. He has no appetite for breaking laws, he says, but that one appeared out of nowhere with little reasoning. He and many other beekeepers began advocating for a change. People lived for a couple centuries in New York with bees and beekeepers, he once pointed out to a radio reporter, and it had never been a big problem. It was only in 1999 that the beehives became illegal in the city.

In 2010, when public pressure caused the city's ban to be lifted every reporter in the world wanted to interview Coté. His work on the city's official guidelines in conjunction with the Department of Health and Mental Hygiene plus his personal history of keeping healthy hives in numerous boroughs made him an instant go-to source for information. He went from being the guy with the yummy honey to being the guy that knew how to keep bees alive on the roof in New York. He was also prepared to answer any criticism people might have of the change in law, and stood by, willing to convince them that the bees added value to the city's landscape.

The criticism never came, though. Most of the city's leadership was behind the idea, hoping it would be one more way the city could be validated as livable, modern and environmentally healthy. And besides, all the other big cities around the world were doing it too. New York hates to be last to get on board with any trend.

Although he's glad the beekeeping regulation was changed, he would have been more comfortable if beekeeping legalization in the city had included some kind of licensing component or educational requirement.

"What we've ended up with are a lot of cowboys and cowgirls who are enamored of the idea of keeping bees without having really learned how to do so," he says. "Legalization has changed things, but I don't think all for the better." He wants beekeepers to be well educated.

Coté has been on television so many times by now he says he's lost count, but a list compiled by an intern who worked with him takes up three full pages. His passion for bees and his ability to articulate the science of beekeeping to the general public have kept his phone ringing. There have been appearances on the Martha Stewart Show, interviews with

ABC News, and feature stories done by CNN's Sanjay Gupta. Coté even briefly appeared in an advertisement directed by Spike Lee and narrated by Robert DeNiro, and had the starring role in another TV spot about Smart Cars which opened with the line: "My name is Andrew Coté and I am a beekeeper in New York City."

There were even rumors that Coté was hired to do a brief stint of modeling; in addition to being articulate, he's kind of ruggedly handsome and obviously comfortable in front of a crowd or in front of a camera. Attention is not something that seems to scare him. But for now he really wants to focus on bees.

At one point in the morning someone asks if he's ever taken containers of bees on the subway and Coté laughs and said yes – although they were safely sealed in protective cases. "But I think I may have really messed with some people's minds – other passengers – doing that."

It's the kind of stunt that would make for interesting television, and not surprisingly, he's also attracted the attention of some television producers who approached with a proposal for a reality TV show. He would probably get good ratings, but Coté turned them down, worried that his group of apprentices would get nothing more than "exposure" and the risk they'd all be made to look like "buffoons" on national networks. He may like to surprise the jaded New York subway rider occasionally, but he sees no reason to lose dignity. Besides, he has learned that the wrong kind of exposure can be very irritating.

During his most recent interview with a major news network, when Coté was asked by the reporter about the health of bees and pollinators and the possible causes of their worldwide decline and CCD, he was unable to actually answer the question before being interrupted. He and his apprentices dissect the interview with a healthy dose of skepticism.

"Did you see what happened after that reporter asked you about the bees dying? As soon as you mentioned it might be pesticides, it seemed like they gave her the cut sign," one apprentice says.

"Yeah," Coté replies, shaking his head. "I started to say pesticides and she interrupted me and changed the subject to talk about her uncle who used to keep bees and I was like, *okayyyyyy*..."

"I betcha one of their sponsors makes pesticides!" another apprentice adds as the beekeepers shake their heads sadly.

"Yeah, somebody selling neonicotinoids!" adds another person, referring to the controversial class of chemicals which were recently banned in the European Union and are suspected by many here in the US to be harming the bees' ability to navigate landscapes.

Even though he began the day by reminding them they can't save the bees with one small rooftop of hives, Coté does think there are ways to improve the status of pollinators like honey bees. CCD remains a mystery. But pesticide use doesn't help, he thinks, and more research could be done on all of the factors that might be causing the bees to die in large numbers across the country.

Sometimes he even wonders if the increase in beekeeping's popularity is adding to the problems of bees. A lot of people have misguided ideas – they think that if they buy a box of bees and build a hive somewhere they alone can solve the mystery that science has been unable to crack. The increased demand for queens from suppliers might be putting a lot of genetically weak bees on the market right now, he thinks, almost like getting a puppy from a puppy mill versus from a shelter. The queens gathered during swarms have shown the ability to winter over and survive New York's environment. But either way, just becoming a beekeeper is not going to save the entire species. He wants his beekeeper apprentices to know that, and reminds them of it constantly.

In a few televised interviews Coté has even gone so far as to wonder out loud if beekeeping is somewhat selfish. These are harsh words for some nature lovers to hear. Some would prefer to think of hobbyist beekeepers and small scale honey producers as gentle shepherds, or saviors who work to preserve a simpler way of life that has disappeared in modern American life. Coté is uncomfortable with such ideas and shirks the mantle of nature hero as quickly as someone might try to put it over him.

Three bees make a star on the back of my yellow, dish-gloved hand. Apprentice Nicole Norton steps over to watch with me, pointing out how they rub antennae to share pheromone information. Her voice is authoritative, serious, and calm.

"They might be from different queens," she explains. They are trying to figure out what is going on, trying to tell each other information."

Norton, like Coté, represents the fifth generation of bee-keepers in her own family – learning the craft first from her late grandfather in Alabama before moving to New York for a career in design. "He had almost an instinctive feel for the bees, for nature."

Recently she was very excited to find an antique smoker among her grandfather's old belongings in storage. She thinks it may be one that dates to the mid-19th century. There's also reason to believe that the original beekeeper in her family brought his hobby and his bees with him when he immigrated from Amsterdam to New Jersey in the 1700s, back when honey would have been an important way to sweeten food in the early colonies.

Some of her relatives back home think she's crazy – not only for wanting to keep bees, but also for wanting to do it in New York. She's tried to explain it to them: something about it seems to make her feel connected to both the natural world and to her family history. But even she herself seems at a loss to describe her motivations. By next year she's hoping she'll feel confident enough to set up hives somewhere in one of the boroughs. Or maybe in Rhode Island or New Jersey. Maybe some in rural locations and some in the city. She's thinking it over, carefully.

"There's so much to learn from the bees," she tells me.

When I asked Coté on the phone a few weeks before my visit if urban beekeeping differs suburban or rural beekeeping, he talked about parking. Parking is hard in New York, and beekeeping always demands heavy lifting. But that's about him, not really about the bees. "When I'm face down in a beehive it doesn't really matter where I am, the bees pretty much behave the same way."

Sometimes, he then conceded, there's more wind to deal with at a place like the Waldorf Astoria – where he gets paid to keep bees and produce honey twenty stories above the ground for the hotel's restaurant. Brooklyn honey has more attitude, Manhattan honey has higher rent and Westchester County honey has higher taxes but better schools, he likes to joke.

The differences between a hive in the country and a hive in the city might be dramatic, but the contrast between what's going on inside the bees' home and outside of it is actually part of the appeal.

"It's just this little box of calm in the chaos of New York," Coté says. "When I'm with the bees its almost meditative – I'm unable to ponder any difficulties or problems that life may be throwing at me... I generally forget my problems."

Although the apprentices thought he might hate the colors they selected for their rooftop colony, Coté stands back now to admire the bright, lively shades of yellow, blue, purple and green. It was only a few years ago, he remarks, that hives had to be camouflaged as air conditioning units or duct work. Until 2010 it was dangerous to paint anything bright like this, since it might make it easier to spot from a distance. It looks cheerful, and everyone notices that the bees are especially attracted to the yellow.

The frames with the drone layers have now been shaken out, cleaned and placed in the newly painted supers. The queens from the swarms captured the day before have also been put into their new homes, along with their attending worker bees. To reduce fighting between the workers who were already there and the new workers from the swarm, the "newspaper method" will be employed. A sheet of *The New York Times* is placed between the older, existing super and the new one where the introduced bees are hanging out. The two sets of bees will acclimate to each other's scent slowly – and one hopes, peacefully – as they also chew away the newsprint. Within a few days they will have removed the paper and left it in small, chewed pieces outside their hive's entrance. With luck they will form one large, peaceful colony together.

Lids are being replaced and secured with ratchet belts to protect against wind gusts. Although beekeepers in some locations use weights, Coté favors ratchet belts in places like Chelsea. It would be very bad indeed to have the lid of a hive sail down from ten stories and hit someone during a storm.

A lot of what Coté does and says is motivated by making sure New York City beekeepers don't get any bad press. He is keenly aware that there are still many people who fear stings and are phobic about bees, although statistics say only one percent of the total population is actually allergic to their venom. Keeping the neighbors happy is important if he wants to keep his hundreds of hives going strong.

The bees have quieted back down and are making sense their new locations and housemates.

Coté is on the phone talking with a worker at a farmers market stall in another neighborhood. The honey collected on this roof won't be sold – the apprentices will get to harvest and enjoy it at the end of the season. But the honey he's produced elsewhere in the city is selling well and he needs to go check on inventory.

The apprentices are making plans to have brunch down the street and I find I'm slightly envious of what they have here – the camaraderie, the view, and, mostly, their relationship with the bees. Next week they'll be back on the rooftop, and I'll be at home wondering how their new bees are settling in and whether or not any more queens at that location will die before spring is over. It feels as if I've become friends with these bees now, but I'm also kind of embarrassed by it – like I got backstage passes and hung out with the roadies for a while. They'll be here for the next concert and I'll go back to being just a groupie.

I've loved insects all of my life, and spent two decades with my face in gardens, gathering information for writing projects about them. But this is the first time I get what it means to have a *relationship* with them. When you tend a hive of bees, it isn't just that you get to know *about* bees; you actually get to know a particular set of individuals, becoming momentarily a guest in their world, their house, their hive. But you are always just a guest.

After I leave the rooftop, I emerge from the freight elevator to find skateboarders zooming by and pizza delivery guys loading up scooters with their doughy pies before zigzagging their way through long strings of yellow taxi cabs. Families with strollers are rolling their way to the High Line, and I follow them, climbing the metallic stairway and pulling out my camera. I want to see if I can find any bees up there.

There are already many groups of people out on this elevated walkway, posing for pictures, or examining flower combinations along this unlikely new city attraction. So many people, in fact, it feels as if I've come to the beach. Some are carrying picnic baskets, others texting on their phones. Many stop every few feet to enjoy incredible views of the skyline around them or glimpses of the Hudson River in the distance. In some places the path narrows so much that people can only walk single file in each direction, making the pace relaxed. If you move to fast you end up accidentally stepping into some stranger's photo.

Only a few short decades back, freight trains ran here on an elevated track which had been built to improve safety in what was then the Meat Packing District. Previous to its opening in the 1930s, pedestrians were hit by trains running on the street level so often that Tenth Avenue – which is a main thoroughfare for this neighborhood – was nicknamed "Death Avenue." A display board in this new park area includes photos of the West Side Cowboys who were hired to ride horse-back in front of the trains along the street and wave red flags, but even this apparently did little to stop accidents.

The track's original designers back then were considered innovative for designing it to run through the center of city blocks here, rather than down the middle of the street as some elevated train lines did in other New York neighborhoods. The entire project, completed at the peak of the Depression, cost more than $150 million. It was heavily used for about two-and-a-half decades.

But by the 1960s trucks dominated shipping and freight train use began to decline, making the High Line archaic. According to official records, the last train to run on the High Line made its run with three carloads of turkeys in 1980.

After the trains stopped screeching down its rails, there were calls for its demolition. Eventually, a group called Friends of the High Line formed with an entirely different idea. They wanted the rail bed to be re-used as a park or open public space. Other places had successful rails-to-trails projects – why not New York, they asked.

By 2002, Friends of the High Line were able to demonstrate the value of such a space to the city. Organizers noted that the High Line "is the future, and it is built on our past," saying also that "a lush urban wilderness, nearly seven miles in total, has seeded itself on the High Line's tracks."

I read through this history on some huge display boards and study grainy photos from the 1980s of shirtless young men standing waist-high in the weeds. I still have bees on the brain and I find myself wondering what kind of plants those weeds were. I squint to see if I can make out any familiar leaf shapes in the picture.

It must have been a bee's paradise. Loads of plants, no pesticides, no humans, loads of sunshine. Air pollution was worse, though. And of course there probably were humans poking around frequently. Maybe homeless people, maybe gangs. It's easy to see all the graffiti in those photos, too. Someone must have put that there. Were there bees among the ruins? Birds? Anything other than rats?

Most of the rails were replaced with curvy, ADA-accessible pathways. The project is like a huge green rooftop park above the streets, complete with porous pavement and garden beds filled with sections of lawn and native plants and trees, turning the former transportation vein of the Meat Packing district into a lush, biodiverse park.

The High Line's success since opening in 2009 has been a testament to the city's ability to re-invent itself as a resilient, livable place. Millions of people have walked along its planted promenade. Real estate prices close by have skyrocketed, and hotel owners have clamored to build near it in order to capitalize on its success.

There are honey bees meandering along the path with me, visiting the purple blooms and blue blossoms up here. Surely some of these are gathering forage for the hives I just watched the beekeepers crack open. It's as if I've walked through the looking glass or entered the other side of a TV screen. I've seen their life from both sides now, and I have the odd urge to tell the two impeccably dressed guys draped next to a magnolia tree, "Hey, I *know* those bees, like really know them." Somehow I know the men would not be impressed, so I resist and move on.

High Line is not a garden, although there are incredible flowers everywhere, including dozens of prized species of native plants such as purple bee balm, amsonia, and joe pye weed. Its not an arboretum, although there are sections of magnolias, red buds, and birch trees. It's like the idea of an art gallery applied to nature: you walk through paintings made of incredible plant mixes where colors and textures are presented as a foreground for bricks, mortar, glass, and steel.

Although I walk from one end of the park to the other, I see only three types of pollinators on flowers I know to be full of nectar: dozens of honey bees, a single hover fly, and a single bumble bee. This is startling, especially to someone like me who writes a lot about urban wildlife. Usually, even the most mundane weed patch in any city plays host to a few species of native bees, flies, and wasps. I've even seen bees buzzing under actively used Amtrak rails in Newark, New Jersey.

Why are the native bees absent here today? Is it because the High Line is elevated? Because it's so new? Or is it just a random bad day for bee-watching in New York? Even though it's cloudy, it's warm. As an urban naturalist I should find a lot more pollinators on these flowers this morning.

Something else begins to bother me while I walk. A couple of days later I call Andrew Coté with a question. Why, I wonder, did he tell us to remember that beekeeping is something we do for ourselves? Why does he sometimes say it's almost a bit selfish?

"I think it would be hubris for us to say that we are saving the world," he replies. In New York there are at least 258 species of feral bees pollinating along with the species that are used in honey beehives like his.

"The honey bees make life sweeter, and they make this a better place. It is pleasurable to have them, wonderful to have them, and I'm a big advocate for them. But I'm skeptical about whether or not we need them," he says.

Later I find out there are others who have been watching the bees along the High Line just like me, such as Sidney Glaser.

"The word I would use to describe them is fascinating." It delights him to know that someone in Chelsea keeps hives as he used to do, before he quit eight years ago. "It became too strenuous and so I stopped when I turned 80," he says wistfully. "But that I had the opportunity to work with bees around the corner from Broadway – I had the best show in town."

Once, he told me, a producer for PBS had him wear a bee beard as part of a show about urban wildlife called *Wild TV*. Bee bearding is an old circus-style trick; by placing the queen of a hive on your face you are instantly surrounded by workers who come to tend their female leader. The producers wanted to demonstrate how gentle bees could be.

In his best year – he thinks it was maybe 2004 or 2005 – Glaser extracted an astonishing 100 pounds of honey from a single hive. He was also the star of an audio feature story for the popular National Public Radio program *All Things Considered* which aired in 2005. Beekeeping was an illegal activity in the city at that point, and Glaser kept the location of his hive out of the story as he described how rewarding beekeeping could be in the city, despite the fact that he'd discovered he was allergic to their venom and working the hives in the summer was often, he confessed, a hot, dirty experience.

"Urban beekeeping is really a labor of love."

In addition to some of the covert hives, he also kept bees in a high visibility location for the Clinton Community Garden in the neighborhood known as Hell's Kitchen, just a couple of blocks west of Times Square.

People like to think of urban farming and urban beekeeping as a relatively new trend, but Glaser and his work at Clinton Community Garden tell a different story.

The garden is one of the oldest of its kind in New York, started in the 1970s when the neighborhood was experiencing one of the city's highest crime rates. There were open air markets for illegal drugs, prostitution, and loads of abandoned, rusting cars along the streets. There wasn't any green space until residents decided to take over an abandoned lot full of rubble, glass, and trash and make it into a garden.

Over time, the space became well-loved and well-tended by its volunteers – to the point where the city decided it was a worthwhile space and ought to be sold to developers. An intense campaign to save the space erupted. Square inches of the place were sold for five dollars a piece by people who were determined to keep it a green garden. Eventually, public outrage forced those in power in the city to concede, and the green space became the first community garden to be granted permanent parkland status in New York.

The front was lined by flower beds, with 108 raised vegetable plots divvied up amongst locals. Concrete blocks and slabs of old slate had been recycled into benches, and things looked beautiful. The plants began to flourish, thanks to the addition of healthy top soil and other amendments.

Veteran gardeners agreed, however, that bees were needed to help with pollination. Hives were built and a colony established, but the bees sometimes languished without consistent care.

"Then Sid showed up, and he was a savior," actress Annie Chadwick remembers.

Glaser had learned beekeeping in order to make himself a more attractive candidate for a job with the Peace Corps. Now he found joy in bringing new life to the raised beds at the center of a neighborhood undergoing a miraculous transformation in the middle of his own city. Under his direction, the hives flourished.

Chadwick tells me that the garden's existence formed an essential component of city life, a way to stay connected to the environment in a very populated, urban place. "Most people in the neighborhood consider this their backyard." Back in those early days she and her daughter spent hours there, finding earthworms, learning about nature. "It's really the backyard of most children who live in Hell's Kitchen, even now."

Like Glaser, she found the bees enchanting. Despite a demanding schedule – her impressive online resume details past roles in movies directed by big names like Penny Marshall, television shows like *Law and Order*, and parts in Broadway plays – she has always tried to find time to devote to the garden and sometimes help with the bees.

"I am so impressed with the bees, their intelligence – and I marvel at their sophistication and their whole structure. It's really almost beyond words how smart and amazing they are. Nothing is as prolific here as the honey bees. They are instrumental and so valuable to the garden. You see the difference in propagation with them there."

Jenny Markovich, the garden's current beekeeper, says keeping bees these days isn't always easy. Three of the four years she's been beekeeping there, she's lost bees and had to buy packages and restart the colony from scratch, and like many others around the country she says it isn't always clear what has caused her bees to fail, even after having them tested and evaluated by scientists at the USDA. She doesn't use antibiotics on her hives because she thinks a natural approach is better for the environment and for the bees. She's also had to battle mice infestations.

Despite the challenges, she's proud of the long history of having bees at Clinton, and the fact that she's part of a thirty year tradition of beekeeping. "We had bees when it wasn't cool, and it was weird in New York City."

The first few years Markovich was there, beekeeping still wasn't legal, although it kind of seemed to everyone in Hell's Kitchen that because the hives at the Clinton Community Garden predated the ban, they were likely to be exempted from scrutiny. "I think in a way it was like don't ask, don't tell," she says, referring to the famous policy of the same time period regarding homosexuality in the US military. The bee ban, she notes, didn't change the garden's policy on bees, so the lifting of the ban didn't either. "But now we can talk more about it on the website."

Because of the bees' health struggles, there hasn't been much honey to share, although Markovich notes with pride that the last time they did have a harvest, they pulled in a tremendous amount of honey from their single Langstroth hive.

"Our honey is unbelievable. When it's posted that we are going to have some, the line goes around the block," she says. Everyone loves that it is natural, unheated, unfiltered, and very fresh.

Hell's Kitchen is no longer the arena for crime and urban decay it once was; it's become quite a desirable place to live, in no small part thanks to the green space that exists at its core. "Real estate agents, they give us donations," Chadwick tells me. "They know how much this adds to the value around here."

Brides want to get married there, and couples often pose for their wedding portraits in the main green space at the front. Every July 4th the neighborhood hosts a huge cook-out there, too. It's a place that beloved by both gardeners and non-gardeners alike.

I love the fact that the bees are part of these scenes — not detracting from the space, but adding to its allure. The bees — once outlawed — are a treasured and respected neighborhood presence, seen by the people here as essential to the green space and to its prosperity. The hives helped turned the neighborhood around. There are places all over the US where others hope to spark similar changes to run-down neighborhoods. This is one of the reasons, I realize, that urban bees are becoming so popular. Urban farmers are clamoring for them.

Chadwick notes that if the land where the garden now sits were ever developed, it would be worth many millions. But to Chadwick and others, as long as it remains a garden, it remains priceless.

Recently, she was at the garden beds weeding when a very well-dressed woman stopped at the fence to exclaim over how beautiful it was, and how surprising. Chadwick paused in her chores to tell the story of the garden, and explain what was being grown there, including the bees and their honey.

The woman gasped in astonishment, saying, "Oh, I'd never eat anything that was grown in the city."

Chadwick quickly replied, "But *you're* growing in the city! This is where *you* live!"

4

Swarms of Gotham with a Cop Named Tony Bees

Finding a swarm of bees is a bit like finding a drop of lava oozing from an unseen volcano: there's a brown mass that moves and wiggles and makes a sizzling sound. You step forward, only to realize it's not lava but in fact thousands of insects moving in a massive ball, fanning each other noisily with their wings.

For most people, it is a shock no matter where it is found. But to find such a large number of stinging insects writhing around in a heap in a place like the Bronx or Soho in New York seems really odd.

To Detective Anthony Planakis, however, a swarm is a beautiful thing. "I don't have kids myself. But seeing a swarm happen – that's almost like what I think it would be like to witness birth."

To understand Planakis' point of view, you have to know a bit about why bees swarm. They don't do it to defend themselves like a squadron of fighter jets. They do it when they need to find a roomier new home. It's not about defense, but about reproduction.

Any hive space – be it made by hand and hammer or found in a hollow tree – has a limited amount of room for new offspring, and healthy bees reproduce rapidly. So when the worker bees determine that there isn't enough space left in the hive they begin to raise a new queen out of the larvae of eggs laid by their current matriarch. Each hive can only have one leader, so once the new queen matures, the old queen exits the hive and a good portion of the worker bees follow her.

In rural areas, they then find a branch ten or fifteen feet off the ground and gather around the queen to soothe and protect her. Scout bees are sent out from the crowd to find a suitable new home – a process that can day a day or even longer. So long as the swarming bees can locate their queen and know she's safe, they stay fairly relaxed.

Once the hollow has been chosen, a signal is sent from bee to bee using dance-like movements, and the entire colony moves en masse to the new location fairly peaceably. It is an event that happens scores of times in forested areas without any human eye ever witnessing it.

But in an urban environment like New York, tree branches are often non-existent. So bees that live in a place such as the

Bowery or Little Italy find other, more interesting locations to roost while they await information from the scouts – like a stop sign, a fire hydrant, or the back of a graffiti-covered mailbox.

A skilled beekeeper like Planakis is trained to handle a swarm and can usually gather it up without the bees becoming defensive. Getting stung a few times is often part of the deal, although not a given if the keeper comes prepared both physically and mentally for the collection.

Planakis, who goes by the nickname Tony Bees, works for the New York Police Department. Although anyone can attempt to capture a swarm, he's the only official working for the city who does it as a part of his municipal job.

To hear him tell it, gathering swarming bees in New York City is a lot like a scene from the 1984 movie *Ghostbusters*. First, a call comes in to the emergency call center. If the swarm lands in a place with lots of foot or car traffic, the street might have to be closed for a while. Sometimes there are screaming and stampeding crowds of people; other times pedestrians gather to gawk, admire, and take pictures with their phones. Planakis arrives and, if need be, suits up, ready to take the bees off safely and quickly.

Most years there are maybe a dozen or so swarms during the city's warmer months. In the spring of 2012, however, something odd happened. Bees began swarming all over the city in great numbers. There were 37 calls to the city's emergency services line about swarms, and Planakis ended up gathering 34 of them for placement into hives.

Swarms make beekeepers feel self-conscious. A veteran knows how to read a hive, how to see that the workers are making ready to leave. Although bees will sometimes swarm unexpectedly from even the most experienced and vigilant of keepers, most consider an unanticipated swarm embarrassing and they try to take care to prevent it. So when the bees started showing up in swarms all over the city and the press began asking beekeepers why, a heated debate broke out. Whose fault was it that all of these bees were escaping in such huge numbers?

Weather might have been the real culprit. To some it felt as if winter never came to the Big Apple that year. It was warm – the official temperature hovered around 40 degrees all season. Only 7.4 inches of snow were recorded in Central Park between December 1, 2011 and February 29, 2012, well below the annual average of 21.

Spring also came very early and flowers began opening well ahead of the normal bloom times, making nectar and pollen available to bees much sooner than normal, creating optimal breeding conditions for bees.

But to some experienced beekeepers, the swarms symbolized a kind of growing pain. Beekeeping's popularity had skyrocketed in the US since the discovery of CCD. The fact that bees were struggling caused more and more people to want to get in on the action and try to help.

New York had also declared beekeeping legal again after a 12-year ban, and attendance at bee club meetings and how-to classes had ballooned into the hundreds. By 2012 more than

200 people had officially registered a hive, and many more were thought to be out there beekeeping in unregistered locations. One organization, NYCBeekeeping, told reporters from the UK's *Guardian* newspaper that their membership had grown to include more than 1,300 people.

Veteran beekeepers from many different quarters and clubs wondered if some of the new beekeepers just weren't ready when spring came that year due to a lack of experience, and their bees reacted accordingly by trying to find less crowded homes.

In the early part of that spring, Planakis says, the calls were mostly about feral hives. Big storms knocked branches down from trees, exposing waxy honeycomb which had been built in the hollow areas inside. But as the season wore on, it was calls about swarms coming from beekeepers' hives.

"This is what we are up against in New York City. All of these – I call them 'havers.' They aren't really 'keepers' yet," Planakis says. A lot of people bought bees without really knowing what they were getting into.

The city is full of odd obstacles for a swarm catcher; it's a fast-paced environment of glass, steel, power lines, and speeding vehicles. Planakis uses a special truck which the police commissioner issued to him a couple of years ago for bee-wrangling jobs. In it he keeps everything ready to go at a moment's notice: a generator, 100 feet of extension cord, chainsaws, loppers, cutters, pruners, ropes, rigging, safety harnesses, extension ladders, cages for queens, bee vacs for getting the swarms that land on hardscapes like hydrants, and enough cages to carry five swarms.

Most swarms are docile, he says, but they don't always stay that way.

One of the most notable swarms of 2012 stopped traffic – literally – when it engulfed a lamp post on Canal Street, making a busy intersection impassable for a time. At three o'clock that afternoon Planakis got the call from the dispatchers. A massive swarm had landed and they'd had to shut the block down. Firefighters arrived with a bucket truck to help.

"I felt like I was fighting nature on that one." The barometer was dropping – he could feel a storm coming in and he knew the bees were going to be edgy.

"If that weather starts changing and these bees get pissed-off because they can't find a home, and you go over there like I've done many job without a bee shirt on – get prepared – because you are going to be in the emergency room because they will go after you."

Once up in the bucket truck that day, his experience as a former Con-Edison employee let him know he had another problem on his hands: the light had a sensor on top. If he wasn't careful, or if either his hands or the bees covered that sensor, the light would come on and the heat would cause the bees to scatter.

The adventure ended peacefully and happily – the bees were secured and placed in his truck to be re-housed in a prepared hive before the storm erupted over his head. Just about all of Planakis' stories seem to end like that – he's worked a lot of swarms and he knows how to get the job done. Even so, you can't help but get sucked in when he starts recounting one. His words fall out at a fast New York pace. It's like listening to a cowboy talk about breaking a bronco, or a deep sea angler talk about reeling in a big fish. He's seen things when he's gone to get those swarms that form a unique picture of urban bees. He's learned to stay cool when others panic.

Planakis became unexpectedly famous when the swarms became so numerous in 2012. It seemed as if the press never tired of covering the topic, sending reporters to photograph him in a bee shirt and veil at the top of a bucket truck or extension ladder over and over again all that season. Taken with his expertise and unusual job description, they wrote feature after feature, delighting in puns and alliterative headlines like the one that flashed across the New York Times on June 16: "As Swarms Startle New York, Officer on Bee Beat Stays Busy."

Jeremiah Budin on a popular blog called NY Curbed declared him "King of the Bees," and made up a very funny – and very fictional – life story for him: he had lived like a bee as a child, "learning to sting, buzz and make honey with his abdomen," like a tall tale about Davy Crockett wrestling bears in Kentucky. Other times, they compared him to Batman, calling his truck the "Beemobile." There were slightly doctored photographs of Tony Bees in a gold crown and donning a gold necklace with a bee pendant.

Planakis says he never read those stories. "I'm not in it for that."

His regular assignment finds him in the very ordinary sounding NYPD Budget and Accounting Office on a daily basis. He was promoted to detective only recently. But his background and finesse with bees was recognized back in 1995, when the force sent him to check out a large number of hives being illegally maintained on public land. They thought maybe he could handle the job because he had listed beekeeping as one of his skills in the paper work he had filled out when he joined the force, along with air conditioning and electrical repair.

His father taught him about beekeeping when he was growing up in Connecticut in the 1970s. While others remember playing around as kids, his father put a hammer in his hand and taught him to build hives. Although it took a couple of years to get up the nerve to put on a suit and work the bees, he eventually became passionate about it. "Now, it's like it's in my blood."

More than anything, Planakis hates to see bees mistreated. There was one time last year, for example, when he was called in to confront someone holding boxes full of live bees in a closed car on a ninety degree day, which he found clearly repugnant. He also worries about someone doing something to harm the bees when they swarm. "I see the bees in a swarm situation as defenseless – that's why I want to get out there as soon as possible."

Being in the public eye has sometimes brought scrutiny and criticism. But after 35 years, he says he knows a thing or two about keeping a hive healthy, happy, and safe, and he stands by his methods. He'd be willing to get up behind a podium and debate bees anytime, any place, with anyone present.

"When you can actually walk up to a hive and listen to it and tell me what's going on in there, then I'll give you a little credit, but 'til then, I'm sorry."

Some of his own hives are in Queens and some in Newtown, Connecticut. He used to keep hives on Long Island, too, but a long time back the spraying of pesticides they did in communities there worried him, so he moved out his bees out. He doesn't treat his bees with chemicals, he says, because he thinks they will adapt to urban conditions better that way.

Maybe one reason he's become a folk hero is because he sees the bees not as a plague upon the city, but as a boon. In New York and its close-in urban suburbs, he points out, there are people who have queens that are lasting, hives that are thriving for years without much intervention. "I think it's fantastic."

In 2013 he was called in to help with the removal of a giant feral hive of honey bees that had become established in the joists of a building's attic. One person on the scene recalled the bees having been there for more than 13 years, and to Planakis it looked as if they had indeed been there for more than a decade. Row upon row of honeycomb draped down from the ceiling, and honey coated the floors and walls. The damage to the building and the health concerns were extensive because rats had found a food resource – their droppings were plentiful, too.

Although such scenes pose health hazards and are not something that makes Planakis happy, in other areas of the US such feral hives – once a common rural occurrence – have all but vanished due to Varroa mites and other parasites.

That bees can establish successful hives in the city without any intervention signals something about the potential the city poses as a habitat for the insect. Planakis wonders if cities are the only places left where bees will survive. Pesticides, he says, seem to be causing so many problems elsewhere. "All these things that are out there in the suburbs, in the country, you don't have in the city."

Planakis loves the way that everything ceases to exist when he's with his bees. "It's the most perfect society I've ever seen. It operates on the caste system, and you know some-thing? There is no jealousy inside that hive, there is no brown-nosing, no ass-kissing or anything like that, everyone from birth knows what their job is, what they have to do to sustain that hive, and to reach their goal. They recognize their one leader, the queen, and should any problems arise they have the ability to handle any problem that comes around. To me it's a beautiful thing."

Planakis worries that too many people are into the bees now just to make money. When a well-known skin care com-pany approached him recently and asked if he'd help promote their line of wax-based lip balms and lotions, he was alarmed by their proposals, which included posing with bees in front of Rockefeller Center in Manhattan. He thought their idea might be dangerous to tourists and harmful to the bees, so he turned them down saying, "Hey, I'm not running the Barnum and Bailey Circus here."

Soon, Planakis will be eligible for retirement, although he's not sure he wants to take it just yet. During a trip to Florida for vacation this spring he found himself checking his phone constantly to see if there were any swarm calls coming through.

"As far as the bees, I told the Commissioner: 'Here's what you do. You pick up every single paper and if you see my name in there in the obituaries, then you know you got a problem. Until then call me anytime, it doesn't matter."

The big swarms of 2012, it seems, were just a fluke. In 2013 the city had a relatively normal winter and a fairly cool spring, and by mid-June there had only been eight calls to the department about bees showing up in strange places.

5

A Night of Honey in the City of Brotherly Love

Most of my life I have not liked the taste of honey.

As a kid, I thought that it tasted worse than medicine. As a mom, when I read aloud from *Winnie-the-Pooh* I laughed along with my kids. But when they asked why the bear liked honey so much I shrugged with puzzlement. And later, when we went to a cute tea party and someone's British grandmother served teeny cucumber sandwiches and decaf Earl Grey tea blended with milk and honey, I quietly demurred as the children exclaimed in delight.

However, when I began interviewing beekeepers and reading about the huge renaissance beekeeping was enjoying in the US, I began to question my distaste.

Everyone everywhere was snapping up the golden liquid. Gourmet chefs exclaimed about its goodness. Newspapers printed details for using it over fresh summer fruit. I watched from the sidelines, interested in the biology behind the stuff, but still not interested in eating any myself. Every beekeeper I met told me to come back later in the season. That would change my taste buds.

The problem, I slowly realized, was not with my taste buds. The problem was my shopping habits. I was buying cheap honey made by huge corporations. More than likely that a lot of processing had been done to it before bottling. In some cases, maybe the company had mixed different honey varietals in a vat at the factory before bottling. It may also have been pasteurized to delay granulation. Both, I've been told, can destroy the unique, complex taste which is naturally present when the golden sticky stuff is pulled from the hive.

I should further confess that although some of the bottles on the shelves next to the boxes of pancake mix at the store were labelled "clover" or "orange blossom" or "blueberry," I had never bothered to try them because they seemed expensive, and I figured it was all just a marketing ploy. If I didn't like the basic honey, why would I like any of that stuff?

Looking back now, it was all reminiscent of my history with apples. For the first twenty years of my life I hated the shiny red fruit because I was only ever offered the mealy, bruised "Red Delicious" varieties at the school cafeteria and at the grocery store where my mom shopped in the 1970s. When

I finally tried a fresh "Gala" at the local farmers market as an adult in the 1990s, it tasted like a whole different kind of food.

Maybe that name thing isn't just a marketing ploy after all – maybe wildflower honey actually does taste different than tupelo. And maybe I should check it out.

So in the name of research, I set off for "Sweet and Savory Science, Hives and Honey" – an evening event during Philadelphia's 2013 Science Festival hosted by the Continental Restaurant and Martini Bar in April.

The Continental sits at the corner of Market and Second in a neighborhood called Old City, which has undergone a massive renaissance in the last 20 years from a graffiti and crime-plagued area to one that is full of people jogging, texting on iPhones and eating in expensive tapas bars.

The Continental was one of the first bars to open in the early years of the neighborhood's rebirth. As I make my way down Market, I notice it still remains a standout, crowned by a giant pole that looks vaguely like a casino swizzle stick topped with giant dice. There are lots of fashionable eateries here now, but none look quite like this one with an abundance of stainless steel, mid-century decor and lampshades shaped like green olives. I have a hunch that the owners were probably more inspired by the huge cars made by the Lincoln Motor Company than they were Ben Franklin and the Continental Congress when they named this place. There's a vaguely Frank Sinatra vibe here.

The smiling manager at the door seems to be dressed in homage to Elvis Costello, complete with wayfarer-shaped, black-rimmed glasses, a checkered 1980s sport coat, skinny jeans, and slightly spiked hair. I have the surreal sensation that I'm talking to the cover of the album *Trust!* I wish I had chosen a more fun outfit. This is really a party scene.

Elvis points me toward a private side room where the Sweet and Savory event is being held. Although pre-paid online tickets were $30, the room is packed with people, and in the back a projector is flashing a rotation of bee photos in time with some groovy music.

I am promptly greeted by a friendly guy in a brown t-shirt emblazoned with the yellow logo of the Philadelphia Beekeepers Guild – a bee in the center of an ornate, medieval-looking flower-covered shield. People in Philly, I think to myself, enjoy trying to straddle as many time periods as possible.

The bar offers honey-flavored martinis – the "Honey Bee," with Maker's Mark whiskey, honey syrup, and lemon juice and the "Gold Rush," with Meyer's dark rum, honey syrup and lemon juice. Honey syrup, the pretty blond bartender says with a patient smile, is really just a simple sugar made from boiling equal parts distilled water and honey. Honey does not pour easily or blend well with the liquor unless diluted. (She also tells me that the drinks are available for one night only; I wonder if that is because she finds the process of making the simple syrup annoying.)

I order the "Bee's Knees" made from Bluecoat gin, honey syrup, and orange juice. It is a tangy concoction served in an elegant martini glass with a fresh citrus slice on its rim. The name is a nod to the era of Prohibition, when honey was apparently a cheap and popular way to spruce up bad-tasting homemade liquor.

Cocktail in hand, I join a table where Don Schump stands next to a glass-paneled observation hive in which honey bees are busily working over their honeycombed wax. The bee-keeper, a big burly guy with a close-trimmed goatee, is animatedly telling a crowd assembled in front of his table that Philly honey is better than any other he's ever had.

When I ask why he playfully shouts, "Because of 200 years of botanical awesomeness! It's just really complex. There are a lot of different plants out there in this city! I sometimes think that honey is really like wine for idiots like me," he adds in a softer, more conspiratorial voice, pausing to tilt his baseball cap back from his face with a tap from his in-dex finger.

Every year his honey tastes different, just like wines do. When spring comes late, for example, Philly honey tends to have an extremely smooth texture and mellow sweetness. Other years it is more bright and crisp in flavor.

Just beyond Schump, I find the current president of the Philadelphia Beekeepers Guild, Suzanne Matlock, who has an array of different honeys in identical white ceramic bowls for people to examine and taste on the ends of pretzel sticks. Some of her offerings are from the Philadelphia area and some have been sent from beekeepers in Maryland.

A fortyish guy in lumberjack-style plaid enthusiastically tries every sample she lays out –Japanese knotweed, blueber-ries, cranberries, and Queen Anne's lace. "I usually don't like honey." He raises his beer glass in a playful toast to Matlock and me, and takes a second helping of each.

"Saying you don't like honey is a bit like saying you don't like soda," Matlock chides him gently. "If someone said that they didn't like soda, you'd wonder which one, wouldn't you? Coke, Pepsi, Seven-Up, Canada Dry, Sprite – there are so many kinds of soda. And there are many kinds of honey each with its own unique taste." Each flower produces a different flavor, and each flower varies depending on where it is grown. Blueberry honey made by bees from flower nectar in Maine might taste totally different from that made by bees in New Jersey.

My favorite is her Queen Anne honey, which Matlock describes as "dark flavor caramel with a tart hint of spiciness." In the bowl it looks as dark as Vermont maple syrup.

Taking up a bit on the end of a pretzel stick to try, I suddenly wish I had a dark beer in my hand instead of a super-sugary cocktail. It is almost as if I had never eaten honey before – the taste of what rolls across my tongue is so different that I don't even recognize it. It seems to sparkle, but is also mellow. The flavor is intense – one tiny dab fills my entire mouth with sweetness. I immediately want to put it on all kinds of food – this honey would be great in a beef marinade or sauce for pork barbeque.

The Japanese knotweed honey, labeled "bamboo" flavor, is even darker, with a finish that Matlock compares to molasses. Although the honey it can produce is tasty and sweet, Japanese knotweed is not usually something American environmentalists think of with affection. The invasive exotic plant was introduced to the US sometime in the 1800s and is almost impossible to remove once it becomes established along stream banks and riversides. Pieces of its hard-to-cut stems can regrow, and its seeds are easily carried by truck tires, shoes, and snow plows from one location to another. In some places it has entirely displaced native plants and made shorelines completely inaccessible for fishing, boating, or hiking.

Part of knotweed's persistence in urban soil is due to its hardiness and its ability to grow in full shade, even in soil high in salinity. Federal officials estimate that removal of the Asian plant costs private property owners and public land managers tens of millions of dollars every year.

And yet, invasives like knotweed form an important part of the story of urban honey. Like knotweed, tree of heaven and purple loosestrife comprise a huge part of the forage used by urban bees, and may be one reason the hives in northeastern cities are able to produce honey so prolifically. The bees in a lot of urban areas have access to a lush, diverse mix of nectar.

"As a gardener, I really hate a lot of these plants. They are bad news," Schump says. "But as a beekeeper I know they make up a lot of the forage in cities." Some of the best-tasting and most available forage plants – such as dandelions – are more annoying than harmful to the environment, he adds.

Anything labeled as "wildflower honey" may include some portion of invasive exotic forage plants along with native flowers and trees. On Matlock's table there are three such bowls. To show how broad the definition of wildflower could be, she has purposefully chosen three very different flavors for sampling; and all three vary in color as well.

Wildflower, she explains, is the descriptive word used for honey when the flowers that the bees forage from is unknown, or from so many different plants that no single type of flower dominates the taste. In fact, most of the honey produced in US cities could be classified as "wildflower," since it is often impossible for an urban beekeeper to know every plant that blooms in their own neighborhood. In a single day a honey bee may visit more than 2,000 plants to find nectar for the hive, and a bee may travel within a three-mile radius of its hive to forage. Many of the flowers a bee visits are not on the ground, either, but on the branches of tall trees.

Listening to this description, I'm reminded of nature writer Sue Hubbell, who in her classic and much-loved 1988 memoir *A Book of Bees* declared that "a beekeeper must be something of a botanist." Walking with a botanical field guide in hand was one of the most enjoyable aspects of beekeeping, she said, but it was also one of the most important. She also confessed that along with a guide book she often went out to classify her bees' forage with a picnic basket, a friend, and a bottle of wine during spring time in order to learn more about her honey for labeling purposes.

Like most rural beekeepers, Hubbell's hives were located in farm fields, tucked next to crops or surrounded by cattle and horse farms, so she could easily identify which blossoms were dominating her own bees' diet.

But here in the city, trees and flowers grow in unexpected locations, colonizing cracks in concrete and utilizing soil in forgotten spots not seen regularly by people. It makes me laugh to think of beekeepers like Matlock or Schump exploring the urban wilds of Philadelphia in the same manner that Hubbell so vividly described. I begin imagining Guild members spreading picnic cloths in the grassy areas in front of strip malls or convenience stores, or scaling security fences around abandoned buildings – like a kind of parkour with bees and their flowers.

Even without such trips to the "urban wild places" to identify the forage flowers, most urban beekeepers love to describe the flavor of honey their own bees produce. For one thing, it is smart business practice. In recent years, some urban neighborhoods have become known for producing certain flavors of honey. Serious foodies like to buy knowing what each kind will bring to their recipes, and are often willing to pay more if a beekeeper can give them a good description of their honey's flavor.

But there's also a certain amount of hometown pride at stake in honey production. Having a jar of honey with a funky urban neighborhood name on it often makes people feel as if they are taking part in the urban homestead movement, or at least supporting it, giving certain brands a cache over others.

Although there is no honey for sale here tonight, I have already discovered in my travels with beekeepers that local brands are not cheap. At one farmers market in the suburbs of DC I had seen premium "basswood" honey priced by a local beekeeper for $15 a pound. In New York, some urban farmers are able to charge – and receive – $40 for their one-pound bottles. Certainly there are far less expensive and less caloric ways to sweeten cereal or tea.

Labels and names have been used by honey makers who wish to send political messages. When they were arguing for the legalization of urban beekeeping in DC, beekeepers presented their City Council members with honey festooned with homemade labels featuring a motif based on the city's famous flag. It was an effective kind of branding that went beyond taste and tried to tap that city's growing sense of reborn municipal pride, and provided a few savvy politicians with some good photo ops.

After trying more than my share of Suzanne Matlock's samples I continue on to a table hosted by her husband, Norman, who is telling listeners what happens during a year in the life of the average worker bee in a Philadelphia hive. Assembled on the table in front of him are various pieces of a beehive super – including wax-filled frames, lids and boxes for transporting queens to new locations.

As he spins out his story with great flourish and humor, one couple right in front is particularly locked into his narrative. The woman, who is about 25, has the same look on her face as a child listening to stories about Santa's impending visit on Christmas. She's a believer – hungry for all of the information he's willing to share, and every few minutes she interrupts him politely to ask for even more details about life in a typical hive.

When Norman Matlock finally takes a break from his story to get a drink of water, I ask the couple if they are going to start beekeeping soon. While the woman shakes her head and smiles sadly to say no, her male companion holds up his hands in mock surrender.

"Not me, not me," he smiles. "This is all her thing."

"No room where we live right now," she says with a shrug and a wistful sigh. "But soon. As soon as I can. That's my dream. I think about it all the time. I have big bee dreams."

The crowd around us is incredibly diverse. Norman is African American, as are many of those who've bought tickets to attend tonight. The couple he's been talking to is white, as is his wife, Suzanne. Both Matlocks look to be in their mid-40s, but there are people both many decades older and many decades younger all around of many different ethnic and racial backgrounds enjoying the bees. Together the crowd forms a fairly good representation of the middle class population currently living in downtown Philly.

The Philadelphia Beekeeper's Guild is a relatively new group. They started as a group of friends who kept meeting at bars around town to talk about their newfound love of the bees. "It was really just a group of us hanging out," says Suzanne Matlock. Someone got the idea to ask a veteran beekeeper who was well known all over Pennsylvania named Joe Duffy to come and talk with them one night.

Duffy, who'd been keeping bees on roof tops and in backyards all over Philly since the 1970s immediately recognized the valuable role a new group could have in fostering both a love for the bees and support for what was becoming an increasingly hard hobby to sustain. When he started out as a keeper there wasn't much to worry about other than a disease called American foulbrood. Now, the mites, the hive beetles, and CCD have made the entire enterprise challenging. After the winter of 2011, for example, he lost about ten of the fifteen hives he was keeping at different locations around the city.

"With these new beekeepers coming in I feel really bad. I mean look-at," he says, using a Philly slang term, "I'm an experienced beekeeper and pretty knowledgeable and I can't keep these darned bees alive!... I mean, it's a nice hobby and I enjoy it for the pollination and things like that but my gosh, it can get really expensive."

So after he gave a talk to the fledgling group about how to get started with bees and how to avoid some of the most common mistakes in urban beekeeping, he opened his own wallet, pulling out a $20 bill and handing it to a keeper named Joe Eckel, insisting he and his friends become more than just a group of friends chatting over beers every once in a while.

Duffy and other veteran beekeepers across the city and all over the country knew something else important about Philadelphia that made many want to support the formation of a new guild. The City of Brotherly Love is also the birthplace of Lorenzo Langstroth, one of the early innovators in beekeeping and the man for whom the most popular beehive design in the world is named. Langstroth was the one who figured out how to turn a painful and often profitless venture into something enjoyable and financially rewarding. His early beekeeping experiments in the 1800s were conducted just a few blocks from tonight's event, near the city's docks.

Although humans had been gathering stores of honey from bees for centuries, the process wasn't easy in the early 19th century. One method involved baskets, known as skeps, which were laid out to entice feral bees inside to set up house-keeping and build their waxy combs. When it was time for the humans to gather honey, leaves were burned to give off a sul-furous gas to kill the bees. A skilled keeper was one that knew how to do the job without tainting the honey.

To many it seemed an inhumane and wasteful process. Each spring a brand new colony of bees would have to be en-ticed to build itself up into the skeps all over again. The amount of honey collected was small and it was almost im-possible for someone to monitor the bees and their progress throughout the year.

Throughout the 19th century, as enterprising inventors set their sites on just about every other aspect of modern agricul-ture, small improvements were made to beekeeping. New, glass-sided observation hives allowed scientists and hobbyists to carefully observe the workings of the hive caste system. Improved field optics also allowed researchers to gain a great-er appreciation of the role that bees played in the pollination of plants – including valuable food and textile crops. Many saw a need to develop a hive which could be maintained without the need of killing the bees.

One early design of wooden hives included bars across the top from which frames hung that allowed bees to build their combs. These new hives could be opened but were not really easy to inspect due to propolis build-up and the fact that the insects often attached their honeycombs directly to the sides and lids. As a result, honey production remained small and often meant many painful stings for beekeepers. With the wooden hives the bees might live more than one season but harvesting the honey also meant removing all of the wax combs, resulting in small honey harvests.

Langstroth found the state of contemporary beekeeping "deplorable," and began to contemplate what changes he might make to improve honey harvesting in order to make it easier, more humane, and more profitable for humans.

Legend has it that he had a sudden epiphany one evening after visiting a   beeyard not far from his home: hives could be made of rectangular frames which would completely surround and encase the combs. Those frames, he further decided, should be spaced so that the bees had enough room to come and go from the box. (Later investigation on his part revealed that hives only needed about a quarter inch of this "bee space" or "dead air" to work well.)

"The chief peculiarity in my hives, as now constructed, was the facility with which these bars could be removed without enraging the bees, and their combination with my new mode of obtaining the surplus honey," Langstroth wrote in a manual he published in 1853 to announce his discovery,

Langstroth on the Hive and the Honey-Bee / A Bee Keeper's Manual.

Langstroth's radical new design was not widely accepted at first. A great deal of debate took place over what he could rightly call his "invention" and what others could claim as their own innovation.

But about 12 years later a jewelry maker in Ohio, Amos I. Root, began mass-producing the Langstroth hives and frames for shipment to rural Americans via the new rail lines that crisscrossed the US. Suddenly, farmers could house valuable pollinators while gaining a sweetener with a long shelf life. Many also gained a second form of income when they sold the honey or made soap from the excess wax. The A.I. Root company still remains one of the largest manufacturers of beehives in the world.

Suzanne Matlock says she knew nothing about Langstroth nor the history of Philadelphia beekeeping when she got started. What she knew was that the in the bees were dying – she and Norman had watched a documentary on public television about CCD in 2007 and both found the everything about the social insects fascinating. They had looked around the city and found the others who had already started getting together to "talk bees."

An idea emerged: the group should erect a historic marker in front of the house where Langstroth was born in 1810.

"Suddenly all of these people were saying, you have to do something to mark that event. And we were like hey, we aren't even a real beekeeping group yet," Matlock recalls.

Matlock says that although she and the other city beekeepers in Philly were overwhelmed at the prospect of hosting the event, beekeepers from other places all over the country offered assistance. Some helped with the extensive and demanding paperwork and legal issues, others with promotion and planning. Someone even helped draft wording for the permanent placard.

At one point Matlock ended up charging the marker to her own credit card, unsure of exactly where the money would come from for reimbursement since the group had not yet even filed its own non-profit status. (Eventually she would get paid back in full, as many donations were made by supporters to cover the expense.)

Finally, September 10, 2010 arrived – the day when the historic marker was to be unveiled. It seemed as if hundreds of beekeepers had come to Philadelphia to be there, standing outside of Langstroth's birthplace, now a private residence along Philly's South Front Street. Pennsylvania's own Secretary of Agriculture, Russell C. Redding, came and gave a speech, and a reporter and photographer from *Bee Culture* magazine were present.

It was then, says Matlock, they realized they had actually done something pretty grand, and they had become a pretty great group of beekeeping friends.

Even though Langstroth's home now has a permanent historic marker, the Guild is still struggling to find a permanent spot to meet each month. For now they enjoy rotating from location to location throughout the city, encouraging more than 100 beekeepers from all over the city to participate. There's a certain breezy friendliness to their website and communications that seems to bridge the gaps between older, more reticent or traditional beekeepers and the younger, urban homesteaders who take up the hobby these days.

Many members, Matlock notes, have a bent towards "natural" beekeeping but she insists that they not judge anyone who does things differently. "But we try to stress that you should let the bees teach you things. We try to be inclusive. We are a support group for beekeepers," she adds.

There are some very real financial benefits to membership in the Philadelphia Beekeepers Guild which are appreciated by both camps of people. At each monthly meeting there are prizes, raffles, and giveaways of "beekeeping interest." Members get discounts to area workshops and events related to beekeeping, and each year they organize a group purchase of woodenware, enabling members to get supplies for their hives at a steep discount. What's more, the Guild also owns a two-frame observation hive which can be used to transport bees to educational events, fairs and festivals, and a motorized extractor which the members can use for a small fee.

Honey extraction is not being demonstrated tonight – this is April and the honeycombs won't be ready until the fall. I make a note to myself to watch someone do an extraction before the season is over. I would like to learn more about how the honey is removed from all of those combs.

Regardless of its color, most of the honey being sampled here at the bar tonight is translucent. Although the color of the honey may vary depending upon the flowers the bees' visited during the season, most of it gleams in the bowl or on the spoon like stained glass. In the US, it seems that most consumers like their honey to look like this, although Canadians tend to think of the cloudy, crystallized versions of the sweet stuff as more prized.

This is where the semantics of honey labelling can get confusing. In the US, the honey that is often labelled at grocery stores as "raw" often crystalizes, becoming more cloudy in appearance than what is offered at the Philly tasting. This has led some US consumers to think that raw honey should always look like that, when in reality it just indicates its been sitting in the jar for a while and was never heated. But there is no official, legal definition of "raw" honey, at least for the purposes of commerce. What people are seeking when they say they want raw honey is generally honey that has not been heated or filtered or pasteurized.

Generally, however, there would be no reason to heat the honey being sold in small amounts by local artisanal producers. Honey is naturally very high in acidity, and also very low in moisture, which prevents it from hosting bacterial growth. Therefore, almost all honey bottled by small-scale beekeepers is uncooked or unheated before being bottled. It goes straight from the comb to the bottle without any kind of treatment.

Most small-scale beekeepers do macro-filter their honey, however, to take out debris that has made its way into the comb. The filters used have relatively large-sized sieves, intended to remove bits of debris or random bee wing and body pieces as well as some broken bits of wax.

When such macro-filtering is not done, the resulting sweetener sometimes takes on a cloudy appearance sooner due to the suspension of fine material including pollen grains and wax.

Macro-filtering also adds air, which helps to slow crystallization. Even though crystallized honey is not significantly different tasting than clear liquid honey, can be harder to pour, making it harder to add to certain dishes. Cooks will sometimes get around this problem by submerging a bottle of crystallized honey in a bowl of hot water. This does not impact taste, but some argue that such heating will reduce the nutritive content or heath benefits of the product or fundamentally change its taste. This is where epicurean debates begin, because taste can be very subjective.

Some consumers also like their honey unfiltered because they feel that there is an added health advantage to leaving the pollen grains in the liquid. Apparently, the science has yet to show this is the case; only a miniscule amount of pollen actually shows up in honey in most cases even if it is unfiltered, since honey is made by bees from nectar, not pollen. Any pollen there is incidental.

Then there are those who prefer their honey to be bottled with a giant piece of honeycomb inside. The wax can be chewed like gum, and it looks like a work of art on the shelf in a sunny kitchen, even it does have a few pieces of random debris stuck in it. Its primitive appearance is part of its charm, and the comb seems to offer visual proof that the honey is raw.

The fact that all of these various forms of honey are available for sale now in the US has only added to people's confusion over definitions. Controversy erupted a few years ago when some honey importers in the US were accused of selling honey that had been "ultrafiltered."

In the food industry, ultrafiltration is a specific term, used to describe a process whereby water is added to honey and then filtered back out again at the molecular level under very high pressure. According to the National Honey Board website, this is a very expensive process which results in a product that the Food and Drug Administration has officially said should not be called "honey" in the US. It is very different indeed from simple macro filtering.

A few years ago, US food safety advocates began accusing foreign honey suppliers of using ultrafiltering in order to remove all traces of pollen, thereby erasing the ability to identify the origin of the liquid in question. Others suspected large grocery store chains in the US were selling low quality honey mixed with high fructose corn syrup and sugar. The inability to identify pollen grains only fueled such accusations.

When several food contamination events connected to Chinese imports began to occur, many Americans began balking at any edible product which wasn't produced in the US. Then, an antibiotic illegal to use in the US was found in some honey which had been imported via illegal importation routes from China, which only increased public distrust of the big honey companies and their mixing methods. Some consumers began demanding local honey because they felt it was safer and more reliable.

Others have also made the case that the importation of cheap legal honey from outside the US is a symptom of how fundamentally changed our agricultural sector has become in this country. By bringing in cheap imported honey, some argue, we've uncoupled a relationship between the pollinators and the crops. Pollination is now often seen as an input to be managed on most large-scale monocrop farms – not a natural process that takes time and patience and a diverse farm landscape. We've become dependent upon the migratory beekeepers who drive their bees up and down the continent because we grow food without pollinators present. Whereas in the past, farmland often included diverse weed patches or even tree-filled hedgerows between crops where bees could thrive, the modern farm is often purged of all weedy space through the use of herbicides and no-till farming methods in order to maximize growing space. Honey bees must be brought in to help pollinate in such locations, and so services provided by the trucked-in bees are often more profitable than any honey such colonies could produce. Honey has become merely a bi-product of this relationship.

Buying local honey could, it is argued, provide small-scale organic farmers with one more source of income. It could also reward and support the growers who tend to the needs their own pollinating insects on site. Therefore, just as other forms of locavore eating have caught on, so has local, artisanal honey.

Frankly, I'm not sure most people understand or are aware of all of those potential economic cascades and theories. Most of the general public also seems to remain unaware of the process of migratory beekeeping. I'm also pretty sure most people don't even think about monocrops and their impact on bees. So I don't think you can blame the long lines that sometimes form at the beekeeper's tables at local farmers markets on any of those forces.

I suspect most people buy local because it seems so damn fun to buy honey made in one's own neighborhood, especially in the city. I've discovered myself how superior the local stuff can taste. I think other people have, too. It is really fun to find out that a neighborhood like Center City or South Street can produce honey that tastes so yummy. It can seem as if the beekeeper has spun gold from urban straw.

I also think that although people may not always understand the intricacies of where honey comes from or how it is made, they do know it is bees that make it. Buying something that might have been made by the insects you've seen on a flower in your own backyard is cool. Besides, the fact that bees can sometimes sting provides a wonderfully odd contrast. What other potentially dangerous thing can also provide you a sugary sweet? It just seems sublime, even to those who aren't back-to-nature, organic gardening types. Its a kind of agricultural poetry.

Beyond the prosaic sweetener, though, there are also a lot of people interested in the healthful qualities which many of the products of the hive have to offer. At a large table near the bar here at the Continental, Bee Guild member Adam Schreiber is telling a rapt audience of about six people what it means to be an apitherapist – someone who uses the products of the hive such as honey, royal jelly, bee venom and propolis for medical use. Laid out in front of him are various books and health care products. He's even brought in some samples he found for sale at a local health food store, including "Botanically Bright" toothpaste from the Tom's of Maine company, which uses a combination of bee propolis and xylitol (a sugar-free sweetener made from birch trees) to whiten teeth.

Schreiber's also brought a dog-eared copy of *The Bible of Venom Therapy,* a book by Bodog F. Beck. Beck was one of the first to try to add some academic examination to the practice of using stings for medical purposes; previous to his 1935 book the practice had sort of existed as a shadowy pursuit undertaken only by those using other folk remedies, and even then it was more familiar to Europeans than Americans. Most conventional medical doctors in the early 20th century often scorned the use of stings due to lack of any real evidence that bee venom might actually act as an anti-inflammatory agent in the human body.

In the last 20 years, however, herbal remedies and traditional healing methods have become much more accepted by both the medical establishment and the public, bringing about a kind of renaissance for the 80-year-old text. More than ever, people are willing to revisit the notion that bees might have something to offer healthcare practitioners.

A lot of modern beekeepers I've interviewed say they regularly get asked about the anti-inflammatory sting therapy. Some report that they are approached by neighbors suffering through the early stages of Multiple Sclerosis who are seeking relief from their disease after having seen reports by a Maryland woman named Pat Wagner, who documented her own sting therapy for the disabling disease in a book entitled *How Well Are you Willing to Bee, The Beginner's Auto Fix-it Guide*.

Others say older relatives with arthritis ask for stings to relieve joint pain. Almost all of the beekeepers I interviewed throughout the 2013 season admitted to the enjoying some of the benefits of occasionally getting stung by their own bees; some talked about the adrenaline rush it brought, or the instant dose of energy, while others said their own stiff fingers were often placated by an occasional accidental sting to the hands.

Despite the new acceptance by the public, there's still a surprising lack of research on the topic of sting therapy, however, which leaves the question of how much one might be willing to experiment on one's own body. Or how much one might be willing to let an apitherapist experiment on you while you seek relief in what may seem like a hopelessly painful situation such as what MS and arthritis can bring. It is a highly personal decision.

Beyond stings and venom, there are other ways that the products of a hive get used by those interested in alternative medicine. Propolis, the sticky glue-like substance that bees make by combining wax and the resins of conifer and poplar trees, is readily available to beekeepers but hard and expensive to find otherwise, Schreiber points out. This can be a really nice benefit to beekeeping for those who want to try it themselves as a way to ward off infections and reduce certain kinds of swelling.

A sixty-something African American woman introduces herself to us and looks over the books and materials Schreiber has laid out and asks him for websites or other sources. He cautions that he is not an apitherapist – just someone who finds the topic interesting, although someday he hopes to be able to offer bee sting therapy through his acupuncture practice. What she is seeking, however, is more information about managing her type 2 diabetes with honey. Is it safer to eat than sugar, she wonders?

Schreiber is careful to tell her to consult her doctor, but I know she's not the only one with this idea. It's something that has become a common question lately as both beekeepers and diabetes patients have both grown in number. The notion that honey is somehow superior for use in a diabetes diet may have come from its strong flavor – perhaps people thought they could use it in smaller amounts. Or perhaps because honey offers a small amount of vitamins and minerals that sugar lacks, it was seen as healthier or more beneficial.

Over and over again many medical professionals urge caution and skepticism when asked about the substitution. Both contain glucose and fructose, but a teaspoon of sugar contains 16 calories while a teaspoon of honey contains 22. Both sweeteners, they often point out, rank very close on the glycemic index. There seems to be no evidence that honey will help in the management of disease.

Honey does have a small advantage over processed sugar when it comes to vitamins and minerals. Most of those micronutrients are removed when sugar is processed, but they can remain behind in honey. But the amount and variety can vary widely based on where and how the honey is processed and what forage the bees visited when making it.

A lot of people, when asked about why they purchase local honey, will also tell you they do it to manage seasonal allergies. The thinking is that because bees gather nectar and eat pollen from local flowers, humans who eat the honey of local bees will somehow be given instant immune system recharges and their allergy symptoms will be alleviated. It seems logical to some that eating honey would provide a kind of immunotherapy, whereby the body would be exposed to the allergen in small, harmless amounts in order to correct the allergic reaction, especially if the honey had been made from forage closest to where the allergy sufferer lives.

As an allergy sufferer myself, I really wanted this to be true, with all my heart and with all of my aggravated sinus passages. Certainly the anecdotal evidence is ample; almost every beekeeper I met during 2013 reported that increasing their intake of local honey had decreased their seasonal allergies or those of a loved one.

But this turns out to be an idea without any scientific backing as of yet. In fact, the only study thus far on the topic of allergies and honey, conducted by researchers at the University of Connecticut's Department of Pathology and published in the *Annals of Allergy, Asthma and Immunology* in 2002, found that honey did not provide people suffering from seasonal allergies with any relief.

But honey, which has been used for curing many kinds of ailments for centuries, is finally getting a bit of use in modern Western medicine for the treatment of other problems.

A team of doctors working at Pennsylvania State University in 2007, for example, found that honey was actually much more effective at calming a child's cough than some common over-the-counter elixirs. It can also be cheaper, doctors noted, and less likely to cause negative side effects than the some of the conventionally produced medicines. (Doctors also caution that honey is not safe for children under the age of one due to a risk of botulism poisoning – and I am obligated to state here for the record that I am merely reporting on research, not advocating or prescribing the use of honey or other products of the hive for treating any type of illness.)

Numerous studies have also concluded that honey is a safe and effective way to treat mild burns because it has some antibacterial and anti-inflammatory properties.

At another display table, Philly Beekeepers Guild Member Edian Rodriguez is showing people his bee suit and smoker.

An older woman seated in front of him is frantically taking down notes. She and her husband both look as if they do not often frequent places like the Continental. Although there were plenty of other people of their age in the crowd – including some of the Bee Guild members – these two seem a bit more suburban than the rest.

Maybe they just remind me of my own suburban parents back in Maryland. Neither has a drink in hand. Neither is eating the gourmet appetizers made with honey, either, like the baklava or the flan served with roasted squash in cleaned-out eggshells. Like my parents, both are dressed in Lands End clothes – comfortable, sensible-looking sneakers and a pink polo crewneck for her and a plaid button-down short sleeve shirt and khakis for him. But both are happy and glowing with excitement, and I find myself enjoying a long round of small talk with them.

When I ask the husband if he has bees at home he laughs.

"Nope, never had them before but after tonight I think it won't be long till we get some. Fantastic stuff," he tells me, straightening his wire-rimmed glasses and pointing to information that someone has given him about getting started with beekeeping. "We are hooked!"

"Oh my gosh," his wife says with a heavy Philly accent, reaching out to grab my sleeve. "I am loving this. I gotta get some bees. I gotta do this."

She asks me if I know of any ways that bees could be used as therapy for children with autism or learning disabilities. At first I'm a bit alarmed, thinking she means sting therapy as discussed over at the apitherapy table. Then I wonder if perhaps she means nutritional products made from the propolis or honey.

No, no, she explains. As a teacher working with populations of such students she wants to figure out a way to introduce her students to some form of beekeeping.

"It just seems as if it would be a connection there," she says. "Like my kids would think those bees were amazing and I think they'd actually find watching them very soothing."

We chat for a while about Temple Grandin's work with farm animals, and the incredibly interesting perspective that autistic people can sometimes provide on life. The woman tells me about her challenging and rewarding teaching work, and how she's always looking for enriching activities for her students, things they can explore and discover. Then we all agree that we love looking at the bees ourselves as they wriggle around in the observation hive. It is hard not to get drawn in by their activity.

Although he's not at the honey tasting event tonight at the Continental, I have met another beekeeper who is teaching kids about beekeeping in this city. Matt Feldman is so proud of being a founding member of the Guild that he has put words about it into his online LinkedIn profile. He also has a thick, brown beard, a big laugh, and a very self-deprecating sense of sarcastic humor, which evidences itself a great deal when he talks to people about the bees he keeps in several Kenyan top-bar hives in a historic, vibrant little neighborhood in the northern section of Philadelphia known as German-town.

A lot of the people start Kenyan top-bar hives because they think it is kinder to the bees. Feldman tells me that he chose the top-bar method for its promise of affordable simplicity, only later to discover later that it is sometimes much more challenging than the Langstroth method. But even despite some challenges, he has found it to be a beautiful way to raise pollinators for various gardens around town.

He wanted to keep bees because he wanted a way to commune with nature while enjoying the convenience of urban living. "The city is just the place to be," he says. Beekeeping would make city living even better. But then he did the math.

"Its like a thousand dollars just to walk in the door," he tells me. "Who has a thousand dollars for a hobby? A thousand dollars is a lot of money."

He began looking over plans for top-bars. A top-bar beekeeper outfits several pieces of wood with lengths of hanging twine upon which the bees attach hexagonal cells that are often measurably smaller in diameter than what is found in a Langstroth hive. Some theorize that the lack of preformed foundation is less stressful for the bees, and more humane, as well.

It all seemed easy to build, which was especially appealing because he is not a very handy guy and he doesn't own a lot of power tools. It seemed like the sort of the thing he could make with inexpensive or borrowed hand saws while he kept an eye on his kids who were both under the age of six when he started out as a beekeeper and a stay-at-home dad. What's more, he thought he could probably make the hives from free scrap lumber, and use the savings to buy more packages of bees in the future.

He was not in the least deterred by the lack of research on how to use top-bars in a city environment, he recalls, laughing at his own hubris. Nor did it worry him that pretty much everyone one told him NOT to start with a top-bar, because it would be more challenging to monitor and maintain over time.

"I'm the guy that says I'm not going do what everyone else does, I'm going do it ten times harder and stupider, cause that's me. I can't do what everybody else is doing cause that just makes so much sense. There's all this research on this other thing, and people know exactly what to do, and I'm like, *meh*, I'll just give it a shot." He tells me this and then laughs dryly.

The majority of his bees live on the raised up berm covering the top of an old Cold War bomb shelter in the backyard of his tiny "twin" duplex-style house, where most of their neighbors can see Feldman do his bee work. He tells me he has yet to get any kind of pushback from neighbors. Some, in fact, have mentioned how glad they are he has the bees. They like having the buzzing insects visit the neighborhood's gardens.

He's grateful for the support, but not too surprised. Philly's a pretty progressive place he says, and there are a lot of gardeners and urban farmers around.

"I envision myself as a fancy farmer, too," he says. "I just don't own my grazing land, and I can't control where my livestock goes." Four years in he's now considered somewhat of a go-to-guy on the topic, simply because he's one of the few who have even tried it – not because he's really a true expert.

"There's a handful of people throughout the nation that do top-bars on a larger scale, but there's very few people that have been doing it for ten or fifteen years. I can name five," he says.

The funny thing is, after four seasons of trying it himself he remains skeptical about whether the method is any better for the bees. His professional training as an oncological nurse causes him to turn towards research, and the data he's seen just doesn't seem to show that top-bars or small cells really benefit their health and well-being, even though a lot of the people who do top-bar hives are adamant that it does.

"I just figure that it is cheap and easy, and I live in a city with a certain socio-economic class, and I'm trying to sell beekeeping to the masses," he says, shrugging. He wants to get more people beekeeping in his city. Telling people they would need a thousand dollars to get started would not go over well.

"So if I tell people: *Yeah, yeah, yeah*, just buy a hand saw for nine dollars and you can make your own hive, and use pallets for the wood, and a hundred bucks for the package of bees about a hundred for the other equipment. It's an easier sell."

Feldman's modesty, however, belies some real success. He's realized his dream of bringing beekeeping to a much larger audience, by starting a beekeeping program at his own kids' urban charter school, which has special environmentally-based curriculum, in order to teach students about bee biology, and give them a chance to learn about harvesting honey.

The venture, he says, began with some online fundraising using the Kickstarter website. Once it went live, he and his fellow organizers were shocked to watch as more than 80% of the money donated was from complete strangers who had never been to the Wissahickon Charter School and did not know either Feldman or the staff. Apparently a lot of people donated because they simply thought the idea of teaching kids about the virtues of bees was a worthwhile idea. With in just a few weeks they made $2,734 – more than $450 over their initial goal of $2,279.

Working with Feldman and the bees is amazing, says teacher Liz Biagioli, because of the enthusiasm he brings to the subject. She's had the pleasure of learning about the art of beekeeping with the students. It was something she had always thought would be exciting to try, but she'd never had the chance until Feldman came along. Now, she's out there every week along side of him, helping to supervise and instruct.

The children who participate are selected based upon a demonstrated interest. Sometimes, they approach her and ask about trying it. Other times, she thinks a kid might benefit from the new experience and she approaches them to ask if they'd like to join in. Often, kids' faces light up when they get that first invitation.

The students' parents have to give permission, and the kids themselves must agree to give up recess one day a week to participate, but nonetheless the program is wildly popular.

"When the kids who are doing it walk out in their bee gear there's this "oooohhh" and "ahhhh" that kind of goes on from the other kids," she says. The bees have generated a lot of school excitement and support.

"Its really exciting to see these kids transition from fear to excitement and really just wanting to delve in," Biagioli tells me.

A majority of the school's 426 students receive free lunch through federal assistance programs. Some have never had a chance to connect with nature. The beeyard has become a key part of the school's large vegetable and flower garden, which flanks an extremely busy road.

Sometimes, Biagioli tells me, the juxtaposition of the road and its traffic can be jarring to her. She grew up an hour north of the city, and always thought of bees and beekeeping as something one did out in the country. Sometimes, when finds herself trying to explain something to the kids and she has to yell to be heard above the sound of the trucks passing by at high speed on the other side of the tall chain link fence, the contrast between nature and the busy cityscape can be sharp for her.

"But we're here in the city and we're doing it, and the funny thing is, the kids don't have that same idea really," Biagioli tells me. "They don't see it that way. For the kids to have that experience is amazing. And that's really a goal for our school, for the kids to get those experiences and those appreciations for the natural world, even though we're in a city. And I think, wow, these things are possible – these kids don't have to be disconnected."

Feldman thinks maybe they could eventually make bee-keeping into an entrepreneurial venture for themselves. He wants to get to the point where he's teaching kids to raise queens which could be sold here in the city to other beekeepers. They could also sell honey, although he concedes that top-bar hives generally don't yield as much excess of the sweet stuff as Langstroth hives typically do. For now, they are simply trying to get to point where money raised through the sale of their own honey and wax candles can be used to sustain their own venture at the school.

Back at the Continental, it's getting late and time to go home. As I make my way out of the restaurant, the Elvis Costello look-a-like that I met at the door tells me he is loving "geeking out" on all the bees.

"I know," I tell him, "and all that sweet stuff to eat and drink ain't bad either."

6

Bee More in Baltimore

"Isn't she pretty?" Steve McDaniel asks me, motioning to the worker bee that is walking its way across the back of his hand.

We are standing in his beeyard, under a generous canopy of trees along a country road about an hour north of Baltimore in Carroll County, Maryland. McDaniel is out marking his queens today, and he's allowed me to come along so I can see how the process works. We are both hoping the ominous, gray clouds will hold their rain until McDaniel can finish his task.

He begins by inserting his metal hive tool carefully into the box and rocking it gently to crack open the propolis seal that the bees have formed underneath. Inside, there's an empty queen cage the size of a toy Matchbox car which was put in about a month before, in June. The queen which was once inside that little box has moved out and has set up housekeeping in his frames.

Her attending worker bees seem unfazed by the removal of the roof of their home and continue working along the frames of their colony. McDaniel pulls out the frame with the most bees – the one where he will likely find the queen. He presents the frame to me as a kind of pop quiz. Dark brown bees scramble all over the wax foundation, like dark, frothy beer spilling over the edge of a pint glass.

"Do you see her? Don't point but describe it to me if you can identify her."

The queen is big and dark and lovely, quite different from the other females working their way along the honeycombed wax, but it still takes me a while to find her. McDaniel does a bit of juggling to balance the frame without his eyes off the queen so that he can carefully pluck her out with his thumb and forefinger. If he puts the frame down in the wrong spot like on top of the opened super, his target will likely drop herself into the box, out of sight and out of plucking range.

"I have to do this very gently," he says in a low half-whisper. "I don't want to crush her or any of the worker bees if I can help it. I have to stay calm, because if I stay calm the bees will stay that way too."

I don't say anything, but the truth is that I am having no problem staying calm; the smell of the hive is almost intoxicating. The only word that comes to mind is cozy — the hive smells cozy. It's sweet, but not sugary sweet. It's warm somehow in the nose, and relaxing. If the color amber had a smell, this would be it. I feel as if I'm being hugged, or as if I've found my childhood teddy bear in the back of the closet. The bees are embracing me with this gentle odor.

The drive out to McDaniel's beeyard took me almost two hours. It was great to put DC's concrete behind me and let the two-lane road spool out in front of the car. I love living in the city, and I have been enjoying my escapades with urban bee-keepers. But in order to understand city beekeeping and comprehend any differences between urban and rural bee-keepers, I'd need to see a big rural apiary. McDaniel, as it turns out, is the ideal guide for this kind of exploration, since he has hives both out here in the county and the heart of Bal-timore City.

Although the sky this morning is heavy, the country color-fully filled my senses with mile upon mile of wildflowers: blue chicory, yellow and black rudbeckia, and white Queen Anne's lace.

Around each corner, new subdivisions full of huge houses with names like Meadowcrest and Hunt's Hollow appeared, but horse farms could still be seen, bordered with white plank fences and signs painted with red fox motifs. Farmland domi-nates the landscape out here, although there are also lush expanses of trees along the edges, and the forests are full and leafy due to this year's abundant rainfall.

At one junction, I waited at a stop light, staring at an enormous farm with a gigantic red barn, where an even bigger house was under construction. While the rest of the nation might be suffering through massive economic troubles, whoever owns that farm seemed to have struck it rich. Corn and soybeans stretched out in tidy alternating ribbons as far as the horizon – the likely source of the wealth in a year when both crops are earning record high prices.

McDaniel does not own a farm out here – he and his wife occupy a small, cheerfully simple place on a few acres which they bought after he spent several years teaching high school science in Baltimore City in the 1970s and 1980s. Since he retired he has pursued a creative dream – selling his stunningly beautiful nature photos at art shows, and photographing special events for schools and other clients.

He began beekeeping in 1979. Fifteen years later he sat for the Eastern Apicultural Society's written exam to become one of only 160 people in the US who can be called a Master Beekeeper. His honey and beeswax always win awards at the Maryland State Fair.

On warm weekends he and his wife Angie often attend festivals and street fairs to sell their wares. He sells the honey varietals, which include some hard-to-find gourmet flavors, such as black locust, blueberry, and basswood with honeycomb while she sells lip balms, hand creams, and candles made from their bees' wax.

McDaniel tells me that the products gleaned from his numerous hives produce a nice side income, but they do more to feed his soul than fill their bank account.

"Its very relaxing being in the beeyard," he tells me. Working the bees is often uninterrupted bliss. Sometimes, when

Angie comes out to tell him he needs to answer some question on the phone he thinks, "Do I have to?"

McDaniel's bees are gentle. Neither of us has put on a protective veil today. I asked McDaniel when I called if I could borrow one of his for this visit, but I have yet to even touch it. When I got out of the car we headed straight for his hives and got to work and the protective gear went unused, draped over the lid of one of the twelve boxes that comprise his beeyard.

Listening to McDaniel I become keenly aware – more than I have with any other beekeeper – that keeping bees is more about farming and agricultural practice than it is about nature and wildlife. This might be because of our setting, nestled as we are in the middle of farms. Or it might be due to the fact we are focusing our discussion on genetics and queens and the management of colonies and breeds.

"I have to mark her very carefully without pushing down." His voice is soft as he takes the cap off a red paint pen and begins to make a mark on the queen's back. "I also have to be extremely careful not to get any paint on her eyes or antennae. That would kill her."

McDaniel has chosen red because this is a year ending in 3. Although its unclear exactly who started the system, beekeepers all over the world who mark queens tend to follow the same pattern, choosing their colors based upon the last number of the calendar year the bee is put into a hive:

White is for years ending in 1 and 6

Yellow is for years ending in 2 and 7

Red is for years ending in 3 and 8

Green is for years ending in 4 and 9

Blue is for years ending in 5 and 0

He also tells me there's a mnemonic that helps newbies remember those colors and numbers:

When You Re-queen Get the Best, as in: **White, Yellow, Red, Green, Blue.**

For a few minutes we wait for the tiny drop of paint to dry in the humid air, watching the clouds and speculating on the chance of thunderstorms. Maryland today feels like a tropical rain forest. It has poured almost every day for a month and dampness permeates everything.

The freshly-colored insect seems comfortable in McDaniel's gentle pinch, and her paint looks like 1940s style lipstick – bright red and flashy. I wonder if her attending workers will notice the color change when she goes back inside. McDaniel says the paint needs to be dry so they won't try to lick it off.

Some beekeepers mark their queens in order to find them quickly when they work the hive, but after decades of bee work, McDaniel can easily find his matriarchs without the need for such visual aids. Besides being bigger, queens behave differently than the other bees, and they are always surrounded by a crowd of worker bees. He paints his queens so that he can quickly determine their age when he checks his colonies.

The drips of rain have become louder, but we are still dry and protected from the downpour under the leafy trees, and so are the bees. "This is a lovely place to have hives because it stays shady on sunny days and you get a few extra minutes when the rain starts," McDaniel tells me.

A lot of people can't work their bees in storms. The insects can get cranky and are more likely to sting as they react to fluctuations in the barometer. They also don't like the droplets of water. One New York City beekeeper, for example, is always easiest to contact on rainy days because, as he puts it, rain turns him into the most useless individual in the world. But McDaniel says he's able to work his bees during stormy days because he is so careful with the genetics of his queens.

Shortly after he finishes that sentence a huge clap of thunder rolls over our heads. While he closes up the boxes, I grab my camera bag and we make our way to the front porch where it is dry and safe. Although we don't hear any more thunder or see lightning, a heavy downpour soaks the entire landscape for the remainder of the morning.

As we sit watching the rain fall, McDaniel tells me more about queens. If one dies unexpectedly or stops producing pheromones, the workers will begin to groom a new queen to take her place. That new queen will then mature, and eventually fly off to mate with as many as 15 drones from other colonies. As a result, the eggs she lays in the hive when she returns will include genetic material from other strains of bee.

While some think that the offspring produced in this way are superior, McDaniel thinks otherwise. Most of the time he prefers to put in a new queen – a type of bee called the Carniolan – about every three years.

"All this stuff about locally raised queens is a crock. Most of our genetics have come from the queens that are coming up from Georgia in the packages the breeders there sell. Thousands come to Maryland every year." Some of the queens being shipped in are just crummy, he says, because so many of the breeders are, unfortunately, just in it for the money. A large percentage of their bees die soon after arrival. This spring, some even arrived dead in the package. The drone bees that are out there breeding with a beekeeper's queens may or may not be high quality. "That's why I always get mine from a professional queen-breeder who knows how to make a really terrific queen," he says with pride.

Sometimes, if bees do happen to re-queen themselves and the brood pattern is good and doesn't show signs of health problems, McDaniel will leave her in place for a short while and mark her with orange, so that he can watch how she does, monitoring the colony for signs of serious health problems like chalkbrood. He also watches to see if the offspring she produces turn out to be "cranky."

I can't imagine this kind, soft-spoken person killing the queens of his hives on a regular basis, although I'm well aware that many beekeepers do when they re-queen their hives – especially those in the large industrial side of beekeeping. I recently watched a documentary which included footage of beekeepers pulling queens out of hives and carefully pinching their heads off. It made me wince and cover my eyes.

McDaniel doesn't like that idea either. He prefers instead to cage the old queen in a small queen cage where she can live for about week. He adds a few workers to feed her, dabbing the cage with sugar water every couple of days.

"Then I might put her in my pocket for a while and take her out to show people at talks I give, or even at the hardware store. I'll ask, 'Hey, have you ever seen a queen bee?' And they really are fascinated. They can't believe anyone can carry bees around in their pocket like that. It's just one more way to teach people about how great bees are."

From time to time he's also given caged queens to kids who want to learn about beekeeping. Because of the screening, they are safe – and he warns them that she'll only live for a week. It has to be a kid who is a little mature, he says, one who is ready for some responsibility and excited about bees or biology.

"You'd think I'd have given them a solid bar of gold. It's just amazing."

McDaniel himself is still in awe of these social insects, too, even after more than 35 years of being a beekeeper. As we work around his frames he points out how incredible it is that the bees can make such mathematically precise honeycomb. They don't waste anything – somehow knowing how to form the shape of the wax cells for holding a maximum amount of honey or brood or pollen using the minimum amount of wax.

"I love the bees, that's all there is to it," he says. "They are fascinating."

Even if McDaniel wasn't interested in genetic strains and keeping gentle bees, he would have had to purchase a lot of new queens this year because, like so many of the beekeepers across the country, he suffered severe losses in 2012-2013.

Wherever there have been large numbers of bee deaths, the toll has been painful. It's not just the money and the lost investment of time. For McDaniel – a man who loves the environment and admires the bees he works with so much – the losses were heartbreaking.

"In 35 years I've never had 70% of my bees just drop dead, especially in warm weather. It started in July and progressed through to October. That's never happened before."

Because McDaniel was trained as a chemist, he often approaches problems scientifically. When the bees started to die so dramatically and so unexpectedly, he thought through every aspect of his beekeeping to see if there was anything different this year from all previous years.

At first he could find nothing to explain the sudden and dramatic deaths. Over the years he's found it harder and harder to keep his bees alive. There seems to be less nectar available in some of the trees that used to be real staples of honey flow, such as the tulip trees that line his property, and he's finding he has to augment his bees' diet of flower nectar with sugar water earlier and earlier each year because of it.

The bees that failed last year had actually looked good up until the week they died. "I had very low levels of Varroa mites, and very few small hive beetles. No disease was perceptible. They were also well-fed colonies... They died with gobs of food available to them. And, they were new queens. Top-notch queens."

One of the colonies was doing particularly well and had produced two supers full of honey before it died. "That's just not normal."

As he speaks, I think of the large tracts of farm land I passed on the way to his place. Most of them were planted in either one or two kinds of crops – far tidier than farms I remembered from past decades. Monoculture farming has been blamed for a lot of environmental problems – there's not much forage in those long, clean strips of corn and soybeans for the bees. Monocrop farms are also often called out for being intensely treated with insecticides, because when a farmer plants one crop for acres and acres it's an invitation for insect trouble. I've always heard they have to treat the crops heavily in order to succeed in that kind of farming scheme.

But just as I'm thinking that maybe cities do indeed provide a comparative safe haven for the bees, McDaniel tells me it wasn't just his rural hives that suffered last year. His hives in downtown Baltimore also began to falter in the middle of the season, as did the hives of many of the beekeepers he knows in the city.

Bees had always done well, for example, at the historic church where he keeps hives near Baltimore's urban Inner Harbor. But last summer, those bees also failed, dying in huge piles outside the hives. He could find no explanation. The bees didn't disappear – it wasn't a case of CCD, which occurs when the workers suddenly leave behind a hive full of honey and a live queen. Instead, they died in place. It sickened him to not know why it was happening.

Speaking about all of this is difficult for McDaniel. "It really burns me up," he says, his voice cracking.

This spring McDaniel began to believe that last year's bees had suffered from pesticide poisoning. They had, he suspects, visited flowers in a garden nearby which had been treated with a class of systemic chemical known as a neonicotinoid.

"And why don't you think that might have come off of the farm fields near here?" I ask gently.

There isn't much in those corn fields to attract his bees, he explains, and the farmers have been using neonicotinoids for years on farms. To his mind, most of them are pretty judicious with the use of those chemicals because they need to keep their costs low.

But this year was the first year he noticed neonicotinoids for sale in the garden section of the Home Depot store near his house.

"I saw this stuff in blue bottles being advertised for rose and flower care," he says. Upon reading the label he was horrified to find it contained imidacloprid, a chemical highly toxic to bees at extremely low levels of exposure. "I mean, this is really nasty stuff, and the rate they are telling homeowners to use is many times higher than what a farmer uses."

McDaniel alleges that every day when his worker bees leave their hives to find forage in the form of nectar and pollen, they are encountering these chemicals on the flowers and plants of some nearby neighbors. Knowing where exactly is next to impossible. Bees, he knows, will travel as far as two to three miles to find their food. His bees could have picked up the toxic pesticides on any one of the surrounding eight or nine thousand acres that surround his apiary here as well as in the city, on the treated blossoms of a neighbor's rose bush or perennial flower.

Proving it would be impossible, he concedes. At the time of the bees' deaths he didn't think to collect any carcasses to send to a lab. Besides, many pesticides are degraded by exposure to sunlight, and neonicotinoids are lethal to bees at such low levels they may not have shown up in lab results anyway.

But, he notes, piles of dead bees in an otherwise healthy bee colony form a classic sign of pesticide poisoning. To him the question is not whether or not it was a pesticide kill, but rather what kind of pesticide kill. The next time it happens to one of his hives he plans to gather the bees as quickly as possible and freeze them until he can send them off for a forensic investigation of sorts. He is determined to get answers.

McDaniel is not the only one raising alarms about neonicotinoids and bees. A lot of beekeepers think neonicotinoid pesticides are to blame for the large number of bee deaths. Its not just that they think the increased incidents of dead bees around formerly healthy colonies are due to exposure to these pesticides. They suspect that even the bees that don't immediately die are weakened by even low exposures.

The American beekeepers aren't the only ones. Across the globe, many people have raised similar questions about this new class of chemicals, which were introduced worldwide in the 1990s for the control of many different kinds of insect problems. In April, just a few weeks before I visited the

McDaniel honey farm in rural Maryland, the European Union voted to ban the use of three of the so-called "neonics" on crops attractive to bees in their member countries. The action followed years of intense protests from European beekeepers and European environmental advocates – many of whom find a strong link between the timing of the chemicals' introduction into agriculture and the emergence of CCD. Beekeepers in France have even taken to the street in their bee suits to protest in the chemicals' usage.

Neonicotinoids work by affecting insects' central nervous systems by binding to receptors of enzyme called nicotinic acetylcholine, which can lead to paralysis and death. The complicated name comes from the fact that they are similar in chemical composition to nicotine. The University of Texas Extension website, *Agrilife*, helpfully states that the name literally means "new nicotine-like insecticide."

The UK-based advocacy group called Pesticide Action Network notes that "bees have a particular genetic vulnerability to neonics because they have more of these receptors than other insects as well as more learning and memory genes for their highly evolved system of communication and organisation."

In 2012 with the help of the Center for Food Safety, a large group of interested parties pulled together to ask the US Environmental Protection Agency (EPA) to suspend use of two neonicotinoids known as clothianidin and thiamethoxam. They argued that the agency knew the chemicals posed harm to honey bees. They also asked that safeguards be put in place to ensure that similar pesticides weren't approved by the agency in the future.

The EPA had granted registration for clothianidin in 2003 under the condition that Bayer, its manufacturer, would eventually submit a field study detailing its impacts on pollinators.

The EPA has officially stated its review of clothianidin's registration should be complete by 2018 – a timeframe that many advocates including the Center for Food Safety – feel is too long. As such, the Center for Food Safety filed a lawsuit against EPA in March 2013, challenging the agency's oversight and registration process, and noting its labelling process for neonicotinoids was deficient. To many it appears the agency is simply stalling.

Chemical companies have meanwhile responded to the suit by asking for the case to be dismissed.

In order to understand why neonicotinoids in particular are causing so much current controversy, it helps to understand a bit about the history of pesticides in general. Farmers have been using chemicals on their crops for centuries, and modern pesticides have been applied to crops for decades.

Many of the same companies which now make chemical treatments for killing crop pests actually had their corporate origins a century ago in Germany during World War I, manufacturing the chemicals used to kill that country's human enemies in warfare.

At the end of the second World War, the chemical warfare industry went civilian and international, focusing on targets like mosquitoes and crop pests instead of people. When DDT was developed in 1939 by a Swiss chemist named Paul Muller, the synthetic chemical was hailed as a modern marvel. It was cheap to produce and easy to apply, and although it was known to be toxic to a wide range of pests it did not seem initially to be very toxic to mammals. It also persisted in the environment – which at the time was viewed as a positive attribute, since that meant it didn't need to be reapplied often and the cost of applications could be kept low. Muller was called a hero, and was even awarded a Nobel Prize in Medicine in 1948 for his work on the chemical.

DDT was incredibly popular and used very heavily through out the 1940s and 1950s in the US by farmers, homeowners and municipalities. One company even began marketing wallpaper imprinted with popular cartoon characters and impregnated with the pesticide. Public health posters showed smiling children singing, "DDT is Good for Me!" Many older Americans also remember a time when trucks circled their small towns spraying out DDT on a regular basis; in the southern part of the US some recall that children often went out and danced in the spray to cool off on hot summer evenings.

Over time, however, ecologists began to ask questions about some of the chemical's lasting power and its ability to kill so many pests at once. What was it doing to fish and aquatic invertebrates? What happened as the chemical made its way up the food chain? Why were birds dying when they ate worms from treated areas? What was its eventual impact on human health?

The most notable of these queries came from biologist Rachel Carson in a 1962 book entitled *Silent Spring*, wherein she questioned the use of chemical and other chlorinated hydrocarbons like it. The book has been credited by many as forming the start of the modern environmental movement.

Although many experts at the time said that the amounts of DDT being used were too small to do much harm to non-target insects and animals, Carson argued that there was ample evidence showing it was toxic to several kinds of aquatic wildlife. She also argued that indirect toxicity could result for other creatures due to the chemical's persistence in ecosystems where it was used.

The use of DDT was eventually banned in the US in 1972, although sadly Carson died after fighting breast cancer in 1964 and so did not live to see the moratorium take place. Many of the concerns about that pesticide and other similar organochlorines were related to their tendency to concentrate in the fatty tissue of mammals and the way they can bioaccumulate in food chains. DDT is a broad spectrum pesticide – so it also kills bees, although it seems that detail was rarely discussed by anyone other than Carson during the time of its use in the US.

But the impact of her research regarding DDT and the reaction of Carson and many other scientists of her time signaled a paradigm shift. Pesticides used in homes and on farm fields were suddenly questioned by a growing number of people; chemical cures were no longer treated as a guaranteed path to salvation and prosperity. Eventually that skepticism would develop into a wider appreciation for the importance of healthy insect relationships in ecosystems.

Some of that sensibility has stayed with the general public to this day and continues to frame discussions about pesticide use and the introduction of new crop treatments and their impact on bees. Over and over again, DDT and the lessons learned regarding its once widespread use are told by advocacy groups as a kind of cautionary tale for all future pesticide usage, and in almost all of the recent documentaries made about bees and CCD have included references to the chemical and to Rachel Carson herself.

In part this is because Carson did more than rail against DDT. What she foresaw and warned against was an economy entirely dependent upon chemicals that would prove harmful to the ecosystem, its humans and its beneficial insects.

But even after DDT was banned, other chemicals continued to be widely used on food crops, and for ornamental landscaping and turf grass. So while some growers moved toward more organic methods for pest control and tried to minimize their use of chemicals on the farm and in the garden, others simply continued searching for alternative chemicals to use.

Organophosphates were developed in the 1940s and 1950s. By 2010 the Natural Resources Defense Council noted that these accounted for about 70% of the insecticides used in the

US. They work by inhibiting an enzyme which controls nerve impulses and are highly toxic to bees.

Many are considered some of the most toxic pesticides currently available today. Exposure to organophosphate pesticides has been linked to increases in diagnoses of attention deficit/hyperactivity disorder in children. Other studies have linked exposure to these pesticides to Parkinson's Disease. They are also known to be endocrine disruptors, and it is believed that exposure to these chemicals may have an adverse effect on male fertility.

Because organophosphates are often used for treating pests on crops such as cotton, peaches, grapes, pears and strawberries, their impacts on human health have caught the attention of both those who argue for food safety for consumers and those who advocate for the well-being of farmers and migratory workers. Many have pushed for a long time to remove organophosphates from the agricultural sector entirely.

In contrast, pyrethrins are derived from the flowers of chrysanthemums, and so they are often thought of as being a bit less harmful by the general public than organophosphates. They certainly are less toxic to mammals, and because of that they are often used for controlling pests on pets and livestock. But their use for controlling mosquitoes and for some other agricultural applications has caused a different problem; run-off in urban areas can do great damage to nearby creeks, rivers, streams and lakes, because these chemicals are highly toxic to fish and tadpoles.

Pyrethroids are synthetics manufactured to be very similar in structure to the pyrethrins, but they persist longer in the environment and are generally more toxic to insects. Like pyrethrins they are not considered very toxic to mammals. In fact, they are often used for the treatment of human head lice in the US, as well as for mosquito control in many dense, urban areas.

But both pyrethroids and pyrethrins are toxic to bees. Some environmentalists have noted with alarm that recent efforts to control the aggressive and recently introduced Asian Tiger mosquito (and the mosquito-borne West Nile Virus) and in parts of the US in the last decade has prompted an increase in the casual commercial use of these chemicals. An untold number of new companies has suddenly emerged, willing to spray suburban backyards with these chemicals in the summer on behalf of homeowners who are willing to pay a premium to rid their lush green, lawn-filled yards of these tiny blood suckers that bite painfully and aggressively and as often in the day as the nighttime.

Summertime in metropolitan DC, for example, is now dotted with signs proudly announcing homeowners' use of such companies – some with cartoonish logos that show giant, dead mosquitos with Xs over their eyes that have just been shot by tough-looking exterminators wielding spray applicators.

Personally, I cannot drive past such signs with out having a flashback to those archives of DDT wallpaper ads from the 1940s. It seems foolhardy to make fun out of pesticide use no matter where and when it occurs, as if we've forgotten any lesson that history might offer us. Spraying chemicals is no joke in my mind, and should never be taken lightly.

In any case, given the known problems and toxic nature of the other pesticides, one might wonder why neonicotinoids in particular seem to have become the target of so many recent advocacy campaigns. There have been chemical threats to the safety of bees for a long time, and many have made the case that neonics are a less toxic alternative than what came before.

But neonicotinoids differ from these various other pesticides because they work systemically; the pesticides are taken into a plant's vascular tissue and can remain as residues for long periods of time in its stems, leaves, pollen, and nectar. While other kinds of pesticides are often only toxic to bees and other pollinators for a short period of time after spraying, a plant or tree which has been treated with a neonicotinoid can be toxic to insects for years. Furthermore, seedlings which sprout from neonic-treated seed contain the chemicals in their tissues from the day they emerge from the soil, and there's increasing evidence that these new pesticides do not stay put in the treated plants – they are showing up even on untreated plants in places close to treated fields.

In a detailed article published jointly in *The American Bee Journal, Bee Culture* magazine and *Bee Health* (a publication produced by the US Extension service), researchers Greg Hunt and Christian Krupke write of beekeepers finding piles of dead bees in front of most of the Purdue University beehives – which had the team had previously considered healthy – during the same week in 2010 that corn was being planted in the area. Krupke and his colleagues were able to test their bee carcasses immediately. What they discovered was that the bees had clothianidin (the aforementioned neonicotinoid widely used to treat corn and other field crop seeds) as well as other seed treatment chemicals either in or on their bodies. The team conducted tests and then published their results in the highly regarded peer-reviewed journal *PLoS ONE*. Many of the bees they found had evidently been gathering pollen from dandelions and other nearby flowering plants.

"Pollen collected by returning foragers and pollen sampled from the cells of those hives had about 10 times the level of clothianidin and thiamethoxam [another neonicotinoid commonly used on soybean plants] as compared to that detected in the dead bees," the scientists write.

The following year, Krupke and his research team went on to study samples of talc – which is commonly used in seed hoppers to keep seeds flowing properly during planting season in the US – and found it could contain very high concentrations of the two aforementioned neonicotinoids. After considering the forage sources of the local bees, the amount of neonicotinoids in the fields and the concentrations of the chemicals in the talc, they concluded that the greatest danger for bees occurs during planting time near farm fields where treated seeds are being used. But they also concluded that bees near areas where corn was planted were being exposed to sub-lethal amounts throughout the growing season due to waste talc from planters.

Krupke's team has since been telling beekeepers how to report their bee deaths to the EPA via the email beek-ill@epa.gov. More data is needed, they urge, and although some keepers are able to keep bees going in areas where corn is heavily planted, dead bees are also continuing to pile up outside of hives in many locations, including Ohio, Minnesota, and throughout Canada.

"This story is like the layers of an onion, that unfortunately require time to peel," the team writes. "However, when we see kills that are synchronized with each other and with corn planting over a wide area, and the pesticide is found in dead bees near agricultural fields, the weight of the evidence points in just one direction."

The authors conclude by saying that although there are many things potentially threatening the health of the honey bee in the US and many factors to consider in the research of Colony Collapse Disorder, "the use of neonicotinoid seed treatments over hundreds of millions of acres annually, coupled with their extremely high toxicity to honey bees and their persistence in plants (including nectar and pollen that bees eat) combine to create an environment where it is very difficult for bees to avoid exposure to these highly toxic chemicals. That in itself makes this topic worthy of further investigation. Another thought that gives us pause is that if we are seeing bee kills in honey bees that have a colony to rely on, what is happening to the many species of native bees in North America that have to go it alone?"

One evening in July, I drive into Baltimore to attend a session of the Baltimore Backyard Beekeepers Network (BBBN), small group that has banded together to discuss all kinds of bee-related issues in the heart of the city. After talking to McDaniel about his hives, I want to know more about the kinds of losses others are experiencing at their hives.

For their meeting, the BBBN gathers in the back room of a small, funky art gallery in Hamilton, a neighborhood straddling busy Harford Road in North Baltimore. As I walk toward the gallery door, I notice some banners suspended from light posts which say: "Main Street, Where Baltimore Happens."

The signs are part of a campaign to invigorate the city, which has been steadily losing people to suburban exodus for six decades. According to recent news reports, such promotional campaigns do seem to be working, albeit slowly. Last year, the city actually gained about 1,100 new residents.

Harford Road does indeed feel and look like a main street of sorts. In addition to the art gallery, there are taverns, liquor stores, some funeral homes, and a few mom-and-pop restaurants with facades that date from the 1950s. You can get a big house here with lots of character for a fairly small price, making this a bit of a hipster haven for young families. Walking from my parking spot to the meeting I pass couples, whose arms are covered in colorful ink, pushing strollers filled with toddlers, and a large group of twenty-somethings heading to a tavern nearby.

Mostly, though, there are lots of cars driving south at very high speeds down Harford Road. It might be a kind of main street, but this is no small town.

One of the first people I meet from the BBBN is Beth Sherring, who tells me she began keeping hives just two Christmases ago. She lives a couple of miles north of here, on the city side of a neighborhood called Parkville.

"I had always talked about *wanting* to do it," she says about beekeeping, laughing and shaking a head full of dark, wavy hair. "But then my husband Henry called my bluff and gave me two hives and all the equipment as a gift."

Beekeeping is very different from her day job in communications at a large Baltimore investment banking firm. Although others have come to the meeting tonight in t-shirts and jeans, she comes straight from work in a black dress and high heels. Many of her office skills come in handy at the BBBN; she's politically savvy and willing to wade through bureaucratic paperwork when needed. She's also feisty and funny and every bit a Baltimore local. So despite being a relatively new beekeeper, she's quickly moved up to become one of the group's leaders, willing to take on City Hall on behalf of pollinators.

The city's regulations, she explains, seem to have been written with exotic animals like reptiles or anacondas in mind, and don't fit modern methods of beekeeping.

"I'm sorry," she tells me, "but these are not Gila monsters we are keeping. They are bees."

As other members of the group arrive, they chime in with agreement. The biggest sticking point for most is the ambiguity regarding fees. Permits, which are gained through Animal Control, are required at a cost of $80. But until now no one has been able to determine if that's supposed to be $80 per beekeeper, per beeyard, or per hive.

Most of the city's beekeepers have simply refused to pay thus far.

"I do know one person who sent in their check," Sherring says. "It has never been cashed."

The city, the members tell me, is claiming the cost is meant to cover inspections, but so far inspections have not been done, and many members are not really sure what the parameters of a possible animal control inspection might be. Most don't want to be inspected regularly anyway, preferring instead to deal only with bee inspectors who are biologists, and only those when absolutely necessary. The idea of an untrained inspector more interested in fees than bees really seems to rile a lot of people in this town.

"It's redundant," Sherring insists.

The state of Maryland already requires beekeepers to register, she points out, and if the city requires an additional registration *and* a fee, new beekeepers might not bother to register with either entity due to the cost. This might lead to problems if a health crisis like American foulbrood breaks out and all the beekeepers in the state need to be notified and inspected by a biologist to control the highly contagious and costly bee disease.

I wonder out loud if the city has been a bit blindsided by the sudden increase in beekeeping. Many members of the group present say they don't think so.

"I feel like they are just milking us for money is all," says one member, sighing. It also seems to many that the city simply doesn't understand the important role bees can play in maintaining urban homesteads, farms or gardens.

"I mean, what the heck does that money cover on their end? Nothing," someone else says.

The regulation's wording is a bit odd, with statements such as beekeeping is permitted only if "the activity is register [sic] with the Maryland Department of Agriculture... No more than 2 hives, each containing no more than 1 swarm, shall be allowed for lots up to 2,500 square feet of lot area; on lots greater than 2,500 square feet one additional hive, containing no more than one swarm may be kept for every 2,500 feet of lot area over 2,500 square feet."

It is entirely unclear what is meant by swarm, and what exactly the authors of the regulation know or don't know about bees, and it does not really seem as if anyone who actually works with bees has been involved with drafting these words. It also seems kind of haphazardly thrown together.

The BBBN describes itself as a diverse group, although the meeting room is filled with eight women and one man, very much matching a trend I've noticed in other beekeeping groups.

Jeavonna Chapman is the only African American here tonight, but I am pretty sure there are many more African

American beekeepers around this racially diverse city. Chapman is a tall, slim woman with a serious expression on her face during most of the meeting.

When the group starts the agenda off by sharing what's going on at their hives, she explains that she still doesn't have her own bees yet, although she's working hard to figure out where she might put a hive up next year.

During most of the week she works as a Computer Network Specialist for the state's Division of Rehabilitation Services, an office that supports the employment and economic independence of those with disabilities. She long ago became a Master Gardener, and loves to pursue all kinds of planting when she isn't sitting in front of the screens at work.

Chapman first began to suspect that there was a lot of danger in the heavy use of pesticides and herbicides when she was pregnant back in the early 1990s. It seemed significant to her that Jim Crockett, the star of the public television show *The Victory Garden*, died of cancer. It struck her at the time that it wasn't uncommon among gardeners to die of various cancers.

"I realized we were just killing ourselves," she says. "And it wasn't just the person doing the spraying, but all the people around them that were affected." She wonders now about increases in things like autism, and can't help but think some of the problems are coming from a contaminated food supply.

The first time she encountered a beehive she was walking through Baltimore's Herring Run Park, on her way to the grocery store. She saw a guy taking a hive out of his car and she was "mesmerized." She began chatting with him, and later began helping him and his wife take care of their 12 hives near an urban homestead in the neighborhood of Lauraville.

She's hoping now that maybe she can actually get a split from them to set up her own beeyard. She's also seen beehives near the huge Baltimore Farmers Market that sets up every Sunday under the Jones Falls Expressway, and she wonders if an extremely urban landscape like that would be optimal. She's keenly aware that bees travel as far as three miles from their hive to forage for pollen and nectar. She has begun to think about any possible beeyard location as the radial point of a very large, very chemically-laden circle.

Chapman is actually better known in her own neighborhood as a woman who fights for the protection and improvement of Clifton Park, a busy, well-used city park south of where we are tonight. Clifton Park's golf course, tennis courts, brand new community pool, and recreation center are always in demand; such amenities are very hard to find in the lower income, blue-collar areas of this particular city.

Chapman has lived all over the country – including Philadelphia, California, and Chicago – but in Baltimore she became increasingly distressed watching residents wrangle with the city over questions of usage and maintenance and environmental impact in the green, open space. There are a lot of people who want to use the park, but their needs sometimes are not entirely compatible. As priorities get set and demands are made, she tries to also keep the environment on everyone's mind.

Clifton Park forms a 267-acre green oasis in a neighborhood where streets full of row homes are often punctuated by abandoned, boarded-up properties owned by absentee landlords who long ago disappeared from anyone's official city records. As an environmental advocate, Chapman has helped to plant many, many trees there and throughout the city. If there's a place she sees where a tree could thrive, she pushes to have one planted. She is passionate about how much good a tree can do for a neighborhood, any neighborhood. It's not just that trees look good, she tells me, it's also their ability to reduce pollution and sequester carbon.

"Trees are just an all purpose wonderland," she says.

But where to put her own bees is now the question. She tells the group that she'd like to find a place where the hive won't be impacted by pesticides. The park guys, she suspects, are out there using heavy chemicals. They must be, she says, because the golf course couldn't look that weed-free unless they were putting out something.

"They say they don't spray, but that doesn't mean they don't treat with other forms, like granules," she says softly, shaking her head. "I've had conversations with them about it. They definitely know who I am."

She's been offered some spots on private property around town for her bees, but some of the most promising places were close to Morgan State University, and she's pretty sure they treat their grounds, too.

Someone in the BBBN suggests that perhaps the historic cemetery which borders Clifton Park's south side would make a good beeyard. She could probably get official permission to do it there, too, they point out. Dead people don't mind bees.

Chapman shakes her head. Nope, she's pretty sure they treat that place with lawn chemicals, as well. "I just don't see the point in setting up a hive if they are just going to be exposed to that stuff and die," she says determinedly.

Members of the BBBN are sympathetic to Chapman's conundrum, even if they don't have an answer for her. Many of them have lost bees in the last year, for unknown reasons.

Maureen Daly was excited to get her first hive up and going last year, after taking a beekeeping class taught by Steve McDaniel. She and her brother got started by sharing a hive in the lush, green neighborhood just north and west of Johns Hopkins University known as Charles Village. Everything seemed to be great until one day in October when she came home to find the entire hive had died in place. It was particularly disturbing to her that they seemed to have plenty to eat, since there was more than 40 pounds of honey in her supers.

"One day they were great," she recalls. "One day, dead."

Daly called in the state bee inspector, Jerry Fischer, to see if he could help to ascertain what might have gone wrong. He found no evidence of mites or disease, and officially listed the cause of the bee deaths as "unknown."

Daly remained upset, however, so she sought out McDaniel's insight and advice, hoping she could learn from any mistakes she might have made. McDaniel was likewise extremely upset to find that the formerly healthy colony was heaping with dead bodies. He could see nothing amiss in her management which would have caused such a complete wipe out. Instead, he thought that her hives showed classic signs of pesticide exposure.

Daly says she remains distressed about not knowing what killed her bees. Even though the two new colonies she got this year to replace the failed hive are now healthy, she finds it odd that someone as experienced as McDaniel saw no indication that anything had been done which would have endangered the bees last year at this time.

If anyone knows bees, she comments, it's McDaniel. He's been doing it for so long.

The BBBN's leader, Beth Passavant, has suggested in the past that they try to take on the pesticide issue by making some kind of statement or taking some sort of protesting action. She has felt from time to time that they need to let people know more about what is happening in their hives, that the bees aren't just disappearing, they are dying in large numbers for unknown reasons. It isn't enough just to watch documentaries and think about the problem. She wants people to know this is happening right now, all around them in their own neighborhoods. The bees are in trouble.

But tackling the issue of pesticides would mean a lot of effort – it feels as if this little group of kindly beekeepers would be instantly gobbled up by the dragon of the big corporate agricultural giants that make pesticides – and everyone here is really just doing bees on the side, after work or when time allows. Passavant herself is about to leave the group because she's moving out of the state soon, anyway, and now they aren't too sure what next steps the organization will take after she's gone. In fact they are scheduled to talk about next steps that very night, right after I leave their meeting.

As I point my car westward and head back across the city towards the highway, I find myself looking around at each stoplight, thinking what the world must look like to Jeavonna Chapman and Maureen Daly and others who seek a haven for their bees. I also think what it must look like to the bees themselves.

This city is marred in many places by rust and decay, empty houses, and storefronts with broken windows. But it also has a lot of lush growth – lots of trees that could offer forage in the spring for the honey flow in the fall. In many areas, native weeds like goldenrod and milkweed can be seen springing up through cracks in the sidewalks, in addition to the invasive exotic vines like porcelain berry and honeysuckle that often braid themselves around telephone wires. And many neighborhoods are thriving under a bloom of renewal, with young families moving in and fixing up the older homes.

Baltimore – like every other major city in the world – also struggles with water pollution. The creeks and streams and rivers here are plagued with sewage, decades old industrial waste, and contaminants picked up on the streets by fast moving storm water. Bees need to drink, just like any other creature, and I wonder where find water, and how clean it is.

A lot of people have compared modern honey bees to the canaries once used to signal poor air quality in coal mines. If the yellow bird in the cage died, the miners knew it was time to leave a cave and find fresh air. Now, we humans are stuck, unable to evacuate but watching the bees die all around. The darkest worry is that perhaps there is no way to escape the unknown danger we are all facing.

I find that the beekeepers' persistence in the midst of these questions to be remarkable. The more beekeepers I talk to, the more I realize how big the pull of the bees is to some. They live with them, placing hives in their own backyards and incorporating their buzzing presence into their family life. It's not just about making a sweet treat of honey, and it's not just about needing a way to pollinate a garden or an orchard. In fact, many of the beekeepers I've met don't even have time to garden because keeping bees is so demanding. It becomes not just a fun hobby but the dominant fact of their life. A few even say they have become defined by their bees – they are the bee guy or the bee woman in their community, and internally some thoughts about their bees permeate their mind every day, all year.

Although for some the desire to beekeep comes from a desire to save the planet, there's something bigger that draws a certain number of people into the world of these social insects, prompting them to forge a bond, make a connection. Over and over again they use words like mesmerized, transfixed, amazed. Over and over again, people talk about wanting to understand the bees, figure them out, gain a greater knowledge of how the bees achieve such an orderly, stable society inside their hives.

Perhaps one reason people are so alarmed about the death of the bees is because they think the bees are privy to an understanding of the natural world that we, as clumsy humans, are not. By losing the bees we would lose pollination services, to be sure. But it also seems as if we might lose the chance to crack a code written in the world all around us, and to understand the power of their propolis, the immunity boost contained in their delicious honey, and the motivation behind the bees' tireless ability to work for the good of the group.

Because everything eventually makes me think of old television shows, this all reminds me of the episode of *The Twilight Zone* where everyone fears the aliens who land from outer space, After they have killed off the visiting creatures they discover the planetary visitors had come with a cure for cancer. For years so many people have feared bees, and some have even fought against their presence in the city. But now, as they struggle to survive, we wonder what message or vital information they have to impart, and whether we are too late to even comprehend it.

It also seems odd to a lot of people – including me – to needlessly harm a creature so capable of self-sacrifice, so dependent upon its brethren. No honey bee can survive on its own for longer than 24 hours. They need each other, and they need a good place to live. So do we.

I decide I need to see a healthy beeyard. I want to know what it looks like when a hive succeeds, partly because I need to be able to hold that positive dream in my own head for the future. But also, I want to know what its like to spend time in an apiary with a beekeeper that isn't suffering from a broken heart. So a few days later, when a beekeeper from Baltimore invites me over to see his thriving urban apiary, I jump back in the car for another trip to Charm City.

From time to time, police officers go door-to-door along Bill Castro's leafy, green street in West Baltimore. Sometimes they come when an incident has occurred. Other times they come to educate residents about ways they can secure their homes and reduce crime.

During one recent visit, the police were standing outside talking to Castro when one of the officers asked if the large wooden boxes with the peaked roofs along Castro's front porch were bird houses.

No, he explained, those are my beehives.

"I showed those guys around – took them to the hives at my backdoor, and those at the side of the house, too," he says. "I was telling them all about bees and then one guy looks around and says, 'Man, this has got to be the most protected house in Baltimore.' "

As he's telling me this story, the bees are zooming in and out of his hives in front of us, heading toward the blue sky above in long arcs of high-speed flight. It's a warm day, late summer, but Castro is ready to work in blue jeans, a plain white t-shirt, and dark work boots. He looks to be in his mid-40s with longish dark hair and wire-rimmed glasses. The pattern and timing of his speech give away his California upbringing – there's not a single trace of Baltimore accent in his languid sentences, and his mannerisms vaguely remind me of Tom Petty. He is one of those rare people who can exude excitement and calm at the same time.

The combined buzz of crickets and cicadas fills the air as we talk. Although I'm enjoying watching the bees come and go, I can see why someone who isn't comfortable around these active insects – like the police officer – would be intimidated.

A beautiful garden takes up all of Castro's front yard. There are orange tomatoes, red peppers, and purple eggplants, along with colorful flowers. Its hard to see the hives behind the large butterfly bush that flanks the front porch. The yard is filled to the brim, but tidy and organized with the veggies in neat rows that make for very lovely sight lines no matter where you stand.

Castro laughs when I tell him how great it looks. Not everyone agrees, he says wryly. The neighborhood has some kind of official historic designation and some members of a local group complained recently about the fact that his lack of lawn stood out too much – and detracted from the uniform appearance of the quaint street.

After thinking over their objections, Castro says he told them he figured they had no real case against him. "These places were built in the 1930s. Right after that, World War II broke out and the government had everyone planting victory gardens. The way I see it, I might have the most historically accurate place in the whole neighborhood, because this is probably what was growing in all the yards around here back then."

In a way, it doesn't actually matter. Castro's garden sits between the border of the new and the old – just out of reach of the rules and restrictions about renovations and landscaping. To one side, the homes are quaint one-of-a-kind cottages. To the other side, it's all pre-fabricated, post-war split levels and ranches.

What unifies his neighborhood – and makes it ideal for bees – are the trees. The diversity of the thick green tree canopy is amazing. There are hickories, maples, and oaks. Lindens line one block and giant tulip trees march through most of the backyards.

To be sure, there's lots of forage here for the bees to choose from in the spring.

"I bribe a lot of my neighbors with honey," he says with a grin. "And that seems to work out just great." Even though he's been beekeeping for decades, he's only been at this particular location for two years. So far the honey has been plentiful enough that he has lots to share. Even when the trees stop blooming, the bees can forage on all kinds of weeds along the busy streets.

"The established colonies here, I don't feed," he says motioning to his yard. He doesn't need to.

His bees, a Russian strain imported by the USDA in 1997 and reportedly highly resistant to Varroa mite, are pretty happy and stay pretty peaceful, so even without the honey bribes it has turned out to be a great place to have hives. Most people don't even know the bees are there, even though they walk by them or drive by them dozens of times every day.

Those that do know often think it is wonderful. As if to provide evidence, a dad and his two young daughters walk by in bathing suits on their way to the neighborhood pool for a swim on this hot day.

"Showing a new friend my bees and my garden," Bill tells them.

"Thanks for the cherry tomatoes yesterday," the dad calls out with a wave from the sidewalk.

"They were yummy!" says his youngest, rubbing her stomach and smiling.

Castro and his wife moved around several times for the sake of her job with the navy – finding homes in Montana, Denver, and Annapolis before landing in Baltimore. Because he is originally from San Diego he still feels a bit surprised by the lushness of the eastern forests in this state.

"I'm just not used to trees this big, or how they just grow so tall all on their own like this," he tells me with a grin. He likes it.

Along the back of his back yard, they form a dense mini-forest. There's a steep ravine back there – and a small, un-known and probably unnamed urban creek runs along a patch of land owned by Baltimore Gas and Electric, the local power company. Deer sometimes make their way through this green corridor, too, although many of Castro's neighbors and friends have told him they had no idea the large mammals lived in-side the city limits.

In addition to the trees, it took Castro a while to get used to the humidity. Actually, he confesses, he's never gotten used to it, and it has made beekeeping a bit more complicated.

He's been working hives most of his life since he was a kid back in the 1970s learning the craft alongside his mom. The first year that he kept bees in Maryland, he was unprepared for the impact that excess moisture would have on his colony. Mold took over, killed the bees, and wreaked havoc with his equipment.

Because he's trained as a carpenter, he approached the moisture problem as a design challenge. His handmade wooden frames have beautiful dove-tailed joints, and the main entrance the bees use is small – smaller than many I've seen on backyard hives. Rather than enlarge that entrance, Castro devised a gabled roof line to sit on top of the supers. At the center of the peak is a vent, just like those you might see on the attic of an old Victorian house in Maryland.

It worked, he says. The very next year his hives began to flourish, the excess moisture vanished and the mold disappeared.

Since then he's tended hives in many locations throughout Maryland. Some were in Annapolis. Some were in cookie-cutter style suburban lots. Some were in gorgeous farmland in Sparks, a horsey small town about an hour northeast of Baltimore. The bees in Sparks did not do well, he notes.

His hives here are doing much better, either despite their urban surroundings or because of it. Like everyone else, he'd love the experts to figure out what is causing so many bees to die and also what is causing CCD. He tries to stay informed by going to bee meetings and by reading articles on the bees' problems. Mostly though, he watches his bees and tries to figure out what's best for each hive in each location. "Beekeeping for me has just been a matter of trying this, trying that to see what works. I try to pick and choose what makes sense to me in my own convoluted way."

And for sure there have been problems along the way that have needed addressing. One of his frames this morning showed evidence of a wax moth invasion which needed to be removed. And there are always Varroa mites to monitor. But, he says, he remains committed to the idea of being "treatment-free."

I'm captivated by the activity of his bees, and it's pleasant in the protective shade of his backyard. I suspect Castro could talk bee philosophy with me all afternoon, but I have come to see what he thinks might be his best beeyard. Since so many others have had catastrophic failures in the last two years, I'm curious to see what a healthy, thriving hive looks like. So we jump into Castro's small pick-up truck and head for the place where he is quietly keeping lots of hives.

It's not a far drive. Castro's old truck, I'm delighted to find, has those hand-cranked windows that I haven't seen since the 1980s. I wind the passenger side window down to let in some fresh air and feel as if I'm travelling back in time. We drive past row homes tightly shoe-horned into city blocks, where linden trees have been beaten by heavy truck traffic. We pass convenience stores offering "fine tobacco products" advertised in worn, old hand-painted lettering. On one corner a woman is selling that summer staple of Baltimore: "Snoballs" made out of crushed ice and colored sugar syrup. Teenagers pop off city busses in small groups, grimacing at the bright sunlight as they line up for a cold treat.

Suddenly we veer to the right, leaving pavement behind to cross onto a huge field covered in weeds. Castro knows the way and drives it without a second thought. It's as if we have switched TV channels from a story about the city to a story about the forest.

Once the truck comes to a stop I open the door and jump out. This place is as different from where we just were as Jupiter is from the Earth. Instead of midcentury row homes covered in aluminum siding we are surrounded by open green space – all grass and trees. There's not a building in sight. Next to me is one of the biggest black walnut trees I've ever seen. It looks like it could compete as a tree champion – and it forms the kind of canopy you might imagine Keats or Shelley sitting under to write lines of verse in the English countryside in the 1800s.

Patches of sun dot the knee-high grass all around us, but along the edges of the lot there are vines and trees, trees, more trees. Along the branches of one gnarled maple we see what look like European hornets – but no, those are cicada-killer wasps, those giant insects which sting and then paralyze noisy cicadas out in mid-flight, mostly uninterested in humans. I watch them do battle in mid-air.

"Here are my honey bees," Castro says, jumping out behind me to head down a slight incline. He's still talking, telling me the details of setting this apiary up and how much honey he harvested last year.

I see the hives with their pretty little gabled roofs. But I am too distracted, too awestruck by our setting to pay attention to bee stuff at the moment.

"Bill," I ask him incredulously. "Where the heck are we? This place is *beautiful.*"

The cicada's crescendo in the tree tops, and neither Castro nor I talk for a moment.

"Look! I exclaim, taking off after a butterfly in flight above us. "It's a spicebush swallowtail. They're a threatened species in this state. They only eat sassafras and spicebush when they are caterpillars. But I don't see any sassafras trees," I tell him.

"Oh, and that looks like one of those commas that I'm not so good at identifying," I add.

"What's a comma?" he asks.

Suddenly we've switched roles, and I'm playing tour guide to Maryland's flora and fauna to the guy from the West Coast.

"An unusual butterfly," I tell him. "Really beautiful. And by unusual I mean that I don't see it that often in city lots."

We stand for a while, watching the breeze move across the tree tops. There are so many species of trees and so many that are huge and very, very old. Each one seems to host a huge amount of wildlife – birds, insects, butterflies.

"This tree gives off a ton of these things," Castro says, picking up a nut from the ground as we walk.

"Hickory," I tell him. "You really can't easily buy and plant a hickory sapling. It has to grow on its own because it doesn't like transplanting. So when you find it in an urban spot it's really a treasure. They are wonderful native trees. Full of wildlife. And you never see them in modern neighborhoods anymore. This one probably is going to turn a gorgeous shade of yellow in a few weeks, when fall comes." We stare up at the mature tree which tops out 60 feet above our heads, maybe more.

Somewhere up in its branches a bird is singing a song that I do not recognize. I wonder if its a kind of warbler, migrating through. It is almost time for that to start, here at the end of August.

"Isn't this great?" he says, making a sweeping motion with his arm.

The ownership of the land we are standing on is a bit of an unknown. What is clear is that Baltimore encompasses a lot of abandoned properties. Vacant lots are, in fact, a massive problem throughout the city. Officials say that there are about 16,000 vacant lots and abandoned houses, but many activists think that number is a gross underestimate. Some of the properties are just small row homes. Some have empty store fronts with smashed windows. Some have been taken over by the city, while others are held by unknown or missing landlords. The city's revitalization efforts seem to be balanced on a fulcrum of such problems. If the lots can't be rehabilitated it will remain hard to attract new young families to settle within the city limits, and without new young families, the city won't likely grow and prosper. There are pockets of prosperity, but also lots of areas than remain untouched by any kind of private economic investment.

Somehow, when Castro told me he had hives on an abandoned lot I had expected something that would be squeezed in between old crumbling brick buildings near congested streets full of crime or possibly drugs. Not this.

"So you are a bee squatter, then," I say.

"Yes," he answers, laughing a bit and dipping his chin toward his chest. "I'm a bee squatter."

There is a huge old home on the wooded 22 acres where Castro keeps his bees. Its an old Victorian beauty, boarded up now and shut down.

"Looks like the Munsters' house, doesn't it?" Castor says, referring to the old TV show about Frankenstein and his fictional family from the 1960s.

"Maybe, but look, there's a whole bunch of stained glass under those plywood boards. I bet it could be beautiful," I say, staring at the big old building.

I have a sudden dream for the future of this lovely piece of land. I envision it transformed from a haunted house to a great urban nature center. The building could be used to house classrooms, and under the trees visiting groups of school children could be led on mini nature hikes.

Castro, though, has a different notion. Wouldn't it be great to try growing a nectar-rich crop up there, along the ridge where the land is flat and mostly weeds and no trees? He thinks it would be fun to try buckwheat because it makes for such delicious honey. In the past the crop was only grown in colder climates or at higher elevations, but many beekeepers as far south as Florida have reported growing it successfully in the last few years. Imagine, Castro says, if you could buy Buckwheat Honey from West Baltimore.

Suddenly I notice a large, muscular, black and brown Rottweiler standing on the very ridge Castro wants to plant. I begin silently calculating how fast I can run to the truck and jump inside for safety when a few seconds later a young guy in his mid-twenties follows. Neither dog nor man seems to be in a neighborly mood. The man doesn't return my meek wave, and the dog is all about smelling the ground in front of him as he ambles past. Obviously both just want to be left alone, to mind their own business and enjoy a peaceful walk in the shade. It dawns on me that Castro understands this and probably knows this guy already, and I feel silly for even worrying about the untethered dog which I now realize is peacefully enjoying the breeze just like we are.

"Everyone loves to come let their dogs off the leash up here," he says. "It's kind of an unofficial park. I've met pretty much everyone that comes up here regularly, and they all know who I am."

"Does anyone ever bother your bees?" I ask.

"Once – a group of kids came around and you could tell they had tried to do something – there were sticks poked into the supers. But I figured out who it was and I explained the bees to them and they never bothered me or my bees again. They were actually okay kids."

Castro is talking about buckwheat again, and his dreams for planting some kind of crop in the future. "If I had a pile of money just sitting around, I guess I'd buy it and fix this lot up," he says, lacing his fingers together behind his head and looking around at the view. "I know a guy who says he could do the planting. He's got the machinery, too."

Beyond his fantasy farm we both notice a lot of discarded furniture – white couches and a plastic laminate dining table – someone's been dumping trash which frustrates Castro mightily. For some reason this triggers a memory for me of the community gardens in New York City, and I realize Castro is no different from those gardeners who started the Clinton Community Garden in Hell's Kitchen. He's just at the beginning – where they were back in the early 1980s. This makes me realize what Castro wants to do isn't as far fetched as it seemed. Maybe he would need to pick a different crop, but planting a few rows of something here isn't all that outlandish. Besides, this city has been giving abandoned lots over to urban farming in other neighborhoods. It might actually work out one day.

Looking at Castro's bees I realize that there's no real indication of why they are flourishing. It's not like I really expected to be able to see anything with my own eyes. Goodness knows if the world's biological experts aren't able to figure out the reason so many bees are dying and the causes of

CCD, I'm certainly not going to be able to ascertain it just by driving around and looking at hives.

But there are a lot of beekeepers and potential beekeepers out there who would love to have a place like Castro's beeyard – a place far from any sprays or chemicals, and in the midst of a grove of huge old trees full of spring blossoms – even if, like this place, it was sometimes used as a dumping ground for old furniture.

I wonder how long it will stay vacant like this. And I wonder how long Castro's bees will continue to thrive.

In September Beth Sherring calls to share some good news. Baltimore City, she says, has decided to drop the fee from the registration requirement for beehives, amending the wording of the exotic animal code to what she feels is far more cognizant of the reality of urban beekeeping.

She sends me a link to the website which states:

> *Recognizing the unique role honey bees play in contributing to public welfare as pollinators sustaining a diverse variety of food crops, the need to increase honey bee populations generally, as well as the need to protect honey bees from disease, beekeepers shall not be required to pay a permit application fee. Beekeepers are, nonetheless, required to obtain a permit.*

Officials have also changed some of the setback requirements so that those with small yards protected by a wall can legally house their bees in a way that won't be bothersome to neighbors.

"I'm really pleased," Sherring says. "And now that the legislation fight is settled, there's room in the BBBN agenda to address pesticides."

7

What *Is* Killing the Bees?

Standing in front of her audience at the Technology, Entertainment and Design (TED) Global conference in June 2013 dressed in plain denim and a dark t-shirt, Marla Spivak seems like a cross between the greatest science teacher ever and the sort of next door neighbor who might knock with extra garden tomatoes at the end of the summer. She's able to deftly mix complex science with a plain-spoken and personal passion for bees. She has a knack – like scientists Carl Sagan and David Attenborough – of making listeners believe they can truly understand the scope of a problem that researchers are struggling to solve. I found listening to her talk at first dispiriting, and then reassuring and inspiring.

Bees, she says, are dying from multiple – and interacting – causes. "The bottom line is, bees dying reflects a flowerless landscape and a dysfunctional food system." This is the "big bee bummer."

Bees need a balanced diet which includes protein from pollen and carbohydrates from nectar. After World War II farmers started using herbicides to kill off weeds which included flowering plants that bees depend upon for survival. Most also stopped planting cover crops like clover to fix nitrogen in soil, instead using synthetic fertilizers, which eliminated another important food source for the bees. Many also began planting things in massive fields containing just one crop, such as soybeans, almonds, or corn.

Now beehives must be trucked in to many locations so the bees can pollinate crops when needed then carted off to a new location and another crop because there would be no other food source for them if they stayed.

While she talks, a photo of a farmhouse flanked by massive and incredibly tidy rows of crops, looking like corduroy, lights up a screen behind her. The photo looks almost identical to the huge farm I saw on the way to Steve McDaniel's place in Carroll County in July, but with even fewer trees.

"We talk about food deserts, places in our cities, neighborhoods that have no grocery stores. The very farms that used to sustain bees are now agricultural food deserts, dominated by one or two plant species."

We are also demanding more of our bees than ever before, she notes, planting more crops that need pollination. Meanwhile, bees have become the target of an increasing number of diseases and pests, including the Varroa mite.

Before the problems of neonicotinoid exposure, other pesticides used since the middle of the last century began taking a toll. Researchers from Pennsylvania State, she tells the audience, discovered that each batch of pollen a honey bee collects has at least six detectable pesticides including herbicides, fungicides, and inert ingredients from pesticides that can be more toxic to bees than the active ingredients themselves.

With a photo of a bee on screen, she asks: "This small bee is holding up a large mirror. How much is it is going to take to contaminate humans?"

In 2010, Spivak was awarded a prestigious MacArthur Fellowship for her work on bee hygienics after she began investigating the abilities of certain strains of bees to detect and then remove infected pupae from their colonies. The award – which is sometimes referred to as a "MacArthur Genius Grant" – is a big deal not only because it acts as a kind of validation of one's lifetime research but also because awardees are given $625,000 to use on research projects, "no strings attached." The foundation proudly states that they like to award people rather than projects.

Lately Spivak has been studying propolis and the role it may play in the health of beehives. The sticky substance the bees make from plant resins to use as the glue of their hives has long been prized by humans for its antimicrobial and antiviral properties. Now, she says, we are beginning to understand its importance to the bees themselves in fighting their own diseases.

Spivak's research team has also been studying the effect of imidacloprid on honey bee queens and ways that urban lawns can be developed as forage for bees. There are also many things, she thinks, that bear deeper investigation in bee science – nutrition, bee habitat, toxicology, and control of Varroa mites without chemicals.

Spivak's TED talk eloquently points to a reality that is often missed by the general public. Although the problem of CCD remains an important mystery to be solved in the realm of biology, many scientists had been discussing the honey bee's diminishing health long before bees began disappearing in large numbers from commercial hives in 2006. USDA statistics show that the honey bee industry peaked in 1947. The bee problem is bigger and encompasses more than just CCD.

The defining characteristic of CCD, according to the US Department of Agriculture-Agricultural Research Service (USDA-ARS), is the disappearance of most or all of the adult honey bees in a given colony, leaving behind honey and brood but no dead bees. While many beekeepers report losses that fit those descriptions, others are now also reporting increasing numbers of colonies that simply don't make it through the winter, and some are also reporting an increase in the number hives that fail in a manner usually associated with pesticide deaths – piles of dead bees outside formerly healthy, vibrant colonies.

The bottom line may be that while we are demanding more and more of the bees through our current agricultural system, they are failing in large numbers each year, whether from CCD or other causes.

At the University of Maryland, researcher Dennis vanEnglesdorp has been heading up the effort to calculate just how many bees are lost each season, in order to better direct scientific investigations. His work is helped by beekeepers and bee researchers nationwide, including Spivak.

Known as the Bee Informed Partnership (BIP), the project began gathering information in 2006 via online surveys which asked beekeepers detailed questions about their management practices and about their winter losses.

Participation has always been completely voluntary – requests are sent out to beekeeping groups all over the country and beekeepers are urged to get online and participate. For the 2012-2013 winter season, a total of 6,287 US beekeepers provided responses. Collectively, that group managed 599,610 colonies as of October 2012 – about 23% of the nation's total.

Survey results released in May of 2013 found that, like previous years, about 30% of the managed honey bee colonies in the US were lost during the 2012-2013 season, representing a increase in loss of 42% over the previous winter's total losses.

Such numbers are staggering. Even among the beekeepers they are considered far from normal; survey participants indicated that they considered a loss rate of 15% acceptable, but about 70% of them suffered losses far greater than that.

Some observers have pointed out that if similar losses were seen among managed herds of cattle, the problem would be considered a national crisis of unheard of proportions and would make the news each night as a food security issue. But perhaps because the bees are tiny, do their work quietly, and are not directly in our diet, their problems have long been overlooked.

The BIP numbers have also served as a way to documenting the extent of colony collapse across the nation. When news of CCD first broke in 2006, some of the veteran beekeepers who heard about it initially dismissed the entire notion of a "crisis" or "disorder" as overblown. Some thought it might simply be the result of poor management, and wondered if a few of the newbies were out there grabbing publicity and looking for someone to blame for their own ineptitude.

It didn't help that the media also treated the entire problem as a bizarre chapter out of a science fiction book or a strange statistical anomaly. Headline writers delighted in making puns about busy bees and focused on oddball, unscientific theories for causes, sometimes trivializing the entire issue. But as the die-offs spread and the numbers began to be reported, the real scope of the crisis became more apparent, even to the skeptics.

vanEnglesdorp is careful to say that the BIP project is not one which he alone invented. "It was an idea that beekeepers, many beekeepers had," he writes on the BIP website. "As I traveled across the country sampling bees to try to find out what was killing [honey bees], beekeepers everywhere said that what they needed was a way to find out what other beekeepers did and which of those things worked."

In 2006 he was working on a PhD at Pennsylvania State University after having served as a state apiarist, and took a class on epidemiology. "I remember that for the first third of the course I thought that this was just the biggest bunch of statistical nonsense I'd ever heard... I was trained as an empirical scientist where you have a control, and a hypothesis, and you test the hypothesis."

Then one day, the professor teaching the course began talking about breast cancer statistics. "It was like the penny dropped. I realized we needed to rethink how I looked at these things. We're not talking about causation, we're talking about probabilities, and when you have these probabilities and you see these consistencies in large populations, even in very dirty data, then you have a chance of asking very informed questions and then going to the empirical process, which is what I had trained for before. "

In other words, by looking at what the beekeepers were doing and experiencing in the field, the team could better direct or inspire research efforts on the bee's problems. The survey was developed, then fine-tuned over time with input from bee experts across the country and beekeepers who were talking to them.

Sometimes the survey's results prove what the scientists already know empirically. "For instance, people who treat for Varroa mites have better survivorship than those that don't, and there are some products that work better than other products," vanEnglesdorp says.

Other times the results point to areas that need further research. "In some cases it is surprising. For instance, we're seeing that people that reuse their [honey]comb right away have lower mortality than those that store their comb – and I would have thought it would be exactly opposite. So we need to take a look at: was that a real effect, was that a correlated effect, or was there something biological going on there."

Beekeepers, he notes, are using the information from the project very differently than the scientists. They are often hungry to know what other beekeepers are doing. There's something inherent in human nature, vanEnglesdorp has noticed, that causes people to listen to advice more if it comes from someone among their own ranks. "Pretty consistently people don't listen to anybody but their own cohorts. And I think that beekeepers don't listen to scientists, and I think they trust each other more than they trust others."

He also tells me that the hobbyists beekeepers – those working on a small number of hives in their backyard – have been much more eager to participate than the commercial beekeepers, partly due to the fact that their problems are so different.

One of the starkest findings makes a good case in point, he tells me. The survey found that people who treat for Varroa mites lose fewer colonies than those who don't, but 60 or 70% of beekeepers don't treat for the mite at all.

"You present that to a commercial beekeeping group and they'll walk out of the room because there's not a commercial beekeeper out there who doesn't treat for Varroa mite." Many see the use of miticide as a necessary trade-off: yes, it may cause some bee losses, but the damage is less than it would be if they left the Varroa mites unchecked. Meanwhile, some of the backyard beekeepers think that if they don't treat their hives at all they will create mite-resistant bees.

"I'd like to say that's not a very sound argument for various reasons. I mean, it's a great ambition, but it's biologically probably not the way we're going to develop resistant populations, and it may actually be counterproductive. So I think how we present to hobbyists or backyard beekeepers is very different from how we present to the other cohorts."

Although vanEnglesdorp doesn't say so, I notice that the survey has also kept the topic of bee health and CCD newsworthy and current. Each year, as the results of the survey are tabulated and announced, news outlets all around the world report on the bees – something that never happened with regularity before 2006. The numbers let people know that the bees' problems are ongoing.

Beyond the BIP and its surveys, vanEnglesdorp has been hard at work on many other kinds of research projects regarding the bees. In 2012 he joined Jeff Pettis, a bee expert from the USDA, to examine how exposure to pesticides and fungicides could aggravate and increase the bees' susceptibility to *Nosema ceranae,* a potentially lethal parasite which has become increasingly common in US hives.

ALISON GILLESPIE

Their research, which was published in the journal *PLoS ONE* in July of 2013, showed that pollen collected by honey beehives in fields from the eastern part of the US contained nine different agricultural chemicals, including fungicides, insecticides, herbicides, and miticides. One sample contained a whopping 21 different pesticides. The most common chemicals found throughout were a fungicide commonly used on apple trees and an insecticide specifically used to control Varroa mites in hives. The food the bees were collecting, it seemed, contained a chemical cocktail.

What was surprising to everyone, however, was that the bees fed the fungicide-laden pollen were nearly three times as likely to be infected with *Nosema* than those which had not.

"We don't think of fungicides as having a negative effect on bees, because they aren't designed to kill insects," vanEnglesdorp stated in a press release put out by the University of Maryland. Furthermore, federal regulations restrict the use of pesticides but not the use of fungicides. "You'll often see fungicide applications going on while bees are foraging on the crop. This finding suggests we have to reconsider that policy."

The study may also have implications for backyard beekeepers who often wonder if some common chemical lawn treatments are safe for bees. I recall sitting through a discussion at a beekeeping meeting where a relatively new beekeeper had asked if golf courses provided safe forage for her suburban bees, and if such locations would make good spots for setting up new hives. Some of the veterans in the room said no, emphatically, while others said yes because lawn treatments were meant only to kill weeds and fungi – neither kind of chemical was aimed at killing insects. While such assumptions are now being questioned more heavily by researchers, the use of chemicals continues unabated by homeowners and land managers near beeyards nationwide.

There are really two big groups in beekeeping, Jeff Pettis tells me when I go to visit the USDA-ARS in Beltsville, Maryland. "One group says we'll manage or treat for these diseases, mites or whatever – we'll intervene. Then there's another group that says they don't want to do much of anything, just let the bees do what they're going to do, we're going to lose some, we're going to gain some – but we're not going to intervene as much. These people can't talk to each other very well. It's an ideological barrier."

Pettis invited me to see his lab and learn more about their research. The facility is located in the middle of a vast tract of federal land just outside of Washington, DC flanked by the Patuxent Wildlife Refuge.

Surrounding these pieces of federal land, there's a massive urban development. Railroad tracks bustling with passenger trains and cargo containers whizz along beside tire warehouses and factories, strip malls, and apartment complexes, and multilane highways bustle with high speed traffic. But here inside the research campus the vistas are absolutely beautiful – crops framed by diverse, forested tracts on distant, gently rolling hills. It's a quiet and calm oasis until I read signs in large lettering that advise visitors to stay out of the fields because they may have been treated recently. There's serious work going on out there – observations are being made, data is being taken, and analyses are being performed by people working in the brick buildings off in the distance.

In 2008 Pettis was named coordinator of a five-year program to improve honey bee health, survivorship, and pollination availability here. A major part of the program examines some of the issues regarding the long-range transport of bees for pollination on large farms – but it also takes into account the needs of smaller-scale beekeepers. CCD has caused big problems for many – and brought forth many questions that bear the need for research. Other labs elsewhere in the country examine genetic issues, pollination, Africanization of bees, and nutrition. The Beltsville lab specifically investigates the management of pests and diseases in honey bees.

Walking through the building alongside Pettis, I notice all of the bee paraphernalia that lines the walls in curio cabinets and glass shelves. There are bee figurines, old scientific models of bee bodies that look like they may have been used to teach graduate biology classes back in the '50s, and incredibly colorful posters – some vintage and some new – lining the corridors in glass cases. There's one whole shelf dedicated to the showcasing and explaining of different varietals of honey from the different regions of the US. And in Pettis' own office, there are more personal tchotchkes – figurines and photos and sketches of bees drawn by children. He asks me if I want something to drink and points to a collection of mugs next to the coffee maker which are also festooned with bees.

Lots of people in his life give him gifts adorned with bees, he says with a grin. They think of him as the bee guy.

Most beekeepers you meet, Pettis says, are pretty passionate about the bees, and with most researchers it's the same thing. "They somehow found social insects or bees fascinating. For me, it was the honey bees."

Pettis has voiced his concerns over and over again about the need to solve the CCD question. "The faint good news," he stated in an article in *Agricultural Research* magazine published in July 2012, "is that CCD does not seem to be getting worse. But – and this is a big 'but' – 33% losses each year are probably not economically sustainable for commercial beekeeping operations."

Pettis has also compared CCD to a jigsaw puzzle with 1,000 pieces – researchers have turned over some of the "blue sky" pieces, but so far that only show us the frame. The center of the CCD puzzle remains illusive and unfinished.

Among almost a dozen theories about the causes of CCD, none seems to have a clear cause-and-effect relationship to the problem. Many scientists who work with the USDA suspect that pathogens are likely culprits. But before any one of the many pathogens impacting bees can be listed as a definitive cause, research must demonstrate that its introduction into a healthy hive causes the syndrome to occur. Neonicotinoids are also coming under increasing scrutiny along with criticism from many parts of the world for their toxic properties, but it is not yet clear that use of the systemics causes bees to leave their healthy hives suddenly and unexpectedly in large numbers. Indeed, France and Germany both continue to report occurrences even though both banned the chemicals several years ago.

Pettis' most recent efforts to turn over more pieces of the CCD puzzle have led him to investigations into queen health and genetic diversity, and the impact that pesticides – including the neonicotinoid imidacloprid – may have on foraging. He's also worked on issues like grooming behavior in hives.

Some critics have said they think the federal government is taking too long to come up with answers on CCD, while others have said they find the low level of funding for CCD research appalling. Pettis has had to navigate a lot of such discussions and keep focused on the bees and how people's actions can benefit their well-being. A huge chunk of the world's food supply depends on pollination. Finding out what's causing so many of them to die each year is of supreme importance. In conversations he constantly describes the US bees as "our bees," and seems to see all efforts to overcome the bee crisis as a team effort – even if they don't originate from USDA labs. To hear him talk, we are all in this together – and given the impact that a complete collapse of the entire honey bee population would have, he's likely right.

Pettis is probably the most famous bee researcher currently working in the US today. He's been in almost every major magazine and newspaper. Yet he remains approachable – an easy-going guy with sandy blond hair and a closely trimmed beard wearing a short-sleeve button down shirt who speaks in a soft, friendly voice to everyone he encounters.

As he and I walk the hallways of the lab, Pettis is often stopped by coworkers to answer questions. There's excitement in the air – some fresh queen bees are due to arrive soon, and each time he runs into a colleague he conveys the news with a smile, sometimes even rubbing his hands together like someone awaiting the arrival of a full-course meal. It is obvious he can't wait to sink his teeth into a new round of investigative questions.

"Queens are failing at a pretty high rate. Part of it seems to be that after they've mated, the sperm starts to die for some reason, and we're not sure why. So we have a florescent scope and we can dye the sperm and it will turn red or green and we'll know if its live or dead. We're doing that next week, we're getting another batch of queens in from California."

Queens, who should live a year or more are only living six to eight months. "There's a lot of things going on. We've got some suspicions, one of them is pesticides."

Pettis also tells me that although there's a fair amount of genetic diversity in the US, he thinks that new efforts to breed local queens are a good thing. "If queens are bred in New York City or upstate Wisconsin or something like that, then they are adapted to that local climate, so they're going to be better than if they were raised in Georgia and a southern bee trying to be maintained in the north... It is nice when people start breeding from their own survivor stock. It really helps out."

People from all over the US also send samples of their failed beehives to this lab for examination. In one room, I meet an undergraduate student from nearby University of Maryland named Katie Jackson who is stretching her neck after spending the morning counting *Nosema* spores through the lens of a microscope. All around her, carefully packaged samples with addresses from all over the US are stacked up in neat piles. Pettis asks her if I can take a turn. I lean over the eye piece and see what look like uniform, cigar-shaped rods. Pettis gives Jackson a few words of gentle, smiling encouragement, telling her that although what she does can be tedious, it's important.

Like a lot of federal scientists I've met over the years, it's plain Pettis wants everyone to see the results and the relevance of the work of the lab he so proudly has helped direct. He wants the public to see how hard his charges work and how earnestly they engage in the important questions at hand about bee health. It would be hard not to see how much he loves the bees and working on this topic.

In one room Pettis introduces me to a man working investigating immune responses in bees. There are five scientists working specifically on bee diseases here, with some also exploring control options such as antibiotics. Although Pettis doesn't mention it, I know the topic is one that is hotly debated; many commercial beekeepers depend upon antibiotics, but research in 2012 showed that US bees were also developing genetic resistance not unlike the resistance seen in agricultural animals such as cows and chickens. Their use has been banned in beehives in many European countries.

Pettis tells me that he and his coworkers often find themselves in the middle of heated debates between beekeepers of different styles and philosophies. Because this lab focuses on diseases and because it is located so close to the epicenter of the federal government, Pettis is also often called upon to answer lawmakers' questions about the problem of CCD, which can be another point of tension.

"On this spectrum of where do we intervene versus where do we not intervene, we have to kind of serve all the beekeepers, so we look at all kinds of options. We look at organic options for Varroa control, we look at straight chemical control of Varroa, too. It's a mixed bag."

*****

The Xerces Society for Invertebrate Conservation is one of many groups asking for more research on the topic of bee deaths. The group thinks that there hasn't been enough on neonicotinoids, and wants more focus on the impact they may be having on invertebrates.

In 2012 the group released a detailed report entitled *Are Neonicotinoids Killing Bees?* In addition to noting that neonicotinoids are present in pollen and nectar of treated plants, in their Executive Summary the authors note that:

- Neonicotinoids can also persist in soils for long periods of time, even after a single application.

Measureable amounts of residues were found in woody plants up to six years after application.

- Untreated plants may absorb chemical residues in the soil from the previous year.

- Products approved for home and garden use may be applied to ornamental and landscape plants, as well as turf, at significantly higher rates (potentially 120 times higher) than those approved for agricultural crops.

Research on honey bees in particular has shown that those exposed to "even sub-lethal amounts of neonicotinoids often experience problems with flying and navigation, as well as reduced taste sensitivity, and slower learning of new tasks, which all impact foraging ability," the authors state.

"Neonicotinoid-treated corn seed is planted on millions of acres annually in the United States," they further add. "Although we do not know the full scope of the impact of this exposure on bees, we do know that bees close to cornfields can come into contact with lethal levels of abraded seed coatings and dust, bees may collect contaminated pollen, and that plants (e.g., weeds) growing around seed-treated fields can become contaminated with systemic insecticides."

The Xerces Society also gives more than 14 bullet points detailing the current knowledge gaps regarding the systemic neonicotinoids, including a lack of data regarding the delayed effects that these chemicals may have on honey. "Because honey bees store food for times of dearth, chemical exposure is likely delayed beyond field study timelines," the authors write.

"What these studies show," says Xerces Society Executive Director Scott Hoffman Black, "is that we should all really be concerned with these chemicals. Whether you are concerned with honey bees, native bees, other beneficial insects, or aquatic organisms – across the board these chemicals, from the studies, seem to be problematic."

It's not just that they are toxic to bees and are so long-lived in the environment – they are now also one of the most used chemicals in the world.

Black and his group are particularly concerned about the impact the neonicotinoids are having on the native pollinators. Honey bees are an introduced species – one that is managed and tended by people. But the impacts on wild invertebrates – the native and non-native solitary bees, the butterflies, the lady bugs and numerous species of beetles – have not been given much attention, despite studies which have documented the tremendous contribution such insects make to agriculture.

"Most insecticides probably impact native bees more than they impact honey bees," Black says. "I would contend that whatever is happening for honey bees, it's probably far worse for native bees that are out there."

Partly this is because native bees can't be moved like honey bees can nor can their hives be closed up during spraying. But also, as his group's reports so graphically detail, the needs of native bees are dramatically different from those of honey bees.

The native bees nest underground or tunnel into the soft, pithy stems of plants. Some use existing tunnels made in trees by other creatures. When making their nests they often use a combination of mud, plant resin, leaves, petals, or plant fibers. This wide range of potential exposure has rarely been studied, even though they may be coming in closer contact with residues from the systemic neonicotinoids than honey bees regularly do. Unfortunately, standardized methods for testing solitary bees and bumble bees do not yet exist.

Black also tells me that his group has received anecdotal reports from many who work with the various *Osmia* species, known by the common name of orchard or mason bees, that these tiny black and blue pollinators are in trouble as well. Many are seeing increasing numbers of dead bees in their mason bee nesting tubes each year. This is a huge concern for those who would like to explore the possibility of using *Osmia* species as viable substitutes for European honey bees in the pollination of crops in large agricultural settings in the US.

When I mention that 2013 was also a terrible year for seeing butterflies, including the iconic monarch butterfly which migrates up and down the continent each season, Black says the situation is really unknown, although the group has summarized the small amount of available scientific research in an additional report released in 2013 entitled *Beyond the Birds and the Bees: Effects of Neonicotinoid Insecticides on Agriculturally Important Beneficial Insects.* "We don't know the impact of these chemicals on butterflies. We just don't because the studies aren't there."

Concerns about neonicotinoids involve urban as well as rural locations, he explains. Although there is no way to gather data about how many insecticides are used by individual homeowners or businesses, stream studies conducted by the US Geological Survey have repeatedly indicated that there are many more pounds of insecticides and pesticides used in the suburbs and in cities than in rural areas.

"People like to point the finger at those farmers who are out there using all those chemicals – but in many urban and suburban areas we're using more. And we're not just using them for economic reasons. We're using them because we want the perfect rose or the perfect lawn. It really has all to do with cosmetics, not economics."

People in cities and suburbs, he points out, are often not trained in the use of chemicals, either. "We need to not give the pass to farmers. Farmers do need to work on using less of these chemicals. But in many cases what we do in urban or suburban areas is just as bad."

Many home gardeners who have always tended their small flower and food plots using organic principles continue to feel insulated from such worries. Since they don't spray the chemicals themselves, they often assume they can continue gardening in a way that will not harm the bees. In some ways it has been an out-of-sight, out-of-mind situation. But in August 2013, a study was released by Friends of the Earth regarding plants sold at three retail outlets – Lowes, Home Depot, and Orchard Supply Hardware – which awakened a lot of home gardeners to the possibility that avoiding neonics wasn't as easy as they thought. Entitled, *Gardeners Beware: Bee-Toxic Pesticides Found in 'Bee Friendly' Plants Sold at Garden Centers Nationwide,* the report indicated that seven out of thirteen samples of garden plants purchased in locations including San Francisco, Washington, DC, and Minneapolis contained the systemic neonicotinoids.

Noting that bees are essential to the human food system, the group and its allies called upon Lowes, Home Depot, and Target to stop selling neonicotinoids and plants treated with the pesticides in their stores, just as several retailers in the United Kingdom had already pledged to do. The group backed their request with copies of online petitions which were quickly signed by more than 175,000 people. Neither of the retail chains had responded by December 2013.

After reading through the reports and interviewing experts about the bees, any illusion that I might have harbored about being able to design organic gardens where bees and butterflies would be protected was scoured away, given the great territory a honey bees forages in the quest for nectar and pollen. In an urban area like mine, where numerous landowners can occupy a single acre, the chances are high that someone has used neonicotinoids. This is the most wretched kind of algebra I have ever attempted, and the odds are stacked against the bees that hum around my flowers even if my blossoms are organic.

Furthermore, the last few years have brought gardeners like me a renewed sense of urgency when it comes to providing a healthy food chain for creatures such as bees, butterflies, and birds. It was only seven years ago that Doug Tallamy published *Bringing Nature Home,* which described his research on the importance of using native plantings in our backyard landscapes. Many of us had known for years we were hosting huge numbers of species in our tiny wildlife habitat gardens, but it was Tallamy who put a number to it, showing that even a humble backyard filled with native plants and trees could play host to hundreds of species of caterpillars, which in turn either turn into beautiful moths and butterflies or feed scores of passing migratory birds. To garden with awareness of such numbers and cycles is to garden with a sense of responsibility.

Knowing that insects such as bees or caterpillars might be killed on plants that I purchased which were sprayed with long-lasting neonics brought me to full despair. All of the avenues that I had been using to try to reverse the lack of wildlife food in my urban habitat garden now seemed darkened with sinister possibilities.

I can rarely afford to go all organic at the expensive garden centers, and most of the time the organic choices just don't exist for common garden annuals. What if the plants I had bought on the cheap at some big box store were killing the bees, the caterpillars, the beneficial soil organisms? What the hell had I been planting for the things visiting my garden — healthy plants or toxic-laced leaves and flowers?

I spent afternoons counting the bees on our basil plants in order to reassure myself, and began making mental notes about places to find organic plants. My whole world order shifted and adjusted to this change in perspective. Every store and nursery that wasn't certified as organic suddenly became suspect – guilty until proven innocent. I began trading plants with friends whom I knew used only organic seeds, and avoided some of my favorite hangouts – the lovely garden centers full of plants shipped in from unknown growers working in unknown locations. When I discovered that a nearby farmers market included a person growing certified organic plants as well as produce, I became her number one customer, buying out her supply of certain annual plants on a single Sunday morning. I also was glad that most of my garden was full of long-established perennials, and began offering as many of my offshoot organic plants and seeds to newbie gardeners as I could possibly manage, telling each person along the way to avoid the neonics when possible.

One morning, while researching pesticides, I realized why it is so many have turned to the words and wisdom of Rachel Carson during such times. I was paging through *Silent Spring*, which is written in a vivid, poetic tone rarely found in modern environmental writing, and was shocked to find the following passage:

> *The world of the systemic insecticides is a weird world, surpassing the imaginings of the brothers Grimm – perhaps more closely akin to the cartoon world of Charles Addams. It is a world where the enchanted forest of the fairy tales has become the poisonous forest in which an insect that chews a leaf or sucks the sap of a plant is doomed. It is a world where a flea bites a dog, and dies because the dog's*

blood has been made poisonous, where an insect may die from vapors emanating from a plant it has never touched, where a bee may carry poisonous nectar back to its hive and presently produce poisonous honey.

It was oddly comforting to know that I had an ally in this woman who died many years before I was born, and her acknowledgement of the change in perspective such chemicals can cause in a nature-lover helped me enormously. I had a coach in my corner, and I would figure out a way to come out fighting this problem.

I found more encouragement and a feeling of camaraderie in Spivak's words, confirming for me that all the effort and caution I was using in selecting plants for my garden was worthwhile. Every one of us, she says in her TED talk, can make a difference by planting bee-friendly flowers in diverse groupings of blooms that will continue for the whole season from spring to fall. We need to put them everywhere we can and we need to make sure they aren't contaminated by pesticides. Maybe it seems like a small solution to a huge problem, she concedes, but it is one way we can give the bees access to better nutrition. "Everyone of us needs to behave a little bit more like a bee society, an insect society, where each of our individual actions can contribute to a grand solution, an emergent property, that's much greater than the mere sum of our individual actions. So let the small act of planting flowers and keeping them free of pesticides be the driver of large scale change."

8

Celebrating Pollinators on the National Mall

"Come learn about the pollinators! Come on over and join us!" a woman in a fuzzy bee costume beckons to me as I emerge from the cool darkness of the Smithsonian Metro stop in downtown DC.

Although it is a broiling summer afternoon, she's very enthusiastic and energetic – just like a real bee – and I'm in awe of her ability to withstand the heat.

Following her across the street, I find what I've been looking for – Pollinator Day outside the US Department of Agriculture (USDA) headquarters building on the National Mall. The street has been closed off and there are rows of information tables tucked away under the shade of some temporary tents.

Lunch hour has just started and everywhere I turn federal employees are wandering around – easy to pick out by the ID cards which dangle from their necks in plastic badge holders. Tourists mill about as well, taking in the monuments and museums, posing for photos in front of famous landmarks. Some of both groups are intrigued by my new friend in the bee suit. She's now been joined by a man in a bright green tomato hornworm costume.

"I turn into a moth," he explains over and over to people. "Moths are great pollinators!"

Maybe so, but bees are definitely the stars of the show today. At one table, a biologist is explaining that most of the native bee species in the US are solitary, and rarely if ever sting people. Some are small, he notes, showing me a photo of a blue and black mason bee. Some are very big, like the carpenter bees people see around wooden playgrounds in the spring.

Bumble bees, perhaps the best known of the native bees in the US, live in colonies like the European honey bees. They don't produce enough honey for people to harvest, but they are excellent pollinators. Four species which were once common in the US are now almost completely absent from their historic ranges, and scientists continue to make concerted efforts to locate them. The USDA even has details on its website for building boxes to attract and house some of the bumble bees, although success with such devices hasn't been too widely tested in backyards.

"If you find one of these bees in your garden, email us," says a man from the Xerces Society. "These are the ones we want to know about." He points to a picture of a Rusty Patched Bumble Bee *(Bombus affinis)* and hands me a card detailing the once common bee's mysterious decline.

At the kids' table, families are working on coloring pages and puzzles. Someone's giving out okra plants elsewhere, and there's honey to taste for free farther down the street. In addition to today's special event, this is also the day the USDA hosts its weekly Farmers' Market on the Mall, and vendors are selling everything from fresh green peppers to sticky balls of hot caramel corn.

At one table, a man from the National Resources Conservation Service of the USDA hands me a folded card about the importance of being a friend to pollinators. We need moths, butterflies, bats, hummingbirds, and bees, it explains. They move the pollen from plant to plant and make the crops flourish.

"Three-fourths of the world's flowering plants depend on pollinators to reproduce... A world without pollinators would be a world without apples, blueberries, strawberries, chocolate, almonds, melons, peaches or pumpkins," the card states.

Most of the educational table space here is focused on native pollinators, since they are often the least understood and least appreciated. But honey bees – those non-native insects brought in from Europe by colonists a few hundred years ago – seem to be attracting the biggest crowd, probably because they are the only ones that can be brought here live for up-close viewing. Every few minutes someone stops at one of the two tables with live bees to talk about honey or ask questions.

"Do you see their tongues?" says Toni Burnham, one of the two beekeepers sitting beside a glass observation hive on a table under the shade. She's talking to a family with two very young girls who have approached with their parents. "If you look closely you can see the bees stick their tongues out," Burnham says, leaning across the table.

One girl hides behind her mom's back – fearful or shy – I'm not sure which. The other squeals with delight. "I see it! It's red! They are licking everything!"

"Hello! Hello!" she calls to the bees, pressing her nose and palms against the glass to get a closer look. Somehow, the fact that these creatures have familiar body parts inspires her to try to communicate with them. "Why do they want to lick everything?" she asks slowly.

Burnham smiles gently, and points out the spot where the queen seems to be hiding under all of her worker bees and explains the bees' work along the honeycombs. The licking is part of how they check on things in the hive. Most of the time they live in dark hives made of wood, not the one here today made of see-through glass. They have to use their senses other than sight to find out what is going on around them.

"Did you know that most of the bees in a hive are girls? They are called the workers," Burnham continues. "And the one in charge, she's a girl too, the queen."

"Hello! Hello!" calls the girl again, softer now. She begs her family to stay longer so she can keep watching.

Burnham's fellow beekeeper, Sean McKenzie, smiles at the scene from under his red baseball cap. He can remember feeling a similar excitement when he was a kid, more than 25 years ago in Jamaica. Cousins would bring gifts of honey still on the comb to his family, he recalls. That was tasty, but it was the social structure of the bees that really intrigued him. He spent hours reading about them long before he was able to get a hive and some bees of his own as an adult living here in the Brookland neighborhood of Washington. There still is no end to his interest in their world, their hives, their habits, he tells me. Friends sometimes jokingly ask if he's the only African American beekeeper in the city, but he's definitely not.

"A lot of my friends say they've changed their attitude toward the bees since they heard me talk about them," McKenzie says. "They tell me: I saw a bee today and I didn't kill it because of you."

The little girl's reaction to the bees in the glass hive is exactly the kind McKenzie and Burnham hope to inspire here today. Love, excitement, respect, enthusiasm – this is what they hope visitors will feel for the bees when the day is done. "Bees are so important," Burnham tells another adult visitor to her table. "Here's a list of ten things you can do to help them," she adds, handing the woman a sheet of paper.

"Do they know what's killing the bees, yet?" a man with a white beard, heavy New England accent, and a Hawaiian-print shirt asks.

He's not the only one wondering. When beekeepers began to report the mysterious disappearance of their bees back in

2006, all bees suddenly seemed horribly vulnerable. What had always been the most ubiquitous of all backyard insects, the honey bee, seemed suddenly akin to the Bald Eagle or the Spotted Owl: vulnerable, fragile, and perhaps threatened by some thing we humans were carelessly doing to our environment.

A year later, in 2007, the US Department of Agriculture (USDA) began holding events like this one, to celebrate the role of bees and other pollinators in agriculture and ecosystems to the general public. Hosting pollinator parties, events and festivals seemed like a way to garner the public's support for bee work, and answer their questions, too.

In truth, however, there had been signals of great trouble for the pollinators of the world long before anyone coined the phrase Colony Collapse Disorder.

Widespread use of pesticides beginning after World War II, and the incorporation of many new kinds of deadly pesticides into the general regime of farming in the US often proved deadly to many bee species throughout the second half the 20th century. And then in the 1980s, two foreign pests began to invade US honey beehives in great numbers and cause even further problems: tracheal mites and Varroa mites.

In 1996, Stephen Bachmann and Gary Nabhan skillfully described the honey bee's troubles in dramatic detail in a book called *The Forgotten Pollinators.* Some of the honey bees' problems, they posited, might be irresolvable.

Even more alarmingly, the two ecologists noted, research was showing that some of the same problems plaguing the heavily-managed honey bees were likewise plaguing wild native bees and other kinds of pollinating creatures like moths, butterflies, and bats. Pesticide use and genetic engineering along with land use change and habitat fragmentation were limiting the number and variety of pollinators available to step into the breech, should the honey bee industry completely collapse. As larger parts of rural North America were turned into farm fields and sprayed with chemicals or transformed into industrial sites and housing developments, pollinators had fewer places to live, and smaller chances of survival.

"The honey bee is faltering... If honey bees continue along their present declining trajectory, what bees or other pollinators will take up the slack in providing essential pollination services for our vast commercial and home agricultural plantings?" the authors wrote. And what were we losing each time a pollinating species disappeared?

It was a terrifying question to contemplate, especially since the general public seemed unaware of how pollination worked or how valuable it was to humans and human food production.

Too little science had been gathered on pollinators, the authors urged. Most of what was known was focused on honey bees, but even that work rarely examined the pollination relationship itself. As a result, conservation efforts rarely protected the native pollinators or promoted their needs. It would take a paradigm shift in conservation to move from protecting individual species to protecting interspecific relationships and landscapes.

What would help, many decided at the time, was an educational campaign. *The Forgotten Pollinators* became the centerpiece of an effort led by the Arizona-Sonora Desert Museum in Tucson where Nabhan was then the Director of Science. Exhibits and a website were designed, and scientific meetings and informational events were held for the public. Pollinators, as it were, gained a PR team.

After the book was published, Bachmann went on to advise a non-profit group called the Pollinator Partnership (P2) whose founding was, in part, inspired by his book and the subsequent attention it received.

P2 now works to promote the health of pollinators critical to food and ecosystems through conservation, research, and education – including the organization of National Pollinator Week activities throughout the US. The group also hosts a website, providing educational materials and backyard guides for anyone interested in learning more about the topic.

Since 1999, P2 has also managed the North American Pollinator Protection Campaign (NAPPC), a collaboration of individuals and organizations from all aspects of the pollinator issue who work to "promote and protect pollinators and the agricultural and ecological services they provide." Members of its task force include beekeepers, native bee advocates, researchers, agency officials from the USDA, the Environmental Protection Agency, and the Department of the Interior, as well as representatives from the pesticide industry and the agricultural sector. Some of their projects have included the drafting of Action Plans to build on current scientific research about pollinators and their habitats. They have also worked to include pollinator-friendly amendments to recent Farm Bills.

Getting consensus among those various stakeholders can be tough work, says Tom Van Arsdall, P2's Public Affairs Officer. The conflicts between some of the differing parties have long and storied histories. One project the group recently tackled went through more than 24 drafts before everyone agreed on the final wording, for example. But he believes finding common ground is the best way to improve outcomes for pollinators.

"They can fight with each other," Van Arsdall quips. "But not at NAPPC. They aren't allowed."

Conflicts between bee advocates and pesticide companies probably get the most press. Many who love both honey bees and natives have been very vocal about their concerns regarding the misuse of pesticides and the role that even properly-used pesticides may be playing in the declining health of the bees.

But there have also been conflicts between those in agriculture and those who advocate for bee health. Although there once was a time when every farmer was also a beekeeper, modern large scale farming has sometimes reduced pollination to just another managed input to be adjusted and addressed – a perception that members of NAPPC have been working for years to change.

Things haven't always been copacetic between native bee conservation groups and beekeepers, either. Even in the *For-*

gotten Pollinators, references were made to some of the negative impacts introduced honey bees might be having on fragile
Southwestern US ecosystems. In some circles, honey bees are
not always thought of as a meaningful part of responsible
wildland management.

When I ask Van Arsdall about some of those potential conflicts, he explains it from an almost anthropological point of
view. "We are tribal as a species, we all like to have our own
tribe, our own identity." There are the native pollinator people, and there are the honey bee people.

"Quite often they have been known to throw spears at each
other – such as when people used to say things like, 'honey
bees don't belong in our landscapes, they're a non-native species!' And then the honey bee people might say, 'Hey, native
pollinators aren't worth anything!'"

That kind of fighting used to be reflected in policies and
programs, he says.

But a major objective of his group is to break down that
kind of tribalism, because so many of the solutions that both
need are the same: good forage, better habitat, and an increase
in sound science related to all of the bees' heath issues.

We know very little about pollinators, Van Arsdall says.
"There's far more that we don't know than we do." In the early
days of P2, that dearth of data helped motivate the group to
push for a report from the National Academy of Sciences
(NAS). Funding was pulled together from various sources,
and NAPPC provided suggestions regarding the researchers
they thought ought to be involved.

The result was a 322-page book entitled *The Status of Pol-linators in North America* which noted – among many other important findings – a downward turn in long-term population trends for the honey bees and a shocking lack of data regarding almost all of the other bee populations on the continent. Just as Nabhan and Buchmann had noted in their book ten years before, the report further outlined the many introduced parasites and pathogens which threatened the bees' health.

"Although honey bees are the most important managed pollinators, other managed non-*Apis* species also require attention," the authors of the report wrote in their summary. "The development of protocols for wild species and the management of agricultural landscapes to sustain wild pollinator populations can create alternatives to honey bees as pollinator demands rise and shortages become likely."

What no one foresaw was that the book's release in 2007 would accidentally coincide with the emergence of CCD. Now bees weren't just dying. They were mysteriously disappearing in large numbers. The mainstream press jumped on the story, outlining the potential for huge crop losses and economic damage. Suddenly everyone was asking for more information about honey bees. Tragedy provided opportunity, in some odd ways.

"Colony Collapse Disorder made the report useful and relevant in a town that often suffers from a short attention span in the face of crises and disasters," Van Arsdall says, referring to DC. "It made pollinator problems visible."

But even without the extra attention, NAPPC never intended the NAS report to be a volume that simply gathered dust on the shelves of government offices. They had always wanted it to be a springboard to action. There were so many challenges facing the nation's pollinators. Even without the honey bee's mysterious ailment, there were problems that needed to be studied and solved.

Furthermore, no one involved felt that a lack of information could justify paralysis, says Van Arsdall, because what was known was that some simple actions could be adopted by people from all walks of life that could make a difference in the life of pollinators.

"I think our actions after CCD also became equally focused on managed pollinators as well as native pollinators, because we recognized there was a need there," he says.

It has astounded him to witness the transformation in both the attitudes of the general public and elected officials regarding all bees in the last eight to ten years. No one used to talk about bees as a positive. They used to be reviled – seen as gross creatures that could inflict pain.

"Bees are warm, fuzzy things now," he says laughing. "Beekeeping classes are overflowing. Everyone wants to keep bees."

Back at Pollinator Day on the Mall, I take a break from the information tables and grab a seat on a shady bench just beside a huge planted area called the People's Garden, where volunteers and USDA employees maintain several raised beds of vegetables and flowers. It's a lovely place – anyone can walk right up to the side of the beds to see all kinds of edibles flourishing in the sunshine. This spot was planted in 2009 to commemorate the bicentennial of Abraham Lincoln's birthday and was named as an homage to the former president's name for this agency, which he called "The People's Department."

Secretary of Agriculture Tom Vilsack used the day of the ground-breaking at the new garden to unveil a nationwide initiative aimed at "incorporating sustainable practices" while encouraging collaborative efforts among community members who maintain them. All of the produce from this and similar gardens is donated to those in need via food pantries, kitchens, and shelters, according to the USDA brochures.

Honey bees are landing on some of the herbs nearby. There are beehives on the roof of the USDA building behind me – established through another initiative undertaken by Vilsack and the Obama Administration. These are the bees that researcher Jeff Pettis mentioned when I talked to him a few weeks before at his lab in Beltsville. I put my hand over my eyes and try to catch a glimpse of the bees coming and going, but I don't see anything other than clear blue sky overhead.

Looking back again at the crowd to my right, I can't help but reflect upon how it is not just our perception of pollinators that's changed in the last twenty years. Our perceptions of cities and our relationship to urban areas have changed as well.

Not all that long ago, urban areas were not the places that anyone went to set up gardens. Industrial air pollution, fed largely by manufacturing plants and factories along urban riv-

ers of the Mid-Atlantic, often blanketed the sky. Lead –
belched from the tailpipes of cars, trucks, and busses – poi-
soned the soil of urban backyards, making it seem healthy to
pour concrete over playgrounds behind city schools in order
to prevent children from exposure to the brain-damaging
chemical during recess. Back in the 1970s it wasn't that unusual to have pollution-induced smog blanketing some urban
bridges in cities, enough to lower the visibility dangerously.

As a result of this and other economic changes, practices
which had long been done as a matter of course in urban places – such as keeping chickens behind the house for the eggs or
a backyard victory garden to provide fresh veggies – became
suspect and were abandoned by the 1950s. Instead, those who
wanted fresh air moved out of the city and found houses in the
newly established suburbs, or bought farms in the country in a
"back to the land" movement.

To a lot of people, Eastern cities became forlorn, damaged
places full of grime, drugs, and crime. They also became
places associated with litter, as was so vividly depicted in a
famous US television ad which showed a Native American
man tearing up at the sight of a city highway full of trash in
the 1970s.

Science, too, had its own bias against the urban environment. Until the 1990s, most of the study of ecology focused
on so-called pristine and undisturbed ecosystems, where the
human population was low and nature remained picturesque
and seemingly more diverse. It wasn't all that long ago that the
USDA itself was thought of as an agency with an almost en-

tirely rural focus. To many who lived in DC in the 1980s, the idea of growing food along Constitution Avenue in the middle of the National Mall outside of the agency's office building would have been a complete joke.

Two big things dramatically changed the cities in this region in the last part of the 20th century, although both are rarely acknowledged. The Clean Air Act, enacted in 1970 and revised in both 1977 and 1990, made city air in the Mid-Atlantic less smoggy, which in turn made many cities in the US seem more appealing, more livable, and quite a bit healthier than they had been.

Meanwhile, manufacturing – especially the heavy industries which often caused the harshest kinds of pollution in many cities – largely disappeared from the American economy. Many of the steel factories, the chromium plants, the canning warehouses, and the chemical producers have either disappeared or downsized in the Mid-Atlantic. The city here is no longer the place dominated by smokestacks and barges and tugboats and coal piles.

Instead Mid-Atlantic city landscapes are dominated by glass office buildings, large computer networks, and entertainment and tourism centers, museums, and fashionable restaurants – and have become places where large ships full of cargo containers dock to unload goods from elsewhere in the world.

A lot of the urban beekeepers I've met so far are recent transplants to their cities, people who have sometimes come to town to work in those glass towers. They often talk about bees as a way to validate the livability of their newly chosen cities. Some even feel a bit defensive about their newly chosen hometowns. Many who live in urban areas face the puzzled looks of older relatives who come to visit and are shocked by their off-springs' desire to live in old, cramped houses full of character in order to gain short commutes to good jobs or close proximity to the cultural and ethnic diversity at the urban core. The places where many urbanites choose to live now are often the very places their parents worked hard to escape decades ago.

Gardens full of bees thriving in the middle of that urban core seem to mean the city is safe, livable, hospitable. Indeed, for some of the people I've interviewed, the bees form an unexpected sign of the urban good life. For centuries the honey bee has symbolized industriousness or selflessness, but now – in a new urban twist – it has become a symbol of a human willingness to acknowledge and connect with the natural, the good and the pure even in the most unlikely places.

I find myself wondering about the role native pollinators are playing in the new dynamic of city living. I still feel as if I don't really understand what other kinds of bees are there in the city, and what I can do to help them. When the man at the Xerces Society table asked me to email him if I saw the Rusty Patched Bumble Bee, I almost began to tell him I probably won't see one in my semi-urban yard. But then I thought back to sitting on the High Line in Manhattan and watching bumble bees. They all looked pretty average – I don't recall seeing anything other than the black and yellow types. But what's really happening on and around city flowers?

If we start thinking that the cities can be places where a honey bee can thrive, we might also have to acknowledge that other bees can thrive there as well. Just as Tom Van Arsdall pointed out, environmental change which is good for the honey bees can often be good for native species as well. The more I learn about having honey bees in cities, the more I want to know about the other bees, too. But what remains unclear to me is how degraded – or promising – urban habitats are for any kind of insect. The skies may be clearer than a few decades ago, and we may have taken the lead out of our gas tanks, but it is not as if cities don't still have their share of environmental hazards. What seems unknown is how those remaining hazards impact various bee populations and their survival rates.

*****

I am immediately charmed by Sam Droege's lab in Beltsville, Maryland when I go to visit him there. There are vibrant, handmade quilts hanging from the ceiling, and strings of colorful plastic beads dangling over the heads of student interns who are counting and mounting bee specimens on a large maple slab table in the middle of the room made from a piece of reclaimed flooring that used to be a bowling alley. Droege tells me he stained it blue himself before bringing it to the lab.

Over the sink where Droege is making me a cup of mint tea, gentle handwritten notes remind visitors to please put the lids back on the glue bottles and wash all dishes because it "makes Sam happy." This is an incredibly pleasant place to sit and talk about science.

While some students chatter cheerfully over a large microscope and debate the most efficient ways to cut out paper labels to be pinned onto the foam board with the specimens they are preparing, Droege tells me he doesn't believe in leaving things government gray. We become what we see, he says with a shrug. Color is good, it enlivens and motivates.

I've come to ask Droege about solitary bees in cities. Just days before we speak, some photos he took made him into a bit of a celebrity. Extreme close-ups of insects, including many colorful bees, were prominently featured in the *Wall Street Journal*.

But I've known about Droege's work at the US Geological Survey for years – long before the WSJ article – having been to hear his lectures on the ecology of bees many times. He's a fascinating guy with a long braid of white hair trailing down his back and a soft, quick smile. He has a wry sense of humor, but he takes his scientific work very seriously.

Droege has been with the federal government since he was a student in 1978, when he came to research bird populations with the famous birding guru, Chan Robbins. Things have changed tremendously since those days – where once the emphasis was on hunting and fishing, there's now a lot of talk of conservation and the value of species richness among native plants and animals. Many in power back in the beginning of his career thought it was strange to study "non-game" birds, and when Droege began working with invertebrates that seemed even odder to some of the old guard. He was warned at one point in the 1980s that studying "bugs" might prove politically tricky.

By contrast, a lot of the biologists doing government field research now tell Droege that they grew up reading things like *Ranger Rick Magazine*. They are far more apt to think there's a lot of value in biodiversity than those who came before. There are more women present, too, he notes, which has changed the dynamic in an enormous and positive way. The sort of "good old boy network" which was in power has been replaced by a much more broad and diverse group of people with varying research perspectives.

Meanwhile, more people in the general public do not see bugs as icky and scary. As a result, Droege has found his work in a kind of unexpected limelight. People suddenly care about bees and want to know more about them. They are learning that bees are more than just pests that can sometimes sting. It is, he concedes, a bit shocking to see how the public's reaction to his work has changed.

Some of the same photographs which appeared in the *Wall Street Journal* article are framed on the walls around and above us. They have become a kind of gateway to the world of the bees, he says – and the public's interest strikes him as almost voyeuristic. Seeing insects so close up through the computer screen is fascinating, but also safe. For many who visit his site, there's an element of otherworldliness to these insects. Because some species can sting, they are dangerous. At the same time, this adds to their mystique.

"Bees are almost more akin to unicorns than they are to bugs, for some people," he says.

The new acceptance and fascination that seem to have blossomed for the insects are very positive, Droege says, even if people do nothing more than look at the pictures online and think they are cool. But it is something he didn't see a few years ago when the only insects people wanted to provide habitat for were butterflies and dragonflies.

Droege does not study honey bees, although I do notice that his lab is only two buildings away from the lab where the USDA scientists like Jeff Pettis are working on those insects. Like any good biologist, Droege is well aware of what his colleagues over there are up to – bee people network a lot and go to a lot of the same professional meetings.

Droege studies the other bees found on this continent, including the solitary native bees, which rarely sting, and the bumbles which live together in small, social colonies.

It is a big topic, but one that has not been explored extensively. There are more than 4,000 bee species known to live north of Mexico and more than 400 of them are still unnamed. In fact, a lack of attention to the topic has led to a taxonomic problem; some of the bees which are on the books have been given multiple names and others remain completely undescribed. Droege and his colleagues are now gathering specimens and developing lists to move the process along.

Some of the species are large and easy to recognize, but many are small and very hard to correctly identify without the aid of a microscope. On the table in front of us, some of the specimens which the students are carefully labeling are the size of marbles, while others are no bigger than grains of rice.

Unlike plants, which people have been cataloguing for centuries, or native birds in North America which started being catalogued more than a hundred years ago, native bees have never really been fully addressed. Droege's lab is charged with developing long-term surveys of plants and animals from around the country, including those which are commonly found on land owned by the Department of the Interior. Every ecologist depends upon these when seeking to explore the changing dynamics of any ecosystem.

But the lack of bee identification guides and methodological manuals was seriously hampering scientist's ability to gather needed data, since only a handful of people could identify the bees accurately.

Making things additionally difficult is a lack of digitized resources; most of the information in museum collections around the continent has not been put into computerized records or made generally accessible. This is one of the things which inspired Droege to put his lovely pictures up for display so publicly on Flickr – it gives many different kinds of people a platform for getting started in the art of identification.

Learning what to look for, how to know one species from the next, is very challenging. Things sometimes have to be puzzled out by a group of researchers, debated, examined, and re-examined. There are times when even the experts stand around and look over a specimen and admit they have no idea what the hell it is, Droege says. "We're way, way behind the other kinds of things." It's a neglected science.

Partly this is due to economics. There isn't a lot of money in the study of the native bees, and until recently there was no agricultural imperative driving the need for more data, no industry pressing for more information or access.

The supplies needed to gather samples are neither exotic nor expensive – you can collect bees in nets or plastic cups and bowls filled with soapy water, and look at them later through a microscope. But the training needed to understand the specimens well enough to identify them is still extensive. There aren't a lot of keys and guides that can reliably take you through the process the way a good bird book can. As a result, there aren't that many "boots on the ground" gathering native bee data in cities or elsewhere, he says. In contrast, ornithologists work with legions of amateur birders who can help provide information and gather data from the field with the help of a good pair of binoculars and a solid bird book.

One thing is certain, though. It is well known that bees are plentiful in many highly urbanized locations.

"There are buttloads of bees out there," he tells me. Honey bees, native solitary bees, non-native solitary bees, and bumbles – all of them can be found in cities.

The natives, he tells me, are known to be great pollinators. Although it is very difficult to study how the natives and the honey bees react to each other, ecologists have found that in most locations, the European honey bees are either a neutral party or a negative party in terms of competition with the native species for floral resources, making life a bit harder for the native bees.

On the other hand, he says, European honey bees have been in the Mid-Atlantic region for more than 300 years, so whatever consequences their introduction would have had has already occurred. The bee species out there have already learned to live with the honey bees and their activities.

City's systems, he also tells me, are dynamic and constantly changing. What he finds when he goes exploring along urban rivers and streets and abandoned train tracks is an ecosystem very much in flux, where introduced species are constantly making new appearances.

This seems especially the case around dock areas where container ships arriving from Europe and Asia are opened and unloaded thousands of times a day. In a study he published in 2011 Droege found an astounding total of 507 bees from 49 different species in some of the most industrialized portions of the Port of Baltimore. Of those, 11 were non-native.

He suspects that bees which have been accidentally packed into the container ships at their docks of origin fly out when the doors are opened at their destination. They find an abundance of blooming weeds exotic to the US but familiar and native to their home continents.

"It's hard to disentangle this from just the general urbanness of these locations. But it is clear that a lot of these introduced bees get their toehold in the Mid-Atlantic."

Droege and his colleagues often caution that the existence of bees in many locations does not justify complacency when it comes to pollinator conservation. It just means that honey bees probably aren't needed in most locations for the pollination of crops, even on urban lots.

Listening to him I realize that in the absence of good data, we gardeners often make assumptions based on our own observations. It also makes me aware of how undervalued and misunderstood some of the smallest insects can be in an urban environment. It is evident that more research into native bees would prove a great aid to those who want to grow food, even in city locations.

Native solitary bees are super good at distributing and establishing themselves. Many of the species do specialize – feeding only one particular kind of flower nectar to their young. But their ability to locate newly planted or sprouted flowers is incredible. If you plant pumpkins in the middle of the city, for example, you'll attract the bees that pollinate pumpkins. Likewise if you plant hibiscus, or ironweed, or any number of other plants, their own pollinators are able to find them, as are many non-specialist bees. "If you want honey, get those honey bees," Droege says. "But if you want that urban garden pollinated, maybe not."

One might assume that Droege's work would prove antagonistic to city beekeepers, or that they would be deflated by this kind of research. Instead, there is a surprising and ever-growing appreciation for the insights he and others have gained into the urban ecosystem. Droege is constantly being invited to give talks to beekeeping associations and garden clubs. In fact, as I researched this book it amazed me how many urban beekeepers urged me to talk to him and include information about his work. He's a very popular guy on the bee circuit.

(For his part, Droege spent a good deal of our time together giving me the names of other bee researchers I needed to speak with – he is extremely interested in getting more people into the mix and seems to like promoting the work of his colleagues.)

Droege also notes that there are beekeepers who have been so intrigued by his work that they have begun to send him specimen samples of natives from their own backyards, hoping to help in the effort to catalogue the species.

All of which leaves me with the big question of conservation. As someone who cares passionately about urban wildlife and especially bees, I want to do something good for the ecosystem. I want to help the bees, and I need to know the best way to do that. I can't say I'm surprised by Droege's answer to this query – because it's the same thing every other biologist has ever told me to do in my own backyard:

Plant native plants, especially those that flower.

"Its a pretty simple equation. You don't have to know which plants are associated with which bee. But if you plant native, you can guarantee you are doing a good thing no matter what, and native plants will bring a lot of interesting things, including a lot of bees."

We can look at suburbs – even those full of houses and sidewalks – as places full of potential if we are willing to plant native street trees and native flowers in the medians. "They can become interesting, open, savannah habitats, ones that just happen to have a lot of odd, hollow, square-looking trees rotting all over the place and a lot of flat rocks. A LOT of flat rocks," he says, referring to houses and sidewalks. "This can be our refuge."

Urban and suburban areas are not just lost areas, and the scale at which insects work is the same as your backyard. "You can make a difference in that space. We don't even know the names of all the species that are out there, but when you plant native, we know you are doing a good thing."

While it's clear that cities can be places where bees can thrive, what remains unknown, it seems, is whether cities are actually superior places for bees to live compared to rural settings, as many beekeepers have argued in the last few years.

Jeff Pettis, the researcher who led me on a tour of the USDA-ARS lab, remains fairly skeptical about any claims that urban bees could possibly be healthier or even more robust than their more rural counterparts. There just hasn't been a lot of published research on the topic, there isn't much data out there, at least not yet. What he's seen hasn't been very conclusive.

Urban bees, he says, do tend to produce a lot of honey. There's some increased plant diversity in cities – especially compared to say, a rural farm field in an area that's essentially planted in one crop and is not surrounded by forests or any other kind of plant life. Monocrops on the super-large modern farms don't offer much to bees once their bloom time is done. Places where there's nothing but huge swaths of corn and soybeans are really not so good for bees.

"But what I think more drives the ability of the bees in a city to make more honey is less competition. You've got this area out in the suburbs where there might be beekeepers managing a lot of hives and there's just not as much forage per hive, so you run into people that outside the city could manage 10 or 15 or 20 hives in an apiary and there you've got a competition issue where you just can't make as much honey," Pettis says. "You put two hives on a rooftop somewhere – there's not as many neighbors around and [the bees] will maximize the stuff."

By way of example, he tells me that the USDA headquarter building on the Mall in downtown Washington has bees that make a lot of honey. Probably their only close competitors for nectar are the bees a few streets over, near the White House – which live in a hive that has also produced a lot of honey. What you would really need to study to get answers about the health of those bees or any bees in the city, he says, is their pollen and whether or not the bees are really getting a diverse diet.

"Nectar gets bees through the winter, and nectar is what turns into honey and gives beekeepers their profit," he explains. "But pollen is what makes colonies grow."

There are many positives to keeping bees in cities, Pettis says, and he thinks the new enthusiasm for urban beekeeping is a good thing.

But some things get brushed over a bit too quickly when it comes to discussing the health of urban bees, he thinks, including air quality. Bees are very hairy, and they actually can pick up things in the air. There also might be pollutants on the surface of flowers that bees could be exposed to in urban places.

Although Mid-Atlantic cities look less smoggy than they once did, the problem of air pollution is by no means solved. One recent study published by a team from the Massachusetts Institute of Technology, for example, found that 130 out of every 100,000 residents of the city of Baltimore are likely to die in a given year due to long-term exposure to air pollution, providing that city with the highest emissions-related mortality rate in the country. The high visibility smokestacks may have disappeared from some parts of our urban landscapes, but the pollution continues to roil out from multiple sources, including coal-fired power plants, vehicular traffic, and the industrial smokestacks on top of the region's remaining factories.

Two studies released in 2013 revealed that bees suffer the consequences of polluted air as well as humans. One, published in the journal *Scientific Reports* by a team working at the University of Southampton in the UK, found that diesel exhaust distorted the smell of flowers for the bees – significant since bees use a combination of visual and olfactory cues when they forage.

Another, published in the journal *Environmental Pollution* by a team from the University of Pittsburgh in Pennsylvania, found that bumble bees could ingest toxic amounts of aluminum and nickel found in flowers that had grown in soil contaminated by exhaust from farm equipment, industrial machines, and vehicles.

What remains unclear is the relative amount of pesticide that a bee might encounter in a city. A few years back Pettis did participate in a study that looked at pollen samples from Staten Island and the borough of Queens in New York – and a variety of chemicals were found. He also knows of a few studies that haven't been published yet. But the pesticide load of cities and bees has not been widely investigated.

On June 15, 2013 – the very first day of Pollinator Week – the discovery of more than 50,000 dead bumble bees outside of a Target department store in Wilsonville, Oregon demonstrated to many just how toxic a suburban or urban environment could be.

The Wilsonville bees were killed when linden trees surrounding the store's parking lot were sprayed with a neonicotinoid called dinotefuran, which is sold commercially under the name Safari. A landscaping company had apparently been asked to kill aphids, which were attracted to the linden blooms; the aphids' honeydew was reportedly dripping on to customers' cars.

After the spraying, dead bees began piling up in alarming numbers. Customers alerted both the local press and the Xerces Society, which happens to have its national headquarters in Oregon. Photographers arrived and began taking pictures. The Xerces Society called it the largest bee kill ever documented and noted that more than 300 bumblebee colonies were impacted.

The event prompted two members of the US House of Representatives, Earl Blumenauer (D-OR) and John Conyers (D-MI), to introduce the "Save America's Pollinators Act" which would restrict the use of certain neonicotinoids throughout the country until a full scientific review could be conducted to determine the chemicals' impact on pollinators. By December the bill counted some 38 co-sponsors, but had little hope of passing in a historically gridlocked and partisan Congress.

After the Wilsonville bee kill, many smaller bee-kill events began to be reported throughout the state. Some said they had also seen such kills in the past, but never thought to report them to any one in authority. Others speculated that perhaps such events are common but often go unseen in grassy areas where the bee carcasses are more hidden. What made the Wilsonville event different was that the bees could be easily seen and counted because the carcasses landed on a paved surface. In response, the Oregon Department of Agriculture (ODA)

issued a six-month restriction on products containing dinotefuran.

Then in late November of 2013, just a month before the
ban was set to expire, the ODA announced it would make it
illegal to use products containing dinotefuran and another neonicotinoid, imidacloprid, on trees in the genus *Tilia* which,
includes basswoods and lindens, trees highly attractive to bees
during the blooming season.

The move was one that the ODA's director Katy Coba described as "aggressive" during a hearing with her state's
legislators. *The Oregonian* newspaper also reported that the
ODA had asked the Environmental Protection Agency if national restrictions were necessary.

Although commercial applicators may be deterred from using the chemicals on the two tree species, the neonicotinoids
in question were expected to be available for sale in stores as
soon as the temporary ban expired, leaving little to deter the
general public from buying them for all kinds of uses in their
own backyards.

I read of the bee kill with a heavy heart. Subtle questions
might remain about the large scale use of neonicotinoids and
their applications on farm fields. But as so many had pointed
out to me on my journey to learn about honey bees, there were
real dangers in urban areas for all kinds of pollinators, even in
places you wouldn't anticipate.

Celebrating pollinators is great. But more needs to be done
to protect them from this kind of application of chemicals for
purely cosmetic purposes. The bees are too important, too

valuable. I want to honor bees as vibrant, and treasured and alive, not attend events to eulogize them after they've disappeared.

9

When Healthy Bees
Must Go

A short time after visiting beekeepers in Baltimore, Bill Castro called me. He'd been alerted to the presence of thousands of feral honey bees in the attic of a very old building in the Hunt Valley area of Baltimore County. He asked if I'd like to come along to watch as he and a fellow beekeeper tried to remove the colony and rehome it.

Hunt Valley, as the name implies, was once the land of grand horse farms, stylish foxhunts and fields full of corn and timothy. In 1981 a huge shopping mall was built on fertile farmland near Interstate 83, angering many locals. Hunt Valley Mall struggled through its first two decades, suffering through numerous retail failures, sometimes being held up as an example of poor urban planning in the region. For a while it looked as if the shopping complex would go completely dark and empty.

On the day I drive to Broadmead, however, the place seems to have successfully re-invented itself as a stop for Baltimore's Light Rail transit system and a mecca for gourmet food lovers. The activity in the parking lot is brisk as people make their way in and out of restaurants and a huge Wegman's grocery store that advertises local produce for sale in its enormous eatery. I chuckle ruefully, remembering when that exact spot used to be an actual farm. I think my kindergarten class may have even gone there to pick pumpkins when it was still a field.

Broadmead, the senior housing complex where Castro has been called to help is a few short miles up the road from the mall. Perched beside the twisty country lane of York Road, it looks like a village nestled in lush, green forest. Staff members in medical uniforms walk between buildings talking on cell phones, which adds a hospital air to everything. Occasionally a man or woman in a business suit strolls by with files or papers in hand.

"Hello down there!" Castro calls in a friendly voice from the top of an industrial lift basket outside of the building called the Holly House. He's wearing a white bee veil, and waves his yellow-gloved hand above his head slowly.

"You might want to stay back for a while," says fellow beekeeper Dan Hemerlein, who is in the lift with Castro and also in a bee suit. "We've just been bothering the bees a bit and they are pissed."

Shielding my eyes to look up at the building's roofline, I'm unable to spot the bees, and a bit surprised that this is the building where they've set up their colony. It's a tight little brick Georgian or Colonial structure three stories high with nine windows looking out to the valley below. It's flanked on one side by a sloped one-story addition and on the other by a much larger, much newer brick building. I am later told it was built before the start of the Civil War, although new parts were added throughout the 20th century. It has been very much dwarfed by the senior housing complex that has been built all around it.

Castro and Hemerlein buzz down to the ground and climb out of the lift. The bees seem to be coming and going from a very small opening in a decorative corbel at the building's roofline, and there's absolutely no way to get to them from inside the building. They have settled in a spot that does not directly connect with the interior of the building which is why, we are guessing, they have been able to go so long without being removed or − for the most part − detected.

"One guy who works here did tell me that he's known for seven years that they were there," Castro says.

"Yeah, but I'm thinking they've been there a lot longer than that," Hemerlein replies. "I think that might be a real big hive under there."

I stand patiently by and listen. Mostly I want to stay out of their way as an invisible observer, but Castro has said he'll loan me a bee veil if I want to go up for a ride up to the top of the building.

Hemerlein is happy to take me, but not such a confident lift driver – he's only used a lift once many years ago. I decide not to tell him I am scared of heights. I also decide to pretend that the bee suit will protect me from harm, and that like Superman putting on his cape, I will be transformed when I put the veil on and will magically become one of those people I always see at amusement parks who loves to fling themselves ever skyward. This leads me to imagine myself wearing the bee veil on a roller coaster, and because I'm nervous I start giggling.

Why not? I think and the lift jerks unsteadily under Hermerlein's nervous and apologetic maneuvers. The bee veil blocks my peripheral vision so I can't see how far I would fall if I tumbled out of the lift.

We stop suddenly and the screen of a third floor window in front of us opens. Castro is inside, grinning. "What do you think?" he asks me.

I am honored that he wants my opinion, so I try to focus on the bees and block the sensation that I might barf up my lunch at any moment. I do not want these two to know how scared I am.

Then the bees are right there, are oozing out like froth from a pot of beans, or a pan of hot water, and I do forget everything else. I begin snapping pictures while Castro and Hemerlein debate their next steps.

Their goal is to get the bees out with as little damage to the brood cells of this feral hive as possible. Those cells are the incubators of this colony, they hold the developing bees which could eventually become either workers or new queens. Although it would be great to get out the existing queen for transfer, Hemerlein tells me this is almost always impossible. The queen often will go deep into the hive to hide, far from where she can be easily captured. Time is of the essence; the Holly House is set for a renovation and a new addition very soon, and the staff wants the bees gone before construction begins. The construction crew apparently wants that too. During a preliminary site visit they were a bit unnerved by the comings and goings of the members of this hive.

In much of the early 20th century it would not have been unusual to come upon a group of bees like this, who were thriving unattended by any human hand. A swarm would leave a beekeeper's crowded beeyard and set up housekeeping in an old hollow tree or an empty attic before being discovered. About 20 years ago, however, biologists noted such "feral hives" had all but disappeared from the landscape of the Mid-Atlantic US.

But hives such as the one that we are inspecting today form one of the great surprises of the modern apicultural world: as CCD has developed into a larger and larger problem, a small but vocal number of beekeepers have noticed that feral beehives like the one at the Holly House have made a bit of a comeback in some locations.

The phenomenon reminds me of AIDS in the 1990s, when the number of deaths from the horrible disease were matched with pleas from those who remained healthy even though they were in the "high risk" groups. Study us, the healthy ones had begged health officials. Find out why we persist in the face of this problem. Presently, bees in these feral colonies almost seem to beg the same.

Today I'm watching Castro and Hemerlein work in the suburbs outside of Baltimore, but beekeepers in urban New York, Philadelphia and Washington, DC have all related anecdotes about removals throughout the last year. Some even make a sizable side income from offering removal services as a part of their apiary's mission. Those who can offer both beekeeping knowledge and construction skills find they are in demand in certain seasons.

The process often begins when a property owner begins finding insects flying inside their house, emerging from light fixtures or window frames. Some even notice honey or propolis stains on interior walls, if the bee colony has gotten sizable.

Although exterminators may be called in to spray feral bees with pesticides to kill them, Castro tells me that increasingly homeowners call beekeepers instead. Some of those homeowners have even told Castro that the exterminators they called refused to kill a hive of bees.

An urban myth seems to have developed since the advent of CCD; many people apparently think that honey bees are now protected by the Endangered Species Act in the US, even though they are a non-native species and therefore would not ever be covered by that law.

Dennis Howard, the chief of pesticide regulation for the Maryland Department of Agriculture, tells me that myth actually predates the bees' current problems. Back in the early 1980s people often called the state offices to inquire about it. It is legal to spray honey bees, he says, provided the correct chemicals are used as directed. But many in his office actively encourage other options when it comes to feral colonies like the one at Broadmead. There's a general appreciation for the role bees play in agriculture.

Howard suspects that pest control companies don't want to deal with bees for a variety of reasons. Many know about CCD, and don't like the idea of killing a beneficial insect. Then there's the potential for bad publicity at a time when so many people are concerned about the bees. It's a competitive business, and many people once known as "spray jockeys" want to encourage a more professional image – they don't even want to be called exterminators anymore, preferring the more understated moniker of "pest control operator."

There's also been a tremendous amount of carry over from other parts of agriculture; as the methods of reducing chemical use through Integrated Pest Management (IPM) entered the mainstream over the last two decades, pest control companies began incorporating IPM principles if only because customers wanted less chemicals used around their homes. The idea of spending money to remove the bees to a new home seems better than spending it to spray and kill the insects.

"I think its a terrific thing," Howard says. "Bees are terrifically beneficial. We'd have trouble eating without their pollination and we don't want to do harm to them unless its absolutely necessary."

The members of the hive being removed today at Broadmead have calmed down, despite the Castro and Hemerlein knocking around on the outside of the building with drills, hammers, and hack saws. The two beekeepers point out that we are probably these bees' first encounter with humans. "We're making the guard bees here actually work, maybe for the first time," says Hemerlein.

Although we can readily see the entrance and exit holes the bees have made in the decorative corbel, it is not apparent where their honeycomb is attached inside the roof. Since the goal of these beekeepers is to rescue as much brood as possible, the exact location is key. From where we are on the lift it looks like the bees are living inside the bricks, which is not possible. They've made use of some holes in the mortar, so propolis and honey can be seen staining the exterior of the metal roof and its decorative fixtures.

Hemerlein uses a special video camera the size of a large TV remote to try to get a view inside the building. The camera has a probe that can be put through the bees' entrance holes. We're anxious to see if a good picture comes on the camera's front screen. Although there's an LED light on the end of the probe, the inside of the hive is too dark to be filmed effectively by Hemerlein, despite twisting and turning. He sighs with resignation and turns off the device.

There's no option but to begin peeling back parts of the roof, with hope that the hive is near the top. It will be much harder to remove vertical sheets of honeycomb heavy with honey and brood without damaging it or causing an enormous mess on the roof. It looks like this project may go on for a few days.

Hemerlein once again fiddles with the toggles of the lift. As we begin our descent I see a crowd of guys in brown uniforms who work for Broadmead down below. They are looking up at the two alien space creatures landing on earth in black and white suits. I wave like the Queen of England with one hand and hold on to the lift's railing for dear life with the other. Always room for a joke, and besides it's a good way to distract myself from vertigo. I'm proud of myself for not throwing up.

For Hemerlein and Castro, today's task is grim. They had both been hoping to convince the building managers to leave the bees in place.

"If I ran the place, I'd say leave 'em," Castro says. At the same time, he knows that construction will involve a lot of vibration along the building, something that can really agitate a beehive and put it on the defensive.

Inside we have some water while Castro and Hemerlein strategize around a small kitchen table. The building has long been used as a guest house for those visiting their family members at Broadmead. It's decorated with ceramic chickens and paintings of pheasants. We take off our bee veils and discover we have all gotten very sweaty. It's not a particularly warm day but the veils get hot and the roof is reflecting a lot of sunshine and heat. Working with bees also demands thick long pants or jeans, and good socks. Castro had even advised tucking my jeans inside thick socks if possible, to avoid any unwanted bee visits up the cuffs.

Hemerlein is tall with gray hair, jeans and a Jerry Garcia t-shirt. His alert blue eyes seem to snap to attention as the conversation progresses, but his voice stays soft and he speaks in a measured, contemplative way, even when he curses.

"Hope you don't mind salty language. Sometimes it gets intense when you do this kind of thing," he tells me apologetically.

I laugh.

Castro takes his veil off and fiddles with his wire-rimmed glasses and run his hand through his hair. The two men are frustrated because this project is probably going to be a lot harder than anyone anticipated. They will need to build more frames to carry the brood out. Castro takes out some wire and some empty wooden frames he's brought. As he works, his staple gun makes a loud rhythmic snap that we have to talk over and around.

I notice there's a tiny decorative bee skep on the knick knack shelf over Castro's head. People here like the idea of bees, they just don't necessary want to share the building with them. Besides fear of anaphylactic reactions, feral hives in walls can attract rats and mice with appetites for sweets, and unlike managed hives they may lack any physical guard or barrier which would keep rodents at bay. Unlike carpenter bees or termites, however, honey bees do not disturb a building's structural integrity and often rarely intermingle with the building's human occupants.

As we watch Castro's hands fly back and forth across lengths of wire, Hemerlein tells me it is a good day to do bee work, according to the biodynamic calendar. He's the first practitioner of the biodynamic method that I've met so far, although I've heard some things about the ideas behind it. Initially conceived and championed by philosopher Rudolf Steiner, biodynamic practitioners see themselves as stewards of the bees more than keepers. Natural combs are used rather than pre-pressed foundations of wax or plastic. Queen replacement is prohibited, as is the clipping of a queen's wings. Beehives must be made of natural materials and the use of pesticides and antibiotics are forbidden. Swarms are also seen as a natural part of colony reproduction, and queens fly free to mate with drones.

Biodynamic beekeeping is more apiculturally-centered, according to Hemerlein.

"Its not about what can I get out of the hive but what can I do to make the hive flourish," he explains.

A lot of people were exposed to the ideals of biodynamic beekeeping in 2010 by the film *Queen of the Sun*. The movie is credited for getting many people interested in beekeeping as a way to save the honey bees from decline. Its gorgeous cinematography shows people living among them harmoniously in both rural and urban settings.

Hemerlein tells me he's completed a two-year course in biodynamic beekeeping, and he continues to try to learn more each year. He never feeds his bees sugar water, nor uses any chemical processes or treatments on his hives, and he never heats the honey – not even with a heated knife for de-capping the honeycomb before extraction. He also follows a set of work days which Steiner laid out long ago according to the lunar calendar.

Most importantly, he does not manipulate the brood chamber – the area where a bee colony houses it developing young. Most of the conventional beekeepers in the US have no problem going down into that area of a hive, he notes, but biodynamic keepers tend to think of that area as absolutely sacrosanct.

"That's their church," Hemerlein says. "Not ours."

Hemerlein was attracted to Steiner's ideas and the ideas of other more modern practitioners like Michael Bush and Dean Lusby because he found the heavy use of chemicals and the intrusiveness of mainstream beekeeping was counterintuitive. The bees, it seems to him, know what to do on their own and need to build strength to fight off problems.

"Whereas in traditional beekeeping, chemicals are used to knock down mites, in biodynamic keeping we are aware that mites are there," he tells me. "But they can co-exist with the bees if the hive is robust enough, and after a while you get to the point where you're not as emotionally attached to your bees as you are, say, your dog. It passes, and hopefully the next generation is stronger."

Castro, who aligns himself with the so-called "treatment-free" beekeepers, says that he and Hemerlein have similar outlooks, even if some of what they do in their beeyards differs. Like many of the hobbyist and backyard keepers I've met, both think that a lot of the problems bees are having are due to issues with poor queens. But they also both think there's just too much being done to hives in the name of production.

"Most beekeeping issues have to do with over-manipulation," Hemerlein says. "I think beekeepers are fucking busybodies, frankly."

"It's human nature – to want to control everything," Castro adds from across the room.

"I try to provide an opportunity for the bees to exist," Hemerlein continues. "And then I stay the hell out of the way. Look, they've been doing this a lot longer than we have, and I don't think we are that intuitive to know what is going on with them. There's a lot of things I look at and I think: *What the fuck?* I have no idea. I don't really know what is going on."

There are a lot of beekeepers who have been going for 30 or 40 years who will tell you the same, he adds.

"You think you might know what is going on, but it doesn't mean you absolutely know. It's a long journey. I didn't think it was going to be that involved when I got into it."

The frames Castro's working with across the room are empty. He says he's rigged this system of using wires and bamboo barbeque skewers over the years as a way to effectively and gently hold the honeycombed brood from feral hives for safe transport. The skewers and wires don't damage the fragile wax and allow him to load up an empty beehive super with the bees. I imagine that it will all be a bit like taking pieces of broken stained glass down from a damaged church window – the wax might be brittle or fragile, and the system he's laid out will help minimize breakage of the honeycomb.

Refreshed and outfitted with more frames, we head back out into the sunshine. It is a gorgeous cool day – you can feel autumn coming. The two beekeepers go up again in the lift while I find a generous patch of shade under a tall pine tree and use the hood of the borrowed bee veil as a pillow under my head. The sky is a crystalline blue color and there are only a few tiny wisps of white clouds above me. Cicadas buzz in the tops of trees, and every once in awhile a cicada killer wasp flies by, too, with a large piece of prey. Butterflies tumble by on their way to the flower garden at the top of the hill. A chartreuse dragonfly almost lands on my shoe then zigs and zags hypnotically over my forehead.

I shake and awaken suddenly. More than an hour has passed since I heard the lift rise up They are still up there, still in bee suits, and still fiddling with hand tools along the roof line.

To avoid falling back to sleep, I page through some promotional materials and learn that Broadmead is managed by the Quaker Friends Services, and "offers a wealth of opportunities to nurture your body, mind and soul. Artists, physicians, educators, CEO's and others from all walks of life bring their diverse backgrounds and unique accomplishments to our community."

Holly House can be rented for parties, complete with catering from an on-staff executive chef. On my way to the bathroom inside the building, I'm impressed by its elegant staircase and grandly decorated visiting rooms – like a Hollywood movie set about aristocratic life in the 1950s. I picture Grace Kelly gliding down to scold me for being here in such dirty, grubby clothes.

I sit on the hill again, and watch a resident take a very well-groomed German Shepherd on a walk. Time passes with aching slowness. Castro suddenly calls down to me: "We got 'em! We found 'em!"

"How many are there?" I shout back.

"It goes from here to here," Castro motions along the roof about six feet. "It's a pretty big hive."

"About how many bees?" I ask again, wanting him to estimate if it is bigger than an average hive. "Like 30,000?"

"31,005!!" quips Hemerlein.

The lift buzzes down and they hop out. The bees are living between and under two expanses of brick – one that forms the exterior of the building and one that forms a kind of rubble line the masons left behind when they finished their work 175 years ago when the building was erected. The two men generously offer to let me go back up again to see it as they carry up some tools.

With Castro on the roof and Hemerlein and me in the lift cage, they gently peel back the tin flashing they've cut open, exposing a lot of propolis and the top edge of honeycombed wax. There is no sign of mite infestation, and absolutely no sign of *Nosema*. They are healthy and vigorous, and also very calm.

I'm struck again by how warm, cozy, and comforting the smell of an open colony is. After a few minutes of deliberation and prodding, we silently watch the bees coming and going as they try to make sense of their newly opened roof.

I understand now why Hemerlein feels sad about what they're doing. I feel as if we are ruining something really beautiful today, poking roughly around in their graceful architecture. It feels different from opening a hive where a keeper has established a relationship with bees they've introduced to a hive. I appreciate now Hemerlein's description of the brood chamber as sacrosanct. We are like vandals busting the windows in a pretty little chapel, though I realize this is better than spraying the bees.

"Sorry ladies," I say out loud from under my veil, "But it's time to go. Holly House can't be your home anymore."

I'm shocked at my own reaction to the whole experience. I wonder once again – as I have when looking in other hives – if there's a chemical that bees give off which causes such reactions in humans. Maybe we are not as immune or oblivious to their pheromones as we think.

I must look a bit sickened. Hemerlein breaks off a piece of propolis and hands it to me. "Eat this. If you ever start to feel sick, just chew on this." I try not to drop it from my gloved hand, the bee veil is blocking my mouth.

On the way back down to the ground I realize I am no longer afraid of being three stories up, although I'm glad I to be back on solid ground and when the lift stops I jump out pretty quickly.

As we reach the sidewalk, a well-dressed man in sunglasses, carrying a clipboard comes walking up the hill towards us. Doug Bareis, who is the Director of Support Services at Broadmead, hired these guys to remove the bees and he's anxious to know how it's going. He's glad to hear that the bees have been located and amazed that we haven't been stung. He asks if the smoker that Castro has been lighting puts them to sleep. Hemerlein's explanation of how it works fascinates Bareis but he keeps glancing worriedly up at the bees directly over our head. Although we've all unzipped our veils and removed them to talk, the bees only seem to be drawn toward Bareis which clearly makes him uncomfortable.

I'm struck by the fact that Broadmead is going to a lot of trouble to remove the bees in this careful manner. I ask Bareis how he feels about what's been done so far.

"Oh these guys are just really perfect," he answers quickly, beginning to fan at a bee that seems to be checking out his scalp. "I am really – this is really great."

He tells me it was Broadmead resident Cliff York who alerted Bareis to the plight of the modern honey bee. York and another resident have been keeping a small hive on a distant hill for about a year with the institution's enthusiastic permission. Removing the feral hive was beyond their abilities, so they referred Bareis to Castro.

"He told me we ought to try to save them, and it has all worked out so well. I have to go now, these bees seem to really want to sting me." Bareis gives a friendly wave while protecting his head with a manila file folder, and heads down the hill. Funny enough the bees did seem to want to chase him off, although they have yet to come near either Castro, Hemerlein, or me, even though we've taken off the protective veils.

I had hoped to be here when they actually began removing the wax filled with brood, but the bees were so well protected in their improvised brick hive that it took far longer to reach them and figure out how to proceed than the beekeepers expected. They are now going to close up the tin on the roof for the night, and come back fresh in the morning. Removal will still take hours, maybe even days. The bees and their brood will be taken to new homes and, although it is late in the year, will hopefully settle in before the cold of autumn really hits Maryland.

As I head back toward the highway, a sign at a local strip mall catches my eye. "Bee Beautiful with an agave facial today!" it says in large black letters, advertising what is supposedly the only "green beauty salon" in the area.

A week later I connect again with Castro, to find out how the mission turned out. The decorative corbel turned out to be made entirely of tin. It seemed pretty small when it was stuck to the building, but in actuality it measured about a foot across and two feet tall. The interior had once been filled with wood which had rotted. The bees had refilled its hollow with their brood cells and the adjoining masonry with their wax combs full of honey. The entire corbel had been held up by nothing more than a few nails and ten years worth of caulking. On their return trip up to the roof the beekeepers noticed it was beginning to tear away from the building. A small tap had sent it falling into Castro's hands, bees, brood, and all.

"The thing weighed about 35 pounds," he said. It was amazing it had never dropped off the building on its own.

The bees were being incorporated into Hemerlein's existing colony in nearby Columbia, Maryland. They had found the queen, but she was dead. Castro wondered if there was another one somewhere in the colony as well, but had not located her before they had to close up shop. Most of the honeycomb had to be left behind after the worker bees tending to it had been removed with a special bee vacuum and transported away.

Cliff York, the beekeeper resident who had been so instrumental in making the removal happen, told me he'd learned to keep bees back as a boy growing up in Appalachia and been keeping bees for years in nearby suburban Towson before he decided it was time to sell his house a year ago and move to Broadmead with his wife. He'd given away a thriving colony to another keeper, but kept his suit and equipment just in case he had the chance to keep a hive again. At 81, he is pleased to have started over, and his first year with his new bees had been a good one.

For years, he told me, people at Broadmead had known about the Holly House bees but not seen any reason to remove them. "They let them be, because that's the Quaker spirit."

10

Catching a Buzz at the Maryland State Fair

At the Maryland State Fairgrounds, a big red sign warns: "All Bags Will be SEARCHED!" I smile patiently while a young guy with an oversized baseball cap looks through my purse. Living in DC I'm used to it – but I didn't expect a search here. I am confident I have nothing to hide.

"Ma'am," he mumbles with an embarrassed smile. "I have to take your mace away."

I blush, realizing that my anti-mugging pepper spray key chain was somewhere in the bottom of my bag. "I'm so sorry, you can just keep it."

"No, you can come back for it. You have to come back for it, actually."

"Oh, okay. I'm so sorry." A seasoned urbanite like me ought to know better and ought to have cleaned out my bag before coming. I feel bad for the young kid who looks like he only recently learned how to shave that peach fuzz growing in around his jaw. He seems afraid of my pepper spray, holding it delicately between his thumb and forefinger while walking towards his boss in a booth nearby.

Through the gate I find myself smack in the middle of the Midway's carnival rides. I'm hit with a wave of sadness. It didn't used to be like this, though, everything else at the State Fair seems exactly as it was the last time I was here – 20 or so years ago. But getting searched at the gate is a new reality.

It has only been a few months since two guys set off bombs at the Boston Marathon. And just one week ago, a guy walked into a school in Decatur, Georgia on the first day of the new semester and threatened to kill everyone with his automatic rifle before he was talked out of it by the building's receptionist.

I feel really embarrassed about having mace in my bag at all, and I wonder what else this young kid has had to collect from people's bags. I cling to the thought that my anti-mugging keychain is the most interesting story he'll have to tell all week. God, I hope no one brought their gun to the fair.

I don't really need the mace anyway – I've just come to see the beekeepers which Steve McDaniel told me will be demonstrating the process of honey extraction every night at 8:00.

For some reason, I assume they'll be in with the farmers, so I search for the smell of manure. That can be tricky at the

State Fair, for there are days when manure comes from many directions even when the Fair isn't in session, and it isn't always from the farm animals. Horses race here daily.

This is Maryland, after all, a state that used to be known for its horse pedigrees and equine estates. Just a few miles south is Pimlico, the track where they hold the second race of horseracing's Triple Crown every April. Timonium and Pimlico are like sister racetracks. The state fair used to feature horses prominently because this area used to be known for its champion breeds.

I know all this because I grew up in Timonium, just a couple of miles from the fairgrounds. My friends and I got our first summer jobs here. My one friend was a tiny daughter of a formerly famous (and formerly rich) Irish jockey and she used her father's connections to get a job exercising the racehorses every morning before school – to the envy of our wealthier classmates who owned their own horses – until a thoroughbred threw her one morning and broke two of her ribs.

There were also summers when we spent long hours selling french fries or taking tickets at the rides. It was a hot, sweaty, thankless way to make cash before school started. And to be sure, it was a great way to get motivated about studying hard in school so we could all get "real" jobs after graduation.

My friends and I lived on the more modest side of town – the side that discovered how smelly horse stalls could be as we made trips to the nearby Burger King drive-thru on a summer night or went with our parents to run errands at the busy corner near the fairgrounds. Humid days were the worst. We couldn't smell it at our house – thank God – but to this day I associate certain banking companies with the strong, grassy scent of horse manure because I often went to the drive-thru window with my dad to deposit checks on summer afternoons.

I stand for a minute and take in the sunset over the carefully tended hedges of the racetrack which has been sprinkled and sculpted and is completely empty and tidy. Tonight it seems too clean, and vacant of even manure. I'm not sure they actually use this track for racing except during the fair. There isn't much interest in betting on horses now that they've introduced Keno and other forms of gambling at casinos. A lot of horse farms have been sold to housing developers in the last 30 years. There are fewer big farms around here than there used to be, and fewer people interested in buying thoroughbreds.

Tonight's manure smell, as it turns out, is coming from some other kind of animal. One of the biggest barns at the back of the fairgrounds is full of beautiful black and white cows, all lined up for milking. They've installed glass windows so that people can watch while machines are hooked up to the cow's udders for milking. A few families with toddlers are trying to explain what's going on – a big cognitive jump from this scene to a milk carton. A couple of the kids seem skeptical. Those machines seem like robots. This does not look like farms in most children's books. But it is, I realize, pretty much what most farms look like now in real life. It's a big cognitive leap for me, too.

Across from the glassed-in barn, the Maryland Foods Pavilion offers a place where you can buy your dinner and watch the cows while you eat food made in this fine state, like chicken, crabs, and barbeque pork. I don't see any one drinking milk, just super-size sodas. Given that a lot of drinks still get bottled by the Pepsi Cola Company in Maryland, that actually seems appropriate.

Inside the barn building college students from the University of Maryland sit next to more black and white cows in the middle of a pile of hay. Sometimes they bring a cow with a glass porthole installed in its side so you can see its digestive process at work. I don't see one tonight, however, and no one else is inside the hangar-sized building but me, a security guard, and the students. The students look bored, uninterested in the cows around them. One of them is pre-occupied with drawing a perfect copy of Testudo, the U of MD's cartoon turtle mascot, on a dry-erase board. Others check their phones for text messages.

It turns out I've gone to the wrong farm building, this is the Cow Palace, not the Farm and Garden Building. "That's where you'll find the bees," the security guard explains.

As I trudge up the hill I pass a great band bringing Beatles' songs back to life but only a dozen or so people are in the bleachers listening. The crowd is so small that the lead singer starts a one-on-one conversation with his girlfriend via the microphone. "Hey Patty, can you go get us some fries?" he asks her. "Yeah, sure," she yells back, giving him the thumbs up from the fifth row.

Just to the left of the stage goats answer him in loud "mahwwww" noises from an enclosure labeled "Goat Mountain" where they are ambling around on concrete cylinders used in urban stormwater ponds. Although goats are almost always a magnet for groups of children, there is only one mom and her young son watching the animals play this evening.

I enter another big building and go inside, which turns out to be the 4-H Display Area, where student work has been hung for judging. Although the room is packed with colorful stuff, the entire place – just like the most of the rest of the Fair – is empty. So empty that the man sitting at an info table visibly brightens when he hears the squeak of the door as I walk in. I feel sorry to tell him that I'm actually trying to find the beekeepers. He sighs and points out the door and up the hill. "Probably in Farm and Garden," he says. "Different building."

4-H used to be all Farm and Garden – the sort of thing kids who wanted to be farmers did after school in rural districts, like shearing sheep and raising rabbits. Now 4-H has grown and changed and adapted to become something bigger. You can still do the agriculture stuff, but there are other kinds of projects, too. Although I need to make sure to get to the bees before 8:00, I take a few minutes to marvel. Unlike so many contests held for kids these days, this is not the "everyone-gets-a-prize-no-matter-what" kind of stuff. These entries are good, really good, and the competition was obviously stiff for the award ribbons. The first prize winners in most of the categories are, in fact, amazing and worth searching out to see if only because they make you realize there are kids who have spent hours and hours working on these projects: self-portraits painted by ten year olds, and incredible action photo shots of someone jumping off a swing set, a close-up of a butterfly, and a sad picture of someone's girlfriend, and quilts in elaborate patterns with modern fabrics that I would be proud to throw on my own bed.

But the bees await.

The Farm and Garden Building is not air conditioned. It's really just a big warehouse with fans and open doors every few feet. At the entrance there are displays from the state agencies. "WE PROMISE!" says one sign in the campaign designed to prevent people from moving firewood from one location to another because doing so might aid the invasion of the destructive Emerald Ash Borers – beetles known to be eating their way through some of the state's prettiest and most valuable hardwood trees. Another sign encourages people to value ladybugs, and another implores gardeners to use "Bay Wise" gardening techniques in order to improve water quality in the Chesapeake watershed.

Past all this, at the back of the building beyond the entries for things like best homegrown table grapes, hot peppers, backyard wine, zinnias, and sunflowers, a huge banner invites people to come visit the "Angels of Agriculture." I have reached my destination.

A glass observation beehive has been set up, and a woman with a kind and enthusiastic voice is showing a group of five burly guys with sleeveless t-shirts and well-worn baseball caps how to find the queen bee. They don't believe her when she tells them the hive is overwhelmingly filled with females; there's a lot of guffawing and joking which she listens to patiently and smiles gently. She is obviously in love with her insects. She's wearing a black t-shirt that says: "Keep Bees and Carry On." The burly guys aren't sure what to make of her, but they also seem mesmerized by the insects. "You mean out of thousands of bees only a few of them are dudes?" one guy says, as if he's trying not to sound too interested. "That is pretty weird."

Above the beehive, there's a copy of a poster made by the Xerces Society and Whole Foods Market which shows two photos: the produce section of the popular grocery store chain with bees and the same produce section without them. After this poster went online in June, it went viral on social networks like Twitter and Facebook, and even Marla Spivak put a copy into her TED talk. "The Whole Foods Market's produce team pulled from shelves 237 of 453 products – 52% of the normal product mix in the department," notes the text.

I make my way up and down the aisles of bee products. There are far more entries are here than any other category in this building. There are handmade candles and soaps, jarred honey which was tasted before being awarded, and beekeeping equipment. I note with pride that a couple of the beekeepers I've interviewed in last few months have items on display. Bill Castro from West Baltimore has won third prize for his gabled hive roof. I feel truly happy for him, knowing how proud he is of that design. A Kenyan top-bar hive has also been given an award – perhaps a nod to some of the less conventional agriculture being practiced now in the state.

At the back of the display area a long table is staffed by seven beekeepers who tell me they are mostly from the Howard County Beekeepers Association. Each night a different group volunteers to be here, promoting their honey, their products, and the good work done by the bees for the state's agriculture and environment.

I notice that one pair of keepers is especially enjoying their volunteer time. Tricia Summers and Mark Boring look like they could be brother and sister – both have light-colored hair and quick smiles and both are eager to talk about bees. After a few questions they confess that they are both "newbies." They got started last year when a swarm took up residence in a hollow wall at the senior center where they work. As they watched an expert beekeeper cut a hole in the dry wall to capture the swarm, they became hooked.

"We signed up for the beekeeping class in our county in late winter thinking there might be a couple of dozen people there," Summers tells me with a laugh. "We got there and there were more than 100!"

The pair has now begun keeping their hives and simultaneously sharing what they learn with the senior citizens they serve.

"Its great, I love it," Summers grins.

"Has the Fair been this empty all week?" I ask.

"You know," Boring says, "they said Tuesday would be the slowest – and this is slow! I mean, when we were kids the

State Fair was a big deal. Everyone went. A really big deal! This place would've been packed when we were kids, just wall-to-wall people. I guess since the kids go back to school earlier, no one comes. It's really awful for these guys."

I wonder who he means – the fair organizers? the farmers? his fellow beekeepers? the bees?

My own kids go to school in a Maryland county that only recently decided to start school the week before Labor Day. I hate it, I tell him. It is so stupid to send them back to school only to have them get a holiday the first week. I know parents who skip the first week because their extended family still vacations at the beach until Labor Day.

It is not just parents who hate it, either. Maryland's comptroller, Peter Franchot, has repeatedly called for the entire state to start school after Labor Day, citing that an extending the summer season to its traditional end would could spell an estimated $74.3 billion dollar boon for the state's economy. More people, he and his staff say, would spend the last weekend of the summer doing things like going to the beach and the State Fair. Other neighboring states are considering similar proposals for the same reasons. Some farmers also say they feel slighted; their kids could participate in more of these late-season exhibitions if the start date was changed and it would help highlight the importance of agricultural education activities if they did.

"You know," Boring says to me, nodding, "the really sad thing is, look how empty the farm displays are. I mean, I was talking to some kids the other day and they thought that carrots came from a bag. The kids had no idea that carrots came from the ground, that someone grew them on a farm. Scary."

I nod in polite agreement. I do agree that kids don't know enough about farm production and food and nature. But as I look over the aisles, it strikes me that in the 1980s we didn't come to the Fair to learn a lot about agriculture, nature, or the environment. We came for the ride crazy rides, junk food, and to hang out with our friends. Sometimes we came to make quick cash as temporary carnies. In fact, I think one reason I couldn't find the Farm and Garden building tonight was because I never went inside here when I was a kid. Why would I? If my friends had seen me in here they would have made fun of me for doing something dorky. And my parents didn't have a vegetable garden back then. Farms were something I visited on school field trips, or when I went to see my relatives in North Carolina, or what we saw out the window on long car trips down I-95.

A few people trickle in the open doors that face the Midway and step up to the table, including a few families with strollers. There are hundreds of bottles of honey on display to sample with plastic spoons. One of the big burly guys gets into an animated discussion with a young male beekeeper who has a heavy Baltimore accent. The burly dude is totally riveted by the bees and wants to know everything about how you keep them and how you harvest the honey.

"You should keep some, man. Get a hive for yourself," says the beekeeper.

"Hey, hey," answers the burly dude. "I don't got no time! But I tell you what, I tell you what: you bring me some of that honey and I'll trade you out for a bushel of crabs. All I got time for is gettin' out in my boat on the weekends. But that damned honey is GOOD."

Everyone in earshot laughs.

"DEAL!" says the bee guy, shaking hands over the bottles of sample honey.

The heat is creeping up. It's humid outside and it looks like a thunderstorm might be brewing to the south of the Fair. The sun has gone down and the Midway lights are bright. I stand at one of the open doors to get a breath of fresh air. Screams can be heard coming from the Zipper, a ride that throws people upside down repeatedly.

I find myself thinking about Kim Flottam, the friendly editor of *Bee Culture* magazine. Back in the spring when I interviewed him, Flottam told me that "as goes agriculture, so goes beekeeping." He was mostly talking about trends – like the fact that more and more urban dwellers and young people are interested in growing their own food and keeping chickens and beehives in their backyards. But his statement is resonating in a different way for me as I look around at the empty State Fair. This event has been so well organized – with signs and maps and information people everywhere. But what really strikes me is how disconnected people are from the farm exhibits. It's too slick, too commercial.

To the right of the main entrance I stumbled upon a beautiful vegetable garden when I had walked through the gates earlier. It was almost invisible, despite some small interpretive signs posted, there wasn't much to highlight the food being grown. It was a fairly traditional garden like I might have found my grandmother tending back in the 1980s when I was in high school.

Wouldn't it be cool, I suddenly realize, if the State Fair was more about how most average urban Marylanders are growing food now? I think of people like my neighbor Eliot, who grows vegetables in a green roof he built on top of his shed. Or the farm people working in downtown Baltimore whom Jeavonna Chapman works with in Clifton Park. Or the churches I've seen that tear up their lawns to put in vegetable gardens for the poor. Or the way farmers markets are packed in both Baltimore City and DC as soon as they open up. Or the pick-your-own places where a lot of the families I know get berries in the spring and apples and pumpkins each fall. I start to count the number of people I know who belong to organic food CSAs – those community supported agricultural farms that promise if you invest in their business, you'll get a delivery of fresh food each week. Those are the most interesting things related to food. Why isn't all that represented here? Why does so much of what's here feel so distant from my own experience of food?

As goes agriculture, so go the bees. So where is agriculture going in my state? Farms – the big ones that sell to grocery store chains – are still things I mostly see through the window when I take a long car trip. And what I see is sometimes startling. A couple of years ago on the way to the beach a bad traffic accident put us on an unexpected detour route deep through two-lane roads flanked by farm fields owned by huge industrial food companies on the Eastern Shore. It felt as if we were on another planet – no trees, no hedgerows full of chicory or other weeds, and almost no room between the rows of corn plants that stretched as far as the eye could see. It was terrifying, dehumanizing, disconcerting.

My kids have asked what the huge, long buildings are for in the middle of the Delmarva peninsula.

"Chickens," I remember telling my son one time on the way to the shore.

"Mom," he said. "How many football fields could you fit in that chicken place?"

"I don't know," I told him with astonishment. "Several... A lot." We drove and drove and drove and still the chicken buildings went on with us.

Where is agriculture going? In two very different directions, I guess. People are more interested in food now than ever – a lot of us want to grow it at home and want to buy it fresh and organic, and to cook it and know about it and share it. People in cities are protesting "food desertification" and demanding access to locally grown produce. Access to fresh, farm-grown healthy stuff has become an issue of equity and environmental justice in some locations.

In the other sense, there are these huge agri-businesses out there now growing food to eat and to make into biofuel, and everyone is alarmed about the hidden sugar put into their food as high fructose corn syrup. Family farms are disappearing –

replaced with industrial outposts. Access to cheap, awful, junk food and really inexpensive fast food is making Americans obese at an alarming rate.

So what does that mean for the bees?

"Hey, everyone, gather around in five minutes," says beekeeper Bill Dickinson from a tiny 10' x 10' stage behind me. "We are going to extract some fresh honey for you, just like we do every night here at the State Fair!"

I am the only one present, and I feel conspicuous with my huge camera and notebook. But I want to take notes and get good pictures, so I belly right up to the front of the stage.

Oh Lord, I think to myself. I hope some other people show up. This really looks forlorn. It's just me and the beekeepers now. Dickinson's microphone is so overpowering that his friends behind the honey table tell him to turn it down.

But then something interesting happens: people start to file into the building. Here comes the crowd of burly guys, back again. Maybe they saw Dickinson's handprinted sign about the demo starting at 8:00. And here comes an African American family with two little girls in tight braids. A man speaking Spanish to his family squeezes in so they can get a good view up front. A handful of couples enter shyly, and stand toward the back. I find myself studying each of them, trying to determine which member of each group wanted to see the honey extraction and made a point to show up here on time. One twenty-something guy in a stingy-brimmed straw fedora tells his girlfriend, "I bet this is going to be sooo cool." (She looks skeptical, but sticks around anyway.)

Within five minutes Dickinson has started the demo, and a good crowd of about 25 people has assembled to watch – easily the most crowded spot I have seen at the Fair all night.

Dickinson begins by explaining the equipment. He's enjoying having an audience and making jokes with the crowd.

One of the female beekeepers I met earlier in the evening nudges me and says, "Doesn't he look like Charlie Sheen? "

"I heard that!" he says with a grimace, shaking a finger at her jovially.

"Before he did the drugs! Before he did the alcohol!" she insists, laughing. But her remark seems to egg him on, and he asks the crowd how they are and if they are having a good time.

Another beekeeper, Henry Lingenfelder from the Hamilton neighborhood of Baltimore, jumps up to help by grabbing a special hot knife for de-capping a frame that the bees have filled with honey. (I realize that I've met Lingenfelder's wife in Baltimore – Beth Sherring who was working with the BBBN to get the fees for beekeeping reduced. Beekeeping is a small world. That's *her* Henry – the one that got her bees and a hive as a Christmas gift.)

"So this is where the bees have stored the honey. We're going to use this heated knife to uncap it," Dickinson explains. "Then we'll put the frame in here." He points to a big, glass cylinder with room for three frames – the extractor.

A wooden super is sitting on the stage as well. Dickinson cracks it open with a hive tool, and a second frame is pulled out.

"Oh folks, isn't that beautiful? That is just perfect – a nice golden color and every single cell is capped and full of honey. That, friends, is what beekeepers dream about. Nice black locust honey from Carroll County."

The beekeepers behind us "ooh and ahh" goofily, but it really is beautiful. Dickinson says it came from Steve McDaniel's apiary. I feel pride and relief for McDaniel, remembering how sad and disappointing his harvest had been the year before. I wonder if the frame being held up right now is one that I watched him inspect back in July. I silently hope that every frame in the super is as beautiful as this one. Seeing it up on stage now feels like a sign of hope that somehow the bees will survive, and can overcome their problems.

"Now I need a volunteer to help me spin the extractor," Dickinson says, and he and Henry begin to ham it up a bit, pretending to be game show hosts. The crowd is enjoying it. A woman in the front excitedly approaches the stage and begins to turn the hand crank in a slow rhythm.

"Do I get the first taste?" she asks, laughing.

"That's right," Dickinson says. "But don't spin it too fast. We don't want to ruin the comb inside because that can be reused for next year once the honey's been drained out."

Honey starts to coat the side of the glass inside the big cylinder, making the side panels of the vessel look like amber-colored stained glass. Meanwhile, Lingenfelder is handing out pieces of the wax he just removed from the frame, mixed with honey. He looks like a waiter at a fancy party, handing out hors d'oeuvres, except that instead of a silver tray he's using a plastic lid from a five-gallon bucket.

"Try some! Try some! Go ahead and chew that wax, it's nature's chewing gum," he tells that skeptical woman I noticed earlier in the back row. Her fedora-clad boyfriend grabs a big piece and chews with gusto. It won't be long, I think, until that guy is keeping bees.

"Do you know how many flowers it takes to make a pound of honey?" Dickinson asks the crowd while the spinning continues. "Who can guess? How many flowers need to be visited to make a pound of honey?"

"A thousand!" a man behind me yells.

"Nope. Anyone else wanna guess?" Dickinson says. "It's closer to 2 million."

"Here's another cool fact. Male honey bees only have grandfathers, not fathers."

This confuses people for a moment or two, but Dickinson continues. "Males are called drones in a hive. Drones only develop from the eggs that have not been fertilized. Therefore, they don't have dads, just the chromosomes of their moms. "

The spinning continues and Dickinson goes on, delving deep into an explanation of the chemicals inside a bee's belly. All around him people are contentedly chewing honeycomb. I'm not sure they are following his science lesson, but they are having fun.

"Man, that is so good," someone says.

"It is good," Dickinson answers. "But it isn't just about the good honey. Bees are so important. A lot of the food you see

at the Fair, a lot of the things being judged in this same building, a lot of the stuff we eat needs the bees. Did you know that
the bees are responsible for about $12 billion worth of our
food?"

Behind me a woman gasps in amazement – she seems to
think he might be exaggerating, but he continues.

"That's right," Dickinson says. "There's a poster over there
that shows you how empty a grocery store would be without
the bees pollinating for us. They say more than 85% of the
plant species on earth require pollinators, including some of
the most nutritious food in our diet."

"Hey, how the bees doing, anyhow? Are they doing better
this year, did they recover from dying last year?" a man at the
side door asks.

"Well," says Dickinson, "most beekeepers report losing
about 30% of their hives and some lost as much as 60%, but
we're still waiting to see I guess."

A second frame is put in for spinning, more honeycomb is
handed out, and another volunteer takes the stage to help with
the spinning, with more questions asked and answers given.
Then a spigot on the side of the cylinder is opened and honey
begins to pour into a clean bucket which is topped by a lid
with a built-in sieve to catch any debris.

"So anything that shouldn't be in the honey is now
screened out by the filter," Dickinson says, showing the crowd
a dead bee that was in the honey.

"Poor little girl," someone says of the dead creature. He doesn't, to my amazement, sound sarcastic. Maybe he's a bee-keeper.

As the demonstration comes to a close, people make their way to the tasting table. They don't want to leave.

After he turns off his microphone, I ask Dickinson where he keeps his bees.

"Oh, I don't have bees of my own. I just love them, and I started to read about them and found them to be the most in-credible thing I ever heard about in my life."

Dickinson helps Steve McDaniel with his urban hives, though, when the chance arises. Most of the time he's at work at the Maryland Food Bank, a charity that focuses on getting donations of food to those in need all over the state. It strikes me that he literally works on ending food deserts on many levels for many creatures.

"But one day soon you'll probably get some bees?" I ask. "I mean, you seem to love the bees so much and you're so ex-cited about them. So maybe one day soon, eh?" I am also guessing that in order to be chosen to lead this demo he must do more beekeeping with McDaniel and other people than he lets on.

He stops and looks me in the eye with a weary smile. "I have to live where I am now," he says. "Know what I mean?"

The sincerity of his words and the change in tone contrasts so sharply with the playful tone he was just using with the crowd that I'm startled. I don't know what to say.

Out of the blue he shakes his head and says to me, "I worry about the bees dying. I think these things we are doing to our yards, our lawns, the things we spray out there – I don't know – I really don't know how you can kill a bad bug without killing a good one." He steps off the stage and goes to help the others clean up their supplies.

It's getting late. The beekeepers are closing down the display for the night, and I need to get on the road for a long drive home to DC.

Out on the Midway I buy a cone of soft serve vanilla ice cream and sit on a bench for a few minutes to gather my thoughts and muster my energy for the trip. There's a thunderstorm brewing, and I don't want to be on the highway in the rain and in the dark, but I'm not quite ready to leave.

I had wondered if I'd feel nostalgic or sad coming here. It's not like I really enjoyed high school, although being here does make me think of old friends who I miss. I realize, as I watch the small trickle of teenagers who are still here waiting for their turn on the rides, that the State Fair wasn't really so much about agriculture when I was growing up either. Maryland's relationship with its farms has always been in flux. Now all of the new energy seems to be swirling around urban farms and suburban homesteading. Why isn't that represented here? The honey demo was one of the best attended events in the whole of the Ag area. Why is that? Why are the bees still resonating with so many people when the other stuff here isn't?

Dickinson's right – it's not just that he needs to live where he is now, all of us need to start doing that.

Maybe the reason the bees are in so much trouble is because we aren't doing that enough. It seems to me that the urban beekeepers and those who live and work in the city on urban farms or tending backyard gardens know this already. They're living where they are, not dreaming of some fictional place in the country where they hope to live one day. The ones I've enjoyed the most are those that love their cities, love their tiny plots of land, and intimately know every inch of ground they walk on each day. Those were the ones that have really inspired me and made me think there's hope for a good, strong future.

Each of the people I met this year was so different, so unique, so divergent from each other in the ways of keeping their bees. And yet they all were truly experiencing the natural environment around them in a very real and up-close way in the present tense, every single day. Almost every one of them could tell me what was blooming any given day of the spring, summer, or fall on their block. Most could tell me how much rain we'd had this year, and what the weather forecast was for the next ten days. They live very much in tune with the natural world in some very "unnatural" locations. Those with hives in the city – they see the promise, they understand that land is land, and that no matter what, it has potential, it has power. Those city beekeepers don't see people outside of the ecosystem. They see the people inside the ecosystem, along with everything else in the city.

People might think urban beekeepers are flakes or dreamers. But to me they were realists, often far more practical and grounded than anyone else living in the city around them.

Maybe the real issue with the State Fair being empty tonight isn't that the schools start early and people don't care about farms. Maybe it's that the school administrators who don't think state fairs matter anymore just don't understand how relevant food is, or how relevant food production could be to everyone's education. Where are the displays on urban agriculture, the celebratory awards for those finding ways to grow food in urban wastelands? Where are the awards to the few schools which serve great meals, or foster great schoolyard gardens full of healthy, nutritious food?

Maybe these fairs need to become more relevant, more representative of what the future of agriculture holds instead of a sentimental pastiche of the past. And maybe too many of us have forgotten how relevant a healthy environment is to our future.

But the bees, they keep trying to show us. We just need to pay attention, and start living where we are now.

References

Agency for Toxic Substances & Disease Registry. "Public Health Statement for Pyrethrins and Pyrethroids." http://www.atsdr.cdc.gov/phs/phs.asp?id=785&tid=153 U.S. Department of Health and Human Services, Public Health Service. 2003 (Accessed November 2013.)

Beck B. *The Bible of Venom Therapy*. Copyright 1935. Reprinted by Health Resources Press. 1997.

Bee Informed Partnership. http://beeinformed.org/

Benjamin A. "New York Beekeepers Quadruple." *Guardian UK* March 16, 2012.

Berfield S. "The Honey Launderers: Uncovering the Largest Food Fraud in U.S. History." *Bloomberg Businessweek.* September 2013.

Beyond Pesticides "Pollinators and Pesticides: Protecting Honeybees and Wild Pollinators."

http://beyondpesticides.org/pollinators/pollinators.pdf. Accessed January 2014.

Black J. "White House Preps for Veggies but Aims to Raise Awareness." *Washington Post*. March 21, 2009.
Broadmead: A Dynamic Lifestyle Community. http://www.broadmead.org/ Accessed September 2013.

Brown T, Kegley S, Archer L. "Gardeners Beware: Bee-Toxic Pesticides Found in 'Bee-Friendly' Plants Sold at Garden Centers Nationwide." http://libcloud.s3.amazonaws.com/93/60/a/3130/Gardeners_b eware_report_8-13-13_final_updated.pdf Friends of the Earth. August 2013.

Buchmann S, Repplier B. *Letters from the Hive: An Intimate History of Bees, Honey and Humankind.* Bantam Books 2005.

Buchmann S, Nabhan GP. *The Forgotten Pollinators.* Island Press 1996.

Budin J. "City Crowns Anthony 'Tony Bees' Planakis King of the Bees." (blog post) NY Curbed (http://ny.curbed.com/archives/2012/08/04/city_crowns_antho ny_tony_bees_planakis_king_of_the_bees.php)

Burnham T. City Bees. (blog) http://citybees.blogspot.com

Burlew R. Honey Bee Suite. (blog) www.honeybeesuite.com

Burros M. "Obamas to Plant Vegetable Garden at White House." *New York Times.* March 20, 2009.

Carson R. *Silent Spring.* Houghton Mifflin 1962.

Caiazzo F, Ashok A, Waitz I, Yim S, Barrett S. "Air Pollution and Early Deaths in the United States. Part I: Quantifying the Impact of Major Sectors in 2005." *Atmospheric Environment.* http://dx.doi.org/10.1016/j.atmosenv.2013.05.081. November 2013.

Colla SR, Ascher JS, Arduser M, Cane J, Deyrup M, Droege S, Gibbs J, Griswold T, Hall HG, Henne C, Neff J, Jean RP, Rightmyer MG, Sheffield C, Veit M, Wolf A. "Documenting Persistence of Most Eastern North American Bee Species (Hymenoptera: Apoidea: Anthophila) to 1990-2009." *Journal of the Kansas Entomological Society,* 85(1):14-22. 2012. DOI: http://dx.doi.org/10.2317.JKES110726.1.

Comptroller of Maryland. (official state website/press release) "Franchot Releases Economic Impact Report of MD Public Schools Starting After Labor Day." http://comptroller.marylandtaxes.com/Media_Services/2013/0 8/15/franchot-releases-economic-impact-report-of-md-public-schools-starting-after-labor-day/ August 15, 2013.

Conte A. "In New York, Seriously Local Honey." Diners Journal, *New York Times* blog on Dining Out. http://dinersjournal.blogs.nytimes.com/2009/09/01/in-new-york-seriously-local-honey/?_php=true&_type=blogs&_r=0 September 1, 2009.

Delaplane K. *First Lessons in Beekeeping.* Dadant Publishing. 2007.

DiPrisco G, Cavaliere V, Annoscia D, Varricchio P, Caprio E, Nazzi F, Gargiulo G, Pennacchio F. "Neonicotinoid clothianidin adversely affects insect immunity and promotes replication of a viral pathogen in honey bees" *Proceedings of the National Academy of Sciences.* 2013 110 (46) 18466-18471; published ahead of print October 21, 2013, doi:10.1073/pnas.1314923110

District of Columbia Mayor's Office. "Sustainable DC." http://sustainable.dc.gov/

Droege S, Shapiro L. "An August Survey of Wild Bees (Hymenoptera: Apoidea) in the Northeastern Port Areas of Baltimore, MD and the Second North American Record of Pseudoanthidium nanum (Mocsary)" *The Maryland Entomologist.* Vol 5 No 3. Sept 2011.

Dresser, M. "Hunt Valley Mall: Troubled Past, Uncertain Future." *Baltimore Sun.* February 1992.

Dvorak,P. "A Growing Buzz Surrounds Washington the Increasing Number of Capital Beekeepers." *Washington Post.* June 3, 2009.

Environmental Protection Agency (EPA). "Pyrethroids and Pyrethrins." http://www.epa.gov/oppsrrd1/reevaluation/pyrethroids-pyrethrins.html April 2013 (Accessed November 2013)

EPA "Overview: The Clean Air Act Amendments of 1990." http://epa.gov/air/caa/caaa_overview.html. Accessed September 2013.

Extension Toxicology Network: DDT (dichlorodiphenyltrichloroethane) http://pmep.cce.cornell.edu/profiles/extoxnet/carbaryl-dicrotophos/ddt-ext.html. Accessed November 2013

Fishel, F. "Pesticide Toxicity Profile: Neonicotinoid Pesticides."University of Florida Institute of Food and Agricultural Sciences - Extension. http://edis.ifas.ufl.edu/pi117. Accessed November 2013.

Flottam, K. "Home Again, Dedicating Langstroth's Birthplace." *Bee Culture.* October 2010.

Frazier J, Mullin C, Frazier M, Ashcraft S. "Managed Pollinator CAP (Coordinated Agricultural Project)." Jointly

published by *American Bee Journal,* and *Bee Culture.* August 2011.
http://www.beeccdcap.uga.edu/documents/CAPArticle16.html
Republished by *Bee Health* January 2013.

Ellis H. *Sweetness and Light: the Mysterious History of the Honeybee.* Harmony Books 2004.

Flottam K. *The Backyard Beekeeper.* Quarry Books 2010.
Friends of the High Line. "Designing the Future." http://www.thehighline.org/competition/about.php. Accessed May 2013.

Friends of the High Line. "History of the High Line." www.thehighline.org/about/high-line-history. Accessed May 2013.

Girling RD, Lusebrink I, Farthing E, Newman TA, Poppy G. "Diesel Exhaust Rapidly Degrades Floral Odours Used by Honeybees." *Scientific Reports.* Doi:10.1038/srep02779. October 2013.

Goulson D. "REVIEW: An Overview of the Environmental Risks Posed by Neonicotinoid Insecticides." *Journal of Applied Ecology,* 50: 977–987. doi: 10.1111/1365-2664.12111 June 2013.

Henry M, Beguin M, Requier F, Rollin O, Odoux J, Aupinel P, Aptel J, Tchamitchian S, Decourtye A. "A Common Pesticide Decreases Foraging Success and Survival in Honey Bees." *Science.* DOI: 10.1126/science.1215039 April 2012.

Hines K. "Hidden Hives of New York." A report for *All Things Considered* on National Public Radio, archive available at
www.npr.org/templates/story/story.php?storyId=4787735. Original air date: August 5, 2005.

Hopwood J, Vaughan M, Shepherd M, Biddinger D, Mader E, Hoffman Black S, Mazzacano C. "Are Neonicotinoids Killing the Bees?" www.xerces.org/wp-content/uploads/2012/03/Are-Neonicotinoids-Killing-Bees_Xerces-Society1.pdf Xerces Society Publication 2012.

Hopwood J, Hoffman Black S, Vaughan M, Lee-Mader E. "Beyond the Birds and the Bees: Effects of Neonicotinoid Insecticides on Agriculturally Important Beneficial Invertebrates."
www.xerces.org/wp-content/uploads/
2013/09/XercesSociety_CBCneonics_sep2013.pdf   Xerces Society Publication 2013.

Hubbell S. *A Book of Bees.* Random House 1998.

Ian MP, Beiler J, McMonagle A, Shaffer M, Duda L, Berlin C. "Effect of Honey, Dextromethorphan, and No Treatment on Nocturnal Cough and Sleep Quality for Coughing Children and Their Parents." Archives of Pediatrics and Adolescent Medicine. 161(12):1140-1146.

Kaplan J. "Colony Collapse Disorder: An Incomplete Puzzle." USDA-ARS *Agricultural Research* http://www.ars.usda.gov/is/AR/archive/jul12/July2012.pdf. July 2012.

Kidd SM. *The Secret Life of Bees.* Viking Penguin 2002.

Kohan E. Obama Foodorama. (blog) www.obamafoodorama.blogspot.com

Krupke C, Hunt G, Eitzer BD, Andino G, Given K "Multiple Routes of Pesticide Exposure for Honey Bees Living Near Agricultural Fields." *PLoS ONE* 7(1): e29268.doi:10.1371/journal.pone.0029268. January 2012.

Krupke C, Hunt G. "Neonicotinoid Seed Treatments and Honey Bee Health." Jointly published by the *American Bee Journal,* and *Bee Culture.* September 2012. Republished online by *Bee Health* July 2013.

Langstroth L. *Langstroth on the Hive and the Honey-Bee/A Bee Keeper's Manual.* Northampton, Hopkins, Bridgman. 1853.

Mayo Clinic. "Diabetes foods: Is Honey a Good Substitute for Sugar?" http://mayoclinic.com/health/diabetes/AN00425. Accessed May 2013.

Meindl G. "The Effects of Aluminum and Nickel in Nectar on the Foraging Behavior of Bumblebees." *Environmental Pollution.* http://dx.doi.org/10.1016/j.envpol.2013.02.017 June 2013.

Miller, J DC Honeybees. (blog) www.dchoneybees.blogspot.com.

National Oceanic and Atmospheric Administration. "National Overview: February 2012." www.ncdc.noaa.gov/sotc/national/2012/2.

National Research Council. Status of Pollinators in North America. Washington, DC: The National Academies Press. 2007

National Honey Board. "Honey Without Pollen is Still Honey." http://www.honey.com/honey-industry/honey-and-bee-research/honey-without-pollen-is-still-honey. Published online April 16, 2012.

Natural Resources Defense Council. "Higher Organophosphate Pesticide Levels Linked to ADHD."
http://www.nrdc.org/living/healthreports/higher-organophosphate-pesticide-levels-linked-adhd.asp Accessed November 2013.

Oertel E. "History of Beekeeping in the United States." Originally a USDA publication, revised October 1980.
Reprinted/posted on Beesource website:
www.beesource.com/resources/usda/history-of-beekeeping-in-the-United-States/ Accessed February 2013.

Pesticide Action Network - United Kingdom. "What Are Neonics." http://bees.pan-uk.org/neonicotinoids. Accessed November 2013.

Pesticide Action Network. "Organophosphates."
www.panna.org/resources/organophosphates. Accessed November 2013.

Pettis JS, Lichtenberg EM, Andree M, Stitzinger J, Rose R, et al. "Crop Pollination Exposes Honey Bees to Pesticides Which Alters Their Susceptibility to the Gut Pathogen *Nosema ceranae*." *PLoS ONE* 8(7): e70182. doi:10.1371/journal.pone.0070182

Rajan, TV, Tennen H, Lindquist RL, Cohen L, Clive J. "Effect of Ingestion of Honey on Symptoms of Rhinoconjunctivitis." *Annals of Allergy, Asthma and Immunology.* doi:10.1016/S1081-1206(10)61996-5

Rudolf Steiner College. "Beekeeping at Rudolf Steiner College." www.steinercollege.edu/beekeeping Accessed January 2014.

Rueb, E. "As Swarms Startle New York, Officer on Bee Beat Stays Busy." *New York Times.* June 18, 2012.

Schneider, A. "Top Pollen Detective Finds Honey a Sticky Business." *Food Safety News* November 2011.

Schreiber A. For the Time Bee-ing. (blog) www.timebeeing.blogspot.com.

Seavey NG. *Capital Buzz.* Institute for Documentary Filmmaking at George Washington University. 2012.

Siegel, T. *Queen of the Sun.* A Collective Eye Production. 2010.

Smart Car Ad: Accessed May 2013. www.youtube.com/watch?v=UlsPmdPkGmY

Sosna, S. "What Winter? NYC had the 2nd Warmest on Record." www.nbcnewyork.com/newslocal/2011-2012-Winter-Warm-Record-Central-Park-NYC-141367583.html. NBC New York. Posted online March 5, 2010.

Southern Integrated Pest Management Center. "UF Researchers Explore the Use of Buckwheat as a Cover Crop in the South." www.sripmc.org/successstory/buckwheat.cfm. Accessed February 2014.

Spivak M. "Benefits of Propolis to Honey Bee Health." *Bee Craft: The Informed Voice of British Beekeeping.* Volume 95 No 3. March 2013.

Spivak M. "Why Bees Are Disappearing." Technology, Entertainment and Design (TED) lecture. Filmed June 2013 in Scotland. Full lecture available online at: http://www.ted.com/talks/marla_spivak_why_bees_are_disap pearig.

Stein S. *Noah's Garden: Restoring the Ecology of Our Own Backyards.* Houghton Mifflin Co. 1993.

Steiner R. *Bees.* Anthroposophic Press. 1998.

Swearingen J, Slattery B. Reshetiloff K, Zwicker S. *Plant Invaders of the Mid-Atlantic Natural Areas.* National Park Service/US Fish and Wildlife Service. 2010

Tallamy D. *Bringing Nature Home: How Native Plants Sustain Wildlife in Our Gardens.* Timber Press 2007.

Tian B, Fadhil NH, Powell JE, Kwong WK, and Moran NA. "Long-term Exposure to Antibiotics has Caused Accumulation of Resistance Determinants in the Gut Microbiota of Honeybees." *mBio* 3(6):e00377-12. doi:10.1128/mBio.00377-12 October 2012.

Traynor J, "How Far Do Bees Fly? One Mile, Two, Seven? And Why?" *Bee Culture.* June 2002.

University of Texas Extension. "What is a Neonicotinoid?" http://citybugs.tamu.edu/factsheets/ipm.what-is-a-neonicotinoid? Accessed November 2013.

Unsworth J. "History of Pesticide Use." http://agrochemicals.iupac.org/index.php?option=com_sobi2&sobi2Task=sobi2Details&catid=3&sobi2Id=31 International Union of Pure and Applied Chemistry. May 2010.

US Census Bureau. "Baltimore City Maryland Quick Facts." http://quickfacts.census.gov/qfd/states/24/24510.html

US Department of Agriculture (USDA) - *Agricultural Resource Service. Colony Collapse Disorder Progress Report.*

http://www.ars.usda.gov/is/br/ccd/ccdprogressreport2012.pdf
June 2012.

USDA- Natural Resources Conservation Service. "Be A
Friend to Pollinators." http://www.nrcs.usda.gov/pollinators.
June 2011.

US Fish and Wildlife Service Environmental Quality Fisher-
ies and Habitat Conservation. "Chlorinated Hydrocarbons
(Organochlorines) – DDT. "
http://www.fws.gov/contaminants/info/ddt.html Accessed
January 2014.

Van Driesche R, et al. *Biological Control of Invasive Plants in
the Eastern United States,* USDA Forest Service Publication
FHTET-2002-04
www.dnr.state.il.us/stewardship/cd/biocontrol/12knotweed.ht
ml. Accessed online April 2013.

Wagner P. *How Well Are You Willing to Bee, The Beginners
Auto Fix-It Guide.* Published by the author. 1994.

Walker L. "Pollinators and Pesticides: A Report by the Center
for Food Safety on Pollinator Health, Research, and Future
Efforts for Pollinator Protection."
www.centerforfoodsafety.org/files/pollinatorreport_final_191
55.pdf March 2013.

Whole Foods Market. "This is What Your Grocery Store Looks Like Without Honeybees." http:/media.wholefoodsmarket.com/news/bees. Accessed Oct 2013.

Wolfe A. "Buzzy Photography: Bees Close Up." *Wall Street Journal.* October 25, 2013.

Zheng Y. "Oregon Agriculture Officials Place Restrictions on Pesticides Implicated in Wilsonville, Hillsboro Bee Die-offs." *The Oregonian.* November 21, 2013.

Thanks to:

Bruce Hall for letting me crash in Brooklyn. Lisa McHenry Bendel for joining me over the Bees' Knees. Bob Fenster for being the world's greatest apostrophe wrangler – really, you rock. Laine Gillespie, Bill Chappelle, Marilyn Gillespie, James Gillespie, Nadine Lymn and David Wacaster for being great beta readers – and enthusiastic cheerleaders. Andrew White who has always been willing to question my nouns, my chapters and my sanity. Craig Gillespie, for his energetic feedback and support. Everyone keeping bees at the Franciscan Monastery in DC for teaching me about honey extraction. David Colin Carr for the editing. Denise Reiffenstein for the fantastic cover design.

And of course Dave, who always believed it could happen – you are my greatest and my best.

I am especially grateful to all of the beekeepers and their beautiful, beautiful bees. It was magical to beek out with you for a while.

ABOUT THE AUTHOR

Alison Gillespie lives in Silver Spring, Maryland. She enjoys gardening, hiking with her husband, and laughing with her children. You can find more of her writing at: www.alisongillespie.com.

24062428R00207

Made in the USA
Middletown, DE
13 September 2015